A FAMILY CONSPIRACY:
Honor Killing

I0125480

A FAMILY CONSPIRACY:

Honor Killing

PHYLLIS CHESLER

Published by New English Review Press
a subsidiary of World Encounter Institute
PO Box 158397
Nashville, Tennessee 37215
&
27 Old Gloucester Street
London, England, WC1N 3AX

Cover Art and Design by Kendra Mallock

ISBN: 978-1-943003-14-3

First Edition

NEW ENGLISH REVIEW PRESS
newenglishreview.org

Contents

Introduction

These articles are the work of an academic turned frontline journalist, one who is covering a very different kind of war. I co-pioneered the study of violence against women in the late 1960s. I focused on women living in North America and Europe who had been psychiatrically diagnosed and hospitalized; were the victims of rape, sexual harassment, incest, intimate partner battering, pornography and prostitution.

I also documented the profound double standards and anti-woman biases which led to good mothers losing custody of children to abusive fathers and husbands; women sentenced to long or life prison terms when they killed batterers in self-defense; and the violence women faced as they fought for their reproductive, educational, economic, political, and religious rights around the world.

My generation of feminists believed in universal human rights. We were not multi-cultural relativists. We called out misogyny when we saw it and did not exempt a rapist, a wife-beater, or a pedophile because he was poor (his victims were also poor); or a man of color (his victims were also people of color); or because he had an abused childhood (so did his victims).

Like other American feminists, I was also active in the civil rights and anti-war movements—but unlike such feminists, I had "once lived in a harem in Afghanistan." This is the opening sentence of my book *An American Bride in Kabul*. I lived with my mother-in-law in a polygamous household in posh purdah; this meant I was not allowed out without a male escort. My father-in-law had three wives and twenty-one children—facts my Westernized husband failed to mention during our American college courtship. I saw women in burqas stumbling around on the streets of Kabul, and forced quite literally to sit at the back of the bus.

Therefore, I was aware early on that worldwide, most women were illiterate, impoverished, and forced to marry men not of their choosing when they themselves were still children. As girls, they were expected to meet impossibly high standards of subordinate behavior—and, if they failed to do so, they risked severe punishment. Thus, for example, women in Afghanistan, Egypt, India, Pakistan, and Saudi Arabia led lives that were far more difficult and endangered than American women did.

In the early 1970s, I was alarmed about the mass gang-rapes of girls and women in the war between Pakistan and Bangladesh. I knew that the victims' families would reject or kill them. By the 1990s and early 21st century, I was, similarly, concerned with the fate of kidnapped and sexually enslaved women in North Africa at the hands of paramilitary units; and in the increasing use of gang-rape as a weapon, not merely as a spoil of war, in Bosnia, Congo, Guatemala, El Salvador, Rwanda, and Sudan.

Given world events, I began to focus on tribal gender and religious apartheid and on the lives of women living in tribal shame and honor societies.

* * *

An honor killing is the cold-blooded murder of girls and women simply because they are female. Being born female in a shame-and-honor culture is, potentially, a capital crime; every girl has to keep proving that she is not dishonoring her family; even so, an innocent girl can be falsely accused and killed on the spot.

A girl's fertility and reproductive capacity is "owned" by her family, not by the girl herself. If a girl is even seen as "damaged goods," her family-of-origin will be responsible for her care for the rest of her life. This is a killing offense. Her virginity belongs to her family and is a token of their honor. If she is not a virgin, the shame belongs to her family and they must cleanse themselves of it with blood; her blood.

Imagine growing up in a family where you are closely monitored, harassed, perhaps even beaten daily; threatened with death if you are seen talking to a boy or if your veil has slipped. Imagine knowing that members of your own family-of-origin might one day kill you for the slightest offense or for no offense at all--and coolly get away with it; imagine knowing that you cannot escape, that no relative, and no legal

12

forum will protect your right to live and to live free from normalized violence.

Becoming too "Westernized," wanting to choose one's own spouse, refusing to marry a first cousin, daring to have infidel friends or allegedly engaging in sex outside of marriage—are all killing offenses.

From a tribal point of view, this shame-and-honor code does enforce social stability but at the price of individual rights and personal freedom.

At first, I did not appreciate the advantages of marrying one's first cousin. However, upon consideration, I realized that one's mother-in-law/aunt might be kinder to a girl whom she has known since birth and whose family-of-origin may live nearby. Perhaps such a mother-in-law/aunt may not prohibit her daughter-in-law/niece from visiting her own mother. (This is sometimes the case).

Keeping money and land within one's own family has always been seen as important. First-cousin marriage maximizes this advantage.

The disadvantages of first-cousin marriage include all the consequences of inbreeding and lifelong misery in a marriage one may abhor.

The institution of polygamy, or so it is argued, allows first, second, third, and fourth wives to remain with their children and to continue family life as usual. Since divorce is unthinkable in tribal societies, this may be seen as a "kindness" to womankind.

Of course, the competition among male siblings for paternal attention and resources and between co-wives can be quite ugly.

Purdah protects privileged women from the lust and violence of non-family men; it does not protect them from boredom or from intimate family rape.

In small, agricultural regions, entire communities, not just individuals, demand that anti-woman honor codes be upheld. Any family that fails to kill a "disobedient" girl or woman will find that no one will marry their other children or deal with them economically. In this context, one can understand (without accepting) the claims made by countless honor killers, namely, that they were only acting in self-defense; that communal norms drove them to it.

When I first began this work, I did not fully comprehend how difficult it might be for a girl or woman to escape being honor killed. From birth on, she has been indoctrinated into believing that she has been born evil and has to cleanse that shame every minute of every day.

Such a girl will have no psychological understanding that she is a human being and entitled to individual or human rights. She will not view herself as an "individual," but as a daughter, granddaughter, sister, niece, and wife—as a member of a family, clan, religious, or tribal collectivity whose welfare she has been born to serve.

Her body does not belong to her but to the collectivity. If her first-cousin/husband beats her very badly, her role is still to remain with him. Her own family will be dishonored if she leaves her marriage.

Therefore, those who escape to save their own lives are among the bravest and most resilient of girls and women. Their families will pursue them forever and thus, they usually require new identities and the equivalent of a witness protection program. They pay a high price for their freedom and survival. They can almost never risk seeing their immediate or extended family again. Some find the price too high and return, most often to their detriment.

Once people with such tribal traditions and psychologies travel to the West, the exacting shame-and-honor codes should no longer apply. But apply they do, at least among Muslims and, to a lesser extent, among Sikhs.

* * *

By 2003-2004, I was writing about honor killings based on newspaper accounts, internet sources, first-person interviews, and on a proliferation of memoirs.

I began to think of such calculated conspiracies as "horror" murders, not "honor" murders. The shame belonged to the perpetrators, not to their vulnerable victims. My understanding of this subject only evolved over time.

By 2005, in my book *The Death of Feminism*, I reviewed the honor killings in the West and was astounded by the fact that so many were torture-murders. By 2007-2008, I called for law enforcement and school officials to recognize the signs of a potential honor killing. In the West, with a few Sikh exceptions, it seemed to be a Muslim-on-Muslim crime.

I also described honor killings in America such as that of Palestina Isa (1989) and Methel Dayem (1999); both were Palestinian-Americans. I wrote about Samia Sarwar/Imran who was honor killed in Pakistan in 1999 and whose case made world headlines. Her mother had arranged for and was present when a contract killer she'd hired murdered her daughter.

There were many more honor killings in Europe than in America, since there was a large immigrant, mainly Muslim, population there.

Thus, in 2005, I wrote about some of the high profile cases such as that of Tulay Goren (1999), Hesha Yones (2002), Fadime Sahindal (2002); Sohane Benziane (2002); Sahjda Bibi (2003); Shafilea Ahmed (2003); and Hatun Surucu (2005).

I could not have written as knowledgeably about honor killing had I not simultaneously embarked on a series of academic studies about such femicide—and had honor killing cases not been reported in the English language media.

In 2009, I published my first academic work on this subject in *Middle East Quarterly*, charting the specific differences between Western domestic violence and honor killing/femicide. While many insist that honor killings are like Western domestic violence, this is not the case.

In honor killings, murders are carefully planned conspiracies and may be perpetrated by multiple family-of-origin members. Brothers, uncles, fathers, and other male relatives usually commit the murder, although mothers have also been known to collaborate in the murders of their daughters; sometimes, they are hands-on perpetrators.

Batterers who murder in the West are usually acting in an unplanned and spontaneous way. They alone are the perpetrators. Their own families do not assist them nor does the victim's family-of-origin. In the West, fathers rarely murder their teenage daughters. This is what happens in a classic honor killing.

Honor killings in the West are sometimes marked by excessive violence, such as repeated stabbing, raping, bludgeoning, or being set aflame. Such killings are similar to what serial killers do to unknown, often prostituted, women.

In the West, batterers and wife killers are not celebrated—they are shunned. If possible, they are also prosecuted. Hindus in India, and Muslims, worldwide, who commit honor killings, are viewed as heroes who have saved their family's honor. Thus, they feel no shame or remorse.

I initially sailed into what was, for me, uncharted territory. Over time, I increasingly made it a point to find and cite all those whose work in this area had preceded mine. Their names are legion and are listed in the bibliographies of my studies.

Researchers in the 20th century, (Ginat, Glazer and Abu Ras), others in the 21st century, (Berko, Brandon and Hafez, Ghanim, Feldner, Kulczycki and Windle, Lasson, Pope, Rosen, Saltzman, Storhaug, Weber, Welchman and Hossain, Wikan), studied the phenomenon of honor killing. Without exception, scholars agree that an honor killing is not like Western domestic violence.

Only those who believe that it is shameful to expose anything negative about Muslims, especially if it is true, silence such exposure by "shaming" it as racist and "Islamophobic."

In the 1990s and into the 21st century, an increasing number of journalists also began to cover honor killing cases, especially if the perpetrators were brought to trial; memoirs and books were written about honor killing and attempted honor killings among immigrants in the West and in developing countries. A number of important films appeared on this subject including: *Banaz: A Love Story; Dukhtar; A Girl in the River: The Price of Forgiveness; The Price of Honor, FOX: Honor Killings in America.*

* * *

There is no way to "measure" the incidence of hidden crimes such as incest or honor killing. One can do so but only imperfectly.

The United Nations still continues to insist that there are only 5,000 honor killings, worldwide. However, in 2010, according to two legal researchers in India, there were roughly 900 reported honor killings in the northern Indian states of Haryana, Punjab, and Uttar Pradesh alone while 100-300 additional, recorded honor killings took place in the rest of the country. According to the Human Rights Commission of Pakistan, 800 women were killed for honor in Pakistan in 2010.

Both figures likely represent only the tip of the iceberg. According to the Aurat Foundation, a Pakistani human rights organization: "At least 675 Pakistani women and girls were murdered during the first nine months of the calendar year 2011 for allegedly defaming their family's honor." Almost 77 percent of such honor cases ended in acquittals.

Although no "true" measure of incidence is possible, I decided to do what was feasible. For my next study, I relied upon the global, English-language coverage of reported honor killings in 29 countries and territories as long as all the variables I wanted to study were known. Given these limitations, it is amazing that I found so many statistically significant differences.

In "Worldwide Trends in Honor Killing" (2009), I studied 230 cases which took place between 1989-2009 in Europe, North America, and in the Muslim world. There were two kinds of honor killings or rather two very different targets. A classic honor killing targeted victims who were an average age of 17; the second, less frequent honor killing targeted victims who were an average age of 36. These age differences were statistically significant.

The younger-age victims were killed by their families-of-origin 81% of the time, worldwide.

The group of older-age women most closely resembled a Western-style domestic violence dispute turned murderous. They were usually killed by their husbands but even here, there were significant differences. Nearly half (44%) the time, murderous husbands were assisted either by their own families or by their victim's family.

Motives were significantly different across continents; in the West, victims were killed for being too "Western;" in the Muslim world, it was mainly for allegedly committing an "inappropriate sexual act." The rate of torture-murders were at their highest in Europe. Perhaps those who were tempted to assimilate had to serve as human sacrifices and object lessons of what could happen to those who "Westernized."

From the time I published this study, my incidence rate of Muslim-on-Muslim honor killing rates, (91%, worldwide), has been used again and again, both with and without attribution, and usually without proper context. After all, this percentage is true in only one study, and in a study limited by whether the honor killing was or was not fully reported in the English language media.

Even as I planned my third study (a comparison of Hindu and Muslim honor killings in Pakistan, India, and the West), I continued to read and write about honor killing cases when and if they were reported.

I began to document such cases in 21st century North America, such as that of Khatera Sadiqi (2006); the Said sisters (January 2008); Noor Almaleki (2009); the Shafia sisters and their father's first wife, (2009). I continued monitoring the American and Canadian mothers who either lured their daughters to their deaths (the 2008 Said case in Texas); assisted their husbands in making a getaway (the 2011 Almaleki case in Arizona); or who knew that their daughter's bones would be broken but who chose to say nothing (the 2007 Parvez case in Canada).

My 2012 academic comparison of "Hindu and Muslim honor killings in India, Pakistan and the the West," documented significant differences in terms of motives. Hindus honor kill when caste violations are committed; Muslims for many different reasons; Hindus often kill the men as well as women, whereas Muslims, rarely do. Hindus do not bring this custom with them when they come to the West; Muslims, and to a much lesser extent, Sikhs, do.

At the outset, I did not understand the role that women played in

17

honor killings as conspirators, collaborators, and as hands-on perpetrators. As the author of *Woman's Inhumanity to Woman*, I should have suspected this, but since maternal filicide is such an unthinkable act, my understanding dawned slowly.

Women have internalized the same patriarchal and tribal beliefs that men have—and in addition, are more responsible for keeping other women in line, especially their daughters. Most mothers want to ensure that their daughters are allowed to live, marry, become mothers, and maintain honorable reputations.

Women are known instigators and collaborators, and are sometimes either the ones who lure their daughters home to certain death or are themselves hands-on perpetrators. Such mothers have rarely been charged in America. I documented this in "When Women Commit Honor Killings" in 2015.

Once I was certain about the probable tribal origin of honor killing, I made a point of stressing that. Surprisingly few Muslim or ex-Muslim dissidents "heard" me; they were too invested in blaming Islam. Some Hindus tried to persuade me that Hindus did not perpetrate such crimes but, even if they did, that they had probably learned it from Muslims. More interesting: Even fewer Islamists understood that my tentative conclusion helped support the argument that honor killings are not necessarily religiously mandated.

This is important because it gives genuine Muslim reformers a basis upon which to condemn it as "anti-Islam."

Ultimately, I held—and still hold—both the Hindu and Muslim leadership responsible for failing to abolish this barbarous custom.

Although people know that the majority of honor killings in the West are Muslim-on-Muslim crimes, the American mainstream media nevertheless persists in focusing on Hindu honor killings in India and rarely on Muslim honor killings in North America. A recent "Islamically correct" pseudo-academic study on this subject ridiculously suggests that Hindus in America bear watching, that they are the problem.

Abolishing human sacrifice will require mass education, consistent law enforcement, and the vigorous assistance of the clergy.

* * *

I may mention the same honor killing case more than once in this volume. I have edited most repetitions out but I've hesitated to remove them all. When one writes an individual article, one has no way of knowing if one's reader today has read all of one's previous articles on the subject or is at all familiar with the subject.

In collecting these writings, I was struck by how my own understanding about honor killing evolved over time, partly as a function of what my research data revealed; in part, based on what became known about the facts of a particular case; in part due to the interviews I conducted—and, of course, as fleshed out by my reading of memoirs, trial transcripts, human rights and Congressional reports as well as by other academic research.

I've been enormously privileged in that I've been able to put my scholarship to good use. Thus, on the basis of my studies, lawyers, and immigrant advocates have asked me to submit affidavits about honor killing in court cases where girls or women, in flight from being honor killed, were seeking political asylum or emancipation from their families.

In 2015-2016, a professor of Law at the University of Arkansas Law School, contacted me about our mutual interest in honor-based violence. She visited, we remained in touch. In 2016-2017, she organized a conference on this subject and invited a small group of grassroots activists—three from the UK, (Rashida Begum, Ruth Beni, Diana Nammi), an American law enforcement officer (Chris Boughey) and myself. I was to be the only academic who had conducted studies of honor killings. This conference was to be hosted in April, 2017, at the King Fahd Center at the University.

It was not to be. A few days before the conference was to take place, the Professor and the Acting Director were forced to disinvite me. Some pro-Palestine and pro-Islam professors warned them that there would be serious trouble were I even to appear via Skype, from afar. This administration-approved dis-invitation led to a small media firestorm.

But the story has a happy ending. One of the feminist activists with whom I work, Mandy Sanghera, based in the UK, said that dis-inviting me had dishonored us all. She vowed to create another conference, probably in the UK. In November, I participated in another conference about honor-based violence at University College London, together with Asma Ashraf, Sabin Muzaffar, Anna Purdie, Mandy Sanghera, and Gwenton Sloley. Sanghera tells me that other universities in the UK want us to present there as well.

One of the many questions with which I wrestle is this: Is an honor killer, by definition, "mentally ill" according to Western standards?

What if he or she has been extremely abused in childhood, suffers from the symptoms of Post-Traumatic Stress, including paranoia, a trigger-temper, and rage-aholism, and believes that such murder is being undertaken in "self-defense?" What if this belief system and psychological configuration is no longer possible to change?

How is an honor killing, which is a family conspiracy and an act of domestic terrorism, different from an act of truck-bomb or human-bomb terrorism? Both are embedded within a system of beliefs which are not compatible with democracy or the rule of law.

My answers to these questions are still evolving.

- 1 -

Forced Female Suicide

Are Arab Palestinian female human homicide bombers active members of a Death Cult, or unwilling participants in it? Are they religious fanatics, Western-style revolutionaries, or clinically depressed human beings facing No Exit lives? Have they been brainwashed by master seducers or have they been brutally forced into it? May we view such women as victims of an honor-based femicide?

These are necessary questions to ask when contemplating female human homicide bombers. Certainly, some female Arab Palestinian human bombers have "freely" chosen the murderous martyr's path: Most likely, some of these women have had close male relatives who died in the war that the Palestinians have declared against the Israelis.

Evidence also suggests that the Palestinians have created yet another form of Arab honor killing. Some Palestinian girls and women have been recruited, seduced, and trapped by older male terrorists in very female-specific ways.

For example, in one instance, the chosen Palestinian girl was unmarried and pregnant. She was offered the chance to "cleanse" her honor by blowing up herself and Jews. I have also been told that some Palestinian masters of mass murder have had affairs with vulnerable young Palestinian girls in order to compromise their "honor" and to season them, pimp-style, for martyrdom. Hard facts are hard to come by, anecdotes abound.

Journalist Barbara Victor, the author of the recent book about Palestinian female human bombers, *Army of Roses,* and playwright Glyn O'Malley, whose play, *Paradise,* is on the same subject, have both dealt with some of the earliest Palestinian female human bombers whose lives were stunted by oppression.

Wafa Idris, the first (known) Palestinian human bomber, was probably in a clinical depression. Her first and only child had been a stillborn and, as a result, she became sterile. Her husband, who was also her first cousin, had divorced her over this and taken a second wife. She was mocked by family and friends; she understood that she had no future in Palestinian society. As a divorced and infertile woman, she was doubly "tainted." Her bleak prospects—due to Islamic and Palestinian misogyny and not to the Israeli-Palestinian conflict—were used to trap her into redeeming her "dishonor" by becoming a murdering martyr.

We cannot say that these women (or, for that matter, their male counterparts) are making "free" choices. No one is offering them the presidency of their country, an all-paid scholarship to a prestigious university—or, as a third choice, the opportunity to kill and die at a tender age. Their choices are "forced." They are probably not political extremists or revolutionaries in the Western sense. They have grown up in a tribal, Islamic society in which women are expected to sacrifice themselves in terrible and medieval ways.

Most recently, the case of Reem al-Riyashi suggests a similar and horrifying scenario. Several Israeli sources have discovered that this young mother of two very young children "was forced to carry out the suicide attack as punishment for cheating on her husband." Allegedly, al-Riyashi's husband was a Hamas activist and her lover was a Hamas operative who had carried out the love affair with the express purpose of recruiting her. According to the British *Sunday Times*, al-Riyashi's husband himself drove her to the border crossing.

This is unbelievable—and tragic. Had these men threatened to kill her children if she refused this mission?

Whatever the circumstances, it is important to understand that the coercion of women by men to become human bombers is not an aberration in the Middle East. Myth aside, Islam is the largest and most savage practitioner of gender apartheid on the planet.

Traditionally, gender apartheid includes compulsory veiling, arranged marriage, sequestration, polygamy, stonings for alleged adultery, female genital mutilation, approved wife-beating, and honor killings in which raped girls and women are killed by their family-origin for the "dishonor" they have brought upon their family.

It is this cultural context that compels us to stop romanticizing such homicide bombers and/or presenting them as heroes.

I understand what the Israeli ambassador to Sweden felt when he saw the exhibit that glorified yet another Palestinian female suicide bomber: Hanadi Jaradat, who killed 22 innocent Israeli civilians, both Christian Arabs and Jews. Jaradat's smiling, serene face floated above a pool of civilian blood. The artwork had been done by an expatriate Israeli artist and installed at the entrance to a building that is to house an upcoming conference against genocide. The Swedes had promised the Israelis that the Middle East conflict was not going to be part of the conference.

But this art exhibit found a way to bring the Middle East conflict into the conference—in a way that justified and glorified homicidal/genocidal human bombers who, upon closer inspection, may be committing a "forced" suicide/homicide as their only way out.

FrontPage Magazine
1/22/04

- 2 -
Mr. and Mrs. Human Homicide Bomber

S ajida Mubarak Atrous al-Rishawi, the sister of al-Zarqawi's right-hand man and the female half of the husband-and-wife team of human bombs who struck in Amman last week, is now in Jordanian custody. Her final act—blowing up a Muslim wedding in progress—demonstrates clear contempt for human bonding and hope.

It is important to understand that, in fighting a war on terror, we are not only waging a war between two different civilizations or worlds. We are also fighting a war between the forces of life (eros) and death (thanatos). All that we hold dear, both instinctively and through religious and social training, is being specifically targeted by jihadists.

Even the concept of motherhood is under attack. For instance, in September, in Tal Afar, Iraq, a woman was photographed holding the hand of a three year old girl. Shortly thereafter, she blew herself up and murdered several others. It would be difficult to find a clearer illustration of the contempt that terrorists harbor for the inclination to protect a small child. That contempt is shared by male terrorists. Anecdotal information also exists about male human bombs who purposely position themselves next to mothers with small children before they detonate their explosives.

Whether this contempt is conscious or not is beside the point. These death eaters emerge from cultures that despise women, locate shame in female genitalia, routinely beat girls and women, or else murder them in honor (horror) femicides. They mock the values of life and the female principle. Their hatred may include motherhood as well as the socialization of men to serve as protectors of women and children.

Jordan has been trying to deal with honor killings. Perhaps that is why King Abdullah condemned these jihadists as "insane." Such denunciations are hardly the norm for the Middle East. In cultures that have normalized—not criminalized—such deeds, there are no such denunciations or concepts of mental illness. Given the level of child and woman-abuse in so many tribal societies, which has been further intensified within radical Islam, few individuals can create a strong sense of self. Jordan is trying to make progress.

Still, the country is not immune from the Middle East's unfortunate tendency to scapegoat others—such as Israel, the Jews, or Americans for Muslim tribal crimes—and this tendency remains rampant. This is one reason why many Jordanians have suggested that either Israel or the Jews were behind the latest bombing of three hotels. They say they cannot believe that a Muslim would do this to other Muslims. To their credit, however, Jordanians immediately protested the attacks on their fellow citizens. Jordanian officials did not hesitate to identify al-Qaeda terrorists as the perpetrators.

As the barbarities committed in the name of Islam become undeniable—expressing the darkest dramas of the Middle East, one can only hope that such terrorists will lose the hearts and minds of the Muslim world by reducing so many of their own to bloody body-parts.

FrontPage Magazine
11/14/05

- 3 -
Honor Murders in the West

The sixteen-year-old girl was "too modern" for her fundamentalist Muslim family. She craved forbidden North American freedoms which, if practiced, would shame her immigrant family. The struggle over this issue was hot and abusive. She was continually attacked and closely monitored. Her own sisters envied and hated her not only because she was allowed to attend school but because her choice of modern dress could harm their own young daughters' future marriage chances.

I am not talking about Toronto's Aqsa Parvez, who was just slaughtered by her father for veiling improperly, but about another sixteen year old: Palestina Isa, who was honor-murdered by her father and mother in St. Louis Missouri on November 5, 1989. Palestina ("Tina") was murdered with primal ferocity. The forensic pathologist reported "thirteen wounds, six of them mortal. The worst one plunged into her chest wall, breaking her sternum and ribs and piercing her heart. A second gash ripped her left lung. Her liver had been slashed five times fatally." Her breasts had been punctured seven times.

Ellen Harris wrote an important book about this case: *Guarding the Secrets: Palestinian Terrorism and a Father's Murder of His Too-American Daughter.* Palestina was being physically abused at home. She attended school with visible bruises. She asked for help. She got none. The only reason her parents were prosecuted and sentenced was this: Her father, Zein Isa, was under federal surveillance. Why? Because he was a member of the Palestinian Abu Nidal terrorist group. The jury actually heard the horrendous twenty minute murder on tape, then convicted her parents.

At one time, the Abu Nidal group had been classified by the American government as the "most vicious terrorist group in the world." On Christmas Eve, 1985, they were responsible for the simultaneous attacks at the El Al counters in the airports in Rome and Vienna in which 18 people died and 101 were injured. In 1986, they attacked an Israeli bus on the West Bank; they also attacked a group of Jews as they prayed in a synagogue in Istanbul, machine-gunning 22 worshippers to death and then killing themselves.

Back then—and even more so today—Islamic terrorists and Islamic fundamentalism is usually correlated with the subordination of women and their even more savage punishment if they stray, by a millimeter, or by accident, from what is expected female behavior.

Zein Isa's second wife (a first wife lived in the West Bank), Palestina's mother, held her daughter down while her husband slaughtered her as if she were an animal, as if she were a woman who had provoked her own murder. Indeed, her parents never showed any remorse. Zein Isa told the police that she "deserved it, that she attacked me."

Each time I wrote about this case, with a few exceptions, most western intellectuals, including feminists, remained uneasily silent. They feared they would be viewed as "racists" or as "Islamophobes" if they criticized such Muslim-on-Muslim femicide. They said that such barbarism was mainly due to historical colonialism and imperialism; that the bikini is as exploitative as the burqa; that western moralism or intervention would only make things worse for women.

I was contacted by a young North American professor, who, when she spoke up for Muslim women, was attacked by other feminists as "racist." A kind friend had slipped her my book, *The Death of Feminism*. She wrote to thank me for writing it and to ask me for advice. Her quandary: She wants to assign the book to her class but fears that doing so might end her career.

Dear Dr. Chesler:

In January 2008 I will be teaching a Masters level course at X University. It is my first experience teaching in a university. In the course of developing my thoughts and syllabus a friend lent me *The Death of Feminism*. The book has expanded my thinking and given me words for another "problem with no name." I feel it will be instrumental in my teaching students how to think.

I have had two recent experiences where I have been shut down by other feminists for launching a critique of Islam and of women wearing headscarves. I have been called naïve, and racism has been implied, despite 22 yrs on the front line as a most outspoken feminist and defender of women's rights and equality rights.

How powerful is this silencing and these accusations of racism. I am not sure, as a new teacher, I could handle the uproar that will ensue if I put your book on my list. Your book, I worry, would end my career before it's started. Isn't this ridiculous, insane, intolerable, to even have this conversation, to have to fear for my career (and my life, let's be clear) for putting a book on a course outline?

I'm sure you are following the case of the 16 yr old Toronto-area girl Aqsa Parvez who was strangled to death this week by her father for being "too western". Talk about being martyred. Her death is causing a real stir here; a very brave woman from a Muslim women's organization spoke on TV last night about how rampant this ideology is and how the Imams here are feeding it.

I was attacked and ostracized by other feminists when I challenged a very liberal approach to the problem of battering in the Muslim community. The speaker said that such batterers needed to be taught that Allah and the Koran do not demand the beating of women. I said it was more complicated than that. Not a single person, many of whom were feminists and long-time activists and have known me and my work for 22 years, agreed with me or came to my support. I was alone, felt I was being seen as racist and it was very traumatic.

The Death of Feminism has affected me powerfully. Unfortunately it is rare that a book really moves one's thinking along. I have never understood why people resist having their minds stretched. I am really appreciative of your hard work and hard thinking and gutsy writing towards a better world for women and for all. Clearly you have paid a heavy price. The price of leadership I guess, though one does not expect to be crucified by one's own community. That hurts.

Pajamas Media
12/13/07

- 4 -

We Will Not Tolerate Honor Killings in the West

Aqsa Parvez, the sixteen year old slain by her father in an honor killing in Canada, was buried secretly and privately. Her teenage friends arrived hours too late at the Islamic Center at the time they had been told her funeral would take place. The kind of family and culture capable of honor murder—she and her family are all Pakistani immigrants—is also quite capable of denying her Canadian friends the opportunity of paying their last respects.

Perhaps Aqsa's family did not want a western-style "scene" at her funeral. Perhaps they viewed Aqsa's westernized friends as enemies who stole their daughter from them. No doubt they are deeply invested in the subordination of women as the very sign and symbol of their religious and cultural identity. A Muslim girl whose hair or face is uncovered is viewed as a prostitute or as an out-of-control female who, for the sake of her family's honor, must be killed.

Her father said: "My community will say you have not been able to control your daughter. This is my insult. She is making me naked."

Thus, while I understand the wrenching, cultural conflict involved, including the rejection of a shallow secular culture which condemns women in yet another way—I must, on behalf of the martyred Aqsa and on behalf of so many other girls who have suffered her fate, still say: Enough! We will not allow such criminal barbarism to gain a foothold in the West.

Aqsa Parvez could have been saved. Apparently, she had twice fled her home and had moved into a shelter. In Aqsa's case, within weeks, she ran away from home a second time.

At this point, she might have been saved—but only if the western shelter had understood that Aqsa needed the equivalent of a federal witness protection program to separate her from her family for the rest of her life. Aqsa would also have needed a warm and understanding alternative family to "adopt" her. Yes—adopt her. Life without a protective extended family is not a life most Muslim immigrants in the West would deem worth living.

Is Canada prepared to invest in such programs? Are America and Europe?

While we may or may not be able to abolish honor killings in Muslim lands, we are absolutely responsible for the proliferation of honor-based violence—or its abolition—in the West.

Forced veiling, daughter- and wife-beating, forced marriages, and honor killing are crimes in the West and must be prosecuted as such.

I favor cultural "sensitivity." However, I know that Islam is a political and military movement and not just a religion. I understand that Islamic religious beliefs may seemingly be at odds with modernity and women's rights, but I also know that other great religions have managed to find a way to straddle the Great Divide between religious belief and modern, democratic public life. Islam must do no less if its followers wish to live in the West or in the modern world. The "sensitivity" must be in both directions.

According to the *Toronto Star*, Aqsa Parvez's friends attended an anti-violence vigil at the Mississauga Civic Centre which was organized by the Canadian Council on American-Islamic Relations. They are actually the Muslim Brotherhood in America. At a CAIR event, "One speaker explained they would say a prayer to comfort those who weren't able to attend the funeral. 'Take mercy on Aqsa,' the prayer went, 'and on us who are left behind.' "

Canadians might consider creating an Aqsa Parvez Shelter for Muslim women who are being battered or threatened with honor killing.

I would go further. It is time for Western democracies to start screening potential immigrants while still in their home countries as to their views about women. If we did so, at the very least, we might have an opportunity to educate would-be immigrants in Western norms and values long before they actually take up residence amongst us.

Pajamas Media
12/17/07

- 5 -
Jailing the Intended Victims of Honor Killings
For Their Own Good

In an attempt to protect high-profile Muslim and ex-Muslim dissidents who have had fatwas issued against them—Taslima Nasreen or Ayaan Hirsi Ali, for example—the "good" people have been forced to jail them, not their attackers. Today, Nasreen says she is a "virtual prisoner" in Delhi where, for her own safety, the Indian government has stashed her after a mob of fanatic Islamists tried to kill her. When Hirsi Ali was similarly threatened, the Dutch government was forced to essentially "jail" her for her own good.

Where will this end? With all the "moderate" and dissident Muslims and ex-Muslims in jail? How big will this jail be? How much will it cost? Can the world's governments afford this? How many people will have to be jailed (or given 24/7 police protection) before the West really understands that a new kind of war has been declared against us—one that we may have to fight in ways other than by jailing innocent civilians?

Hint: There are no civilians in this new kind of War.

What is the price of dissent? How much will governments be willing and able to pay to protect women from their own families who intend to honor-murder them? Or who control them in extreme ways? Today, a Saudi woman and her advocates are appealing to the Saudi King to save her from her own brothers who forced her to divorce her husband and the father of her children because the husband was deemed tribally unworthy. The woman is now distraught and threatening suicide.

The British government announced a new program that would

better protect and prosecute honor killings in the West. The approach will follow an anti-Mafia model in that the British police now understand that the equivalent of a federal witness protection program will be required for both intended victims and for witnesses who might be willing to testify on their behalf.

I recently saw Marjane Satrapi's film *Persepolis*. Her heroine, "Marjane," is a child when Khomeini comes to power. She is a very young adult when she leaves Teheran first for Vienna, and then for Paris. Marjane is a feminist warrior. (And so is her grandmother!) Both are portrayed as daring and sophisticated. The jailing, torture, and agonizing deaths of the regime's political opponents, both male and female, is rendered in a soulful and heartbreaking way—as is the regime's diabolical persecution of women.

The West, where women are not punished for how they dress or because they dance or even sleep with men, is still not a welcoming place for a young Muslim immigrant entirely on her own. The young Marjane ends up homeless on the streets of Vienna, where she nearly dies. The difficulty of integrating into a Western-style life, without any family protection or connections, sends Marjane back home to Teheran where at least she has family. Grim Iranian political reality ultimately returns her to the West.

When Westerners fight about Muslim immigration and about alleged "racism" towards Muslims, they are often talking about two distinct populations. Those who argue for an open door policy are thinking about Muslim and ex-Muslim immigrants in flight from Islamist persecution who require and may deserve asylum in the West. Those who argue against open immigration are thinking about their Islamist persecutors and about those Muslim immigrants who intend to practice Islamic gender and religious apartheid in the West.

Pajamas Media
12/27/07

- 6 -

Bhutto's Assassination May Be Viewed As a Political and Cultural Honor Killing

Benazir Bhutto was the first woman Prime Minister of a Muslim nation, and she symbolized an unacceptably Western form of female ambition and achievement. She had attended Harvard/ Radcliffe and Oxford. She spoke English—perhaps more fluently than she spoke her native Sindi or Urdu. She had once dressed as Western women do. Indeed, many Muslim women from wealthy families, including educators and feminists, have done so for a long time. They may not be able to do so now.

Although male politicians and dissidents are assassinated with impunity, still, in a sense, Bhutto's assassination may have also been a political and cultural version of an honor killing. Indira Gandhi, was the first and only female Prime Minister of India; accused of both corruption and cruelty, she was assassinated by Sikh nationalists. Bhutto's assassination was a Muslim-on-Muslim murder. Taliban fanatics decided that, in addition to allegations of normalized corruption, Bhutto was also--and unacceptably, publicly, too-Western, and they sentenced her to death for this sin.

Pakistan is known for its many bloody honor murders.

In 1999, in Lahore, Pakistan, Samria Imran was shot dead in her feminist lawyer's office by a man whom her parents had hired to kill her. Her crime? Having dared to seek a divorce.

In 2001, in Gujar Khan, Pakistan, Zahida Perveen's husband wrongly suspected her of adultery. He attacked her, gouging out both of her eyes and severing her nose and her ears. His male relatives honored him for doing so. A team of American doctors subsequently fitted Zahida with glass eyes and prostheses for her ears and nose.

In 2002, a tribal council in the Punjab sentenced eighteen-year-old Mukhtaran Bibi to be gang-raped. This was a punishment for something her twelve year-old brother had allegedly done: Walking with a girl from a higher-status tribe. (Actually, he had been sexually abused by Mastoi men who sought to cover up their crime in this way.) Mukhtaran Bibi's father was forced to witness her gang-rape, after which she was driven naked through the streets. Mukhtaran Bibi took the matter to court; amazingly, the gang-rapists were eventually arrested and convicted. Mukhtaran Bibi was given round-the-clock government protection. The rapists have vowed to kill her anyway.

Did Benazir Bhutto think that her membership in a historic dynasty would protect her from the war against women that jihadists are currently waging? Did she think that the government could protect her from such woman-haters who would vote al-Qaeda into power if they had the chance?

Although both privileged and corrupt, Bhutto was still one of the "moderate" Muslims for whom the West yearns. Al-Qaeda and the Pakistani Taliban murdered her. Al-Qaeda commander Mustafa Abual-Yazid claimed responsibility and was quoted as saying: "We terminated the most precious American asset which vowed to defeat the mujahideen." Her assassin's willingness to die in order to kill, terrorize, and impose his ideology upon others is precisely what keeps other "moderate" Muslims silent.

Pajamas Media
12/28/07

- 7 -

Honor Killings in Dallas: Made in the USA

On January 1st, 2008, an Egyptian Arab Muslim father in Dallas, Texas shot his two teenage daughters to death because he disapproved of their American ways. Their names were Amina and Sarah Said and their father's name is Yasser Abdul Said. They were 17 and 18 years old and their friends considered them "geniuses." Yasser was a taxi driver.

Perhaps the way in which Amina and Sarah dressed, and how they thought, shamed their father, Yasser. He was no longer in control of his women, which provoked his need to kill them. Perhaps their flowering sexuality enraged him because it made him desire them—and from this he concluded that other men might desire them too—and if he could not have them, no man could.

Blogs, (*Hot Air, Atlas Shrugs, Jihad Watch*), and the local Texas media (the *Dallas Morning News*) were all over this. The only national coverage of this story was contained in the *Washington Times*. Why did the national and international media stay clear of this story? Perhaps they chose to dig deeper first, or maybe they were waiting for an arrest to be made. But one also wonders: Were they afraid of being accused of "Islamophobia" if they reported the story? Did they not want to use the word "Arab" or "Muslim" lest they be attacked as "racists"?

Earlier, on January 3, 2008, the hardcopy edition of the *New York Times* carried a story about a non-Muslim (probably Hindu) honor killing in Chicago, in which a father, Subhash Chander, killed his pregnant daughter, son-in-law and 3-year-old grandson "because he disapproved of his daughter's marriage" to a lower-caste man. All the protagonists are from India or are of Indian origin. So far, I can find no coverage of

37

the Texas honor killing by a Muslim father in the pages of the Paper of Record.

Amina and Sarah Said also had unacceptably non-Muslim boy-friends. They told their friends that their father was angry with them for "not acting like proper Muslim girls." Thus, these sisters feared for their lives. They told people that their father was threatening them.

They could have been saved if a school or police official had been trained to pre-emptively recognize and rescue the girls and women in danger of being killed by their families in honor killings.

Yasser Abdul Said has made the Most Wanted List. However, I am told that the police have described the murder as senseless, baffling, puzzling, etc.—as opposed to as an obvious, old-fashioned honor killing. Perhaps I'm wrong, but has anyone thought to look for him in a mosque?

Pajamas Media
1/3/08

- 8 -

The Story is Bigger than an Honor Murder in Dallas, or, What Happens in Dallas Stays in Dallas

D ays after the shocking and shameful double honor murders in Dallas took place, the mainstream media continues to maintain its enormous and profound silence. The murderer remains at large and is strongly suspected to be the father of the slain girls: Yasser Abdul Said. I have been told that both the AP and Fox affiliates put the story on the wire but it has not traveled beyond Dallas.

Thus, the story is now also about the national media's utter failure to cover the Dallas-based honor murders of two teenage sisters, Sarah and Amina Said—and it is also about their father Yasser, an Egyptian-born taxi driver, who has managed to avoid capture for five full days. As of this writing, he has still not been found.

Is there connection between these two stories? I fear there might be, at least in this sense: If Yasser Said's photo had been plastered all across our television screens and on the pages of our morning newspapers maybe—just maybe—someone might have recognized him or maybe—just maybe—someone at a mosque might have been shamed by this dishonorable act and been encouraged to mount a Muslim religious campaign to find and turn him over to the police.

Authorities have offered a $10,000.00 reward for Yasser Said.

As I've previously noted, on January 3rd, the *New York Times* covered a daughter's murder in Chicago—but the murder was committed by a drunken and abusive Hindu father which subliminally is meant to "prove" that non-Muslim fathers also kill their pregnant daughters, sons-in-law and grandchildren.

It's not as if the mainstream media is quiet about Muslim Matters. In fact, the January 5th-6th issue of the *New York Times Book Review* is entirely devoted to Islam. The lead essay is a sterling example of the subtle disinformation campaign being waged by the overly glamorized Tariq Ramadan and is titled "Reading the Koran." Is this title a play on or a playful admonition towards Azar Nafisi's best-seller *Reading Lolita in Tehran*—a far more comprehensible and literary piece of writing but one which is highly critical of Islamist Iran?

And just today, the Paper of Record has a piece about domestic violence in the Muslim communities but the headline reads: "Abused Muslim Women in U.S. Gain Advocates. Sympathetic Clerics Ally With Activists." All's well, Islam is not the problem, Imams to the rescue. (Would that this were so.) According to this article, one brave mullah (truly, peace be upon him) and some religious Muslims are "saving" abused Muslim women—not only from murderously violent Muslim men—but also from the female and feminist staff at domestic violence shelters (read: secular feminists) who are too spooked by hijab and halal eating requirements to be of much use. Or perhaps their western and modern ways spook abused Muslim, tribal women.

Earlier today, the Said girls had two funerals: one was a large Christian Baptist-style funeral (!) at which a Catholic priest presided and the second took place in a mosque. (Is Mrs. Said a convert to Islam from Christianity or did teenage schoolmates wish to be consoled by a Christian service?) Mrs. Tissy Said and her teenage son has gone into hiding. The family was, allegedly, plagued by domestic violence. The deceased teenagers (may Sarah and Amina rest in peace) had both been very smart and also afraid of their father. They had intellectual and professional ambitions and they had non-Muslim boyfriends. This passes for a capital offense in many Muslim families.

Only a few honor murders may need to take place in order to intimidate and humble an entire generation of Muslim women. Honor murderers might be doing the "dirty" work for tribal Islam.

This might be one reason why Muslim religious and community leaders do not step forward to denounce honor murders and ostracize the honor killing families for doing so—but perhaps they also fear losing a certain advantage. Both Osama bin Laden and Yasser Said profit psychologically and economically when women are willing, not rebellious, slaves.

Pajamas Media
1/3/08

- 9 -

Human Sacrifice in Dallas

This story out of Dallas is an awful one. The mainstream media has certainly failed their task but so have the local police and social service agencies—at least according to the (still only local) report published yesterday in the *Dallas Morning News*.

In 1998, when they were 8 and 9 years-old, these slaughtered girls accused their father of sexual abuse. Their mother swore it was true. The girls then said that they had lied. The authorities believed them.

The same authorities never intervened against this father who, according to unnamed family members, "was given to fits of violence, threats and gun-waving rants about how Western culture was corrupting the chastity of his daughters."

No one saved these girls, no one—no child protection agency--stopped the life-long violence against them, no one arrested their father—because he was only violent towards his wife and daughters. He was not violent towards anyone else. He did not disturb the peace. Thus, he was allowed to prey on his own flesh and blood.

We are talking about America, not about Egypt—where Yasser Abdul Said came from and where he may now be hiding. We are talking about America where American feminists have revolutionized our understanding of domestic violence. The police, the judiciary, and social services have tried to keep up—but it is a huge problem. Even feminists have been cautious when it is Muslim men who sexually abuse their female children. They fear that condemning it might be seen as "racist."

Still, there are some real Western heroes who have saved tortured Muslim women. Often, they had to put such victims into federal witness protection programs because nothing else will stop the entire Muslim family from coming after them.

Yasser Abdul Said was a violent man who used brutal force against his wife and daughters. People in Texas knew about it. People cared about it but no one cared enough—or were willing to risk death by daring to come between a man and his prey. Non-tribal battered wives who are held hostage long enough are reluctant to press charges, and they have been too beaten down to feel they can start life on their own; some come to identify with or to serve their tormentors.

Yes, this happens in non-Muslim families all the time and people rarely stop it. Usually, the beaten-down woman is the one who alone finally decides to try and save her own life—or the lives of her children. Often, when wives leave violent men, that's when they are killed. Or, if they kill in self-defense, the women often get life sentences, sometimes with no parole.

According to the Dallas paper, the father, who is still missing, has a long history of family violence. He married his wife, Patricia, ("Tissy"), when Patricia was only fifteen years old. Patricia's sister, Connie Moggio, "said his controlling and violent nature gripped the family from the start." According to Moggio, "once, he shot out the tires on his wife's car to keep her home." Another time, he blocked Moggio's car when she was trying to help Tissy and the children escape. Amina was seen at school with red welts and bruises and she once confided that her father had kicked her in the face. Everyone knew about the threats. He threatened to kill her.

According to the Dallas paper, the day after Christmas the girls ran away—and they ran away with boyfriends who were trying to save them. Their mother talked them into returning; to this day, their brother, Islam, and their mother, Tissy, insist that what happened has nothing to do with Islam (the religion) or with the Arab Middle East (the culture).

America failed these two daughters, bright with promise. Did we fail them because we don't care about dark-skinned Muslim (girls)—or because we are so afraid of interfering with any dark-skinned man's religious and cultural right to subordinate, torture, and ultimately sacrifice "his" women that we choose to look the other way?

Why is the mainstream media still silent? Perhaps if one of the many Presidential candidates would comment about this case, the media would follow suit.

Pajamas Media
1/10/08

43

- 10 -
Jihad Comes to Dallas

"I have been warned to shut up. But when Yasser Abdul Said killed those girls he did not just spill Muslim blood on American soil. He shed my blood. I am not going to be quiet. I made a promise at their funerals that I would speak out."

I am talking to Gail Gartrell, the great-aunt of Amina and Sarah Said who were honor murdered by their father, Yasser Said, on New Year's Day, 2008. As of this writing, Yasser Said has not yet been captured.

The girls were murdered in Irving, Texas, an area with a large Muslim population that is also known to some experts as a place where Hezbollah and the Muslim Brotherhood may be active. Gail and the other female relatives with whom I have spoken believe that Yasser Said is "possibly some kind of terrorist...Yasser always seemed to have a lot of guns, machineguns—they're illegal here—but handguns too." Gail tells me:

"It's another face of jihad. These men come here from Egypt, they marry American women in order to become American citizens. The American wives convert to Islam. Then, they have Muslim children who are natural-born American citizens—but who are raised to hate America and to want to live under Sharia law. Then, these men expect their teenage American daughters to marry much older Muslim men from Egypt in arranged marriages. I know that Yasser wanted Amina to marry someone from Egypt."

On March 8, 2008, nine relatives who live in Texas and are Christians, gathered on the spot where Amina and Sarah were murdered to "celebrate their lives." The spot is right near a shooting range and shots continued to ring out as they and their Minister spoke. (Gail told me that here is another example of Yasser knowing "exactly what he was doing. He did not want anyone to pay attention to a gun going off when he shot his daughters dead.")

The girl's own mother, "Tissy" Said, was not at the March 8th Celebration. She is the one who effectively lured her daughters to their deaths. Their brother, Islam, was also not there; Islam is Yasser and Tissy's first-born son.

Gail is proud that her great-niece Amina refused to accept an arranged marriage, glad that they were both brave enough to run away. Both girls had non-Muslim boyfriends. Neither girl wanted to wear hijab. Clearly, these American-style choices are all capital crimes to someone like Yasser Said.

After my original articles ran, Gail Gartrell, Amina and Sarah's great-aunt, reached out to me. I have now talked with her, with two other great-aunts: Joyce and Jill, and with Connie, who is Tissy's sister.

Gail, Connie, Jill, and Joyce are all risking their lives in speaking out. Here's an idea of what they are saying.

That Yasser is probably still hiding out in Texas; that his brothers are hiding him; that Yasser and his brothers may have committed another honor murder in the past. They were allegedly heard plotting to kill their own sister when she threatened to leave her husband; that Yasser beat and sexually assaulted his two daughters; that Tissy, their mother, both denied and enabled the sexual and physical abuse.

Since the double honor murder, Tissy has been living with a brother-in-law (the murderer's brother). She has broken with her Texas female relatives and has warned them to shut up. Here's what Gail Gartrell has to say:

"Tissy is a dead woman, no matter what happens. They will kill her if she leaves. But they will also kill her even if she stays. Why? Because she once dared to run away with the girls, if only briefly. But she came back to Yasser and she convinced the girls to come back. I believe that they will kill her because she ran."

Pajamas Media
3/10/08

45

- 11 -
An American-Muslim State of Mind

Islam Said blames his sisters' deaths on their boyfriends. On March 8, 2008, the Lewisville High School celebrated the lives of the honor murdered Amina and Sarah Said. Local media was there. I watched as Islam grabbed the microphone and characterized his sisters' boyfriends as "gang members" who "killed his sisters." He also said: "They pulled the trigger, not my dad. My dad is the victim here."

It is absolutely crucial for Westerners, especially Americans, to understand his mind-set. This is a cultural and political mind-set which has nothing to do with the color of one's skin and everything to do with one's tribal ideology. Despite heated denial and much controversy, it is also a mindset which is correlated with the practice of Islam in its current, highly politicized, jihadic mode.

Thus, when anyone tries to describe the crimes against humanity which are committed in the name of Islam (the religion, not the man whom I quote above), both Muslims and politically progressive non-Muslim Westerners cry "racism."

But this is a totalitarian tactic used to silence those who dare to expose injustice and who wish to resist terror and tyranny. The charge of "racism" is a rallying cry which is first used against dark-skinned Muslim and ex-Muslim dissidents. The lovely dark-skinned ex-Muslim feminist freedom-fighter, Ayaan Hirsi Ali, has been characterized as a "racist" in Holland and in the pages of America's *Nation* magazine. This tactic works best among guilty, liberal Westerners who really do want to atone for or abolish, finally, the West's awful history of racism.

However, the West crusaded against and finally abolished slavery. Many of us remain ashamed of and conflicted about its terrible legacy.

Muslims have never launched a campaign against their own anti-black racism. The Arab Muslim and African use of slaves continues to this day in many forms, both in the Middle East and in the West, especially among United Nations diplomats who are posted here.

Muslim employers in Saudi Arabia are not apologizing to their Philippina servants whom they imprison and routinely force to work around the clock both as domestics and as sex slaves. Ethnic Arab Muslims in Sudan are not guilty about gang-raping black African girls and women in Darfur—no more than they are guilty about genocidally exterminating black Africans who are also Muslims, Christians, and animists.

It's the same mindset that inspires Islam Said to view his father, Yasser Abdul Said, the honor murderer, as the true "victim." The defender of the faith, (whether that faith is conceived of as one's religion or as one's family "honor"), is always the "victim." Yes, even human homicide bombs who blow up innocent civilians in Iraq, Pakistan, and Afghanistan and who gun down Jewish children in religious schools in Jerusalem are viewed as victims and martyrs. Their supporters do not view them as murderous aggressors, nor do they view their indoctrinators or themselves as such.

While I would like to attribute Islamic gender apartheid to a cluster of factors including normalized childhood abuse, poverty, and a lack of education, it is also increasingly clear that wealthy and well-educated Muslims, who live in Muslim majority countries and in the West, share the same views. Based on extensive interviews that I have done with the female relatives of the murdered Texas teenagers, it is clear that:

a) Amina and Sarah were expected to wear headscarves. Their failure to do so, their "hidden" lives as normal American teenagers, doomed them.

b) Amina and Sarah were expected to enter into arranged marriages against their will to much older Egyptian men whom they had never met. Their refusal to do so doomed them.

c) Amina and Sarah were expected to keep quiet about the horrific sexual, physical, and psychological abuse which was heaped upon them by their father, mother, and brother. Their failure to do so doomed them.

d) Amina and Sarah were not supposed to have "boyfriends." At the very least, their friends, both male and female, were not supposed to be Christians. The fact that they were friendly with Christian male teenagers doomed them.

e) Amina and Sarah were supposed to hate America and to choose Sharia law. Their failure to do so doomed them.

These are only some of the "rules" that Amina and Sarah were expected to obey. One of my informants has quoted their brother Islam, who often stalked his sisters, as saying: "They knew the rules. They broke them." Islam is saying that it is their fault that his father had to kill them.

Thus, whenever you see a woman in a face veil, headscarf, or burqa, it is very likely that these rules also apply to her.

For the record: Allow me to repeat what I have written before, namely, that there are many individual Muslims who are personally peaceful and who favor human rights for everyone, including women and infidels. There are also individual Muslims who oppose and who have fled Islamic apartheid regimes. However, most Muslims do not publicly condemn the barbarism committed in the name of their religion. Only a brave handful do.

There were also individual Germans in the Nazi era who did not personally hate the Jews, gypsies, anarchists, or homosexuals; a few even risked their lives to save such targeted "enemies." However, most Germans (and Poles, Austrians, Ukrainians, etc.) chose to opportunistically profit from the persecution of the Jews and refused to risk anything in order to resist Hitler. Their failure to do so meant that they enabled and collaborated with him. To quote Edmund Burke: "All that is necessary for the forces of evil to win in the world is for enough good men (and women) to do nothing."

I stand ready and willing to honor and to work with all those Muslims and non-Muslims who oppose Islamic gender and religious apartheid. Our lives depend upon such heroic collaborations.

Pajamas Media
3/12/08

- 12 -

Murderous Mothers

Texas-born Patricia (Tissy) Said, formerly of the Owens family, is the mother who lured her two teenage daughters, Sarah and Amina, to their deaths at the hands of their own father this past New Years Day in Dallas. How can a mother do such a thing? Even if her own life was threatened, even if her husband Yasser had literally held a gun to her head and told her to trick her daughters into returning, isn't a mother supposed to sacrifice herself for her children? Or at least to protect them? What can explain such a perversion of maternal instinct and of the life force itself?

Tissy Said is not the first mother to have participated in an honor killing on American soil. In 1989, in St Louis, Missouri, Brazilian-born second wife, Maria Isa, held her daughter Palestina ("Tina") Isa down for twenty minutes as her father, Zein Isa, a Palestinian Abu Nidal terrorist operative, viciously and repeatedly stabbed her to death. Zein Isa had the same mind-set that Islam Said, the brother of the honor murdered Dallas girls has. Isa said that "he had stabbed his daughter in self-defense, that she had so shamed him, that he had to commit a crime to restore his honor."

Palestina tried very hard to please her parents. She was overworked, treated "like dirt," chronically beaten and constantly abused, both verbally and psychologically. But, like Amina and Sarah Said, Palestina also had academic ambitions—and she had a non-Muslim and African-American "boyfriend," who was merely a friend, not a beau. Such Americanized behavior doomed all these honor murdered girls.

Both research and anecdotal evidence document that women collaborate, both directly and indirectly, in honor killings. According to a

49

study which I cite in my 2002 book, *Woman's Inhumanity to Woman*, Arab girls and women gossip about and slander others girls and women in a way that demands that the men "do something" to restore their families' honor. Palestina Isa's three sisters kept pestering their father to "do something about the nigger-loving whore."

Sometimes, a mother might physically murder her own daughter on her own, by herself, directly, not indirectly. For example, in 2003, on the West Bank, Amira Abu Hanhan Qaoud, brutally murdered her 13-year-old daughter Rofayda who had been raped and impregnated by her two brothers. Amira was quoted as saying that "I had to protect my children. This is the only way I could protect my family's honor." Her sons were her children—not her daughter.

I am not saying that this mother in Texas murdered her own daughters physically, with her own hands, am I? In Tissy's favor, let me note that, in late December, she ran away with her girls, whom she also calls her "angels." At that time, Tissy also admitted to one of my interviewees that Yasser had threatened to kill the girls. In addition, she paid two months rent up front for a place in Tulsa, Oklahoma, where she and the girls were going to live.

Once, long ago, Tissy had also admitted that Yasser had been sexually abusing Sarah and Amina when they were seven and eight years old. But she didn't turn him in—her mother, the girl's maternal grandmother, did that. And, according to her Owens relatives, Tissy laughed it off, "giggled," minimized it all. Tissy stood by her man and she helped the children recant their sworn testimony because otherwise, "daddy would go to jail." The girls subsequently told relatives that their recantation was false.

After Tissy's own mother had turned Yasser in to the police, Tissy kept all the relatives on her side of the family far away from the girls. She and Yasser kept moving, roving, "like nomads," (or like sociopaths), to escape school or child protective agency scrutiny.

According to my interviewees, Tissy also went to jail for her man when she was caught collecting welfare and a housing subsidy based on Yasser's presumed absence. (In reality, he would sneak into the government subsidized housing at night.) Tissy also worked as a store clerk, as did her daughters. According to my interviewees, Tissy, not Yasser, was the main support of the family. Yasser only worked as a taxi driver "when he felt like it." And he kept his money to himself—or so they think.

Even now, when her daughters are dead and her man is still on the run, Tissy has chosen to live with one of Yasser's brothers and has warned her great-aunts not to speak out and not to call this cold-blooded murder an "honor killing." She claims that her first-born son Islam needs her, and that he has grown up with his first cousins on his father's side. Indeed, Islam's need for her—perhaps her need for Islam—is the reason Tissy gave for having to return to Yasser, leaving her girls behind somewhere in Oklahoma.

According to my informants, "Islam bosses his mother around. And he stalked his sisters, he spied on them. But Islam also spends all his time at home with his mother. That's where he's been ever since he dropped out of school when he was 14. There is something wrong with him." My informants tell me that Tissy could never control her son; that she minimizes, denies, and forgives his "weird, frightening, anti-social behaviors." He is her wounded child. He still needs her. None of my interviewees are clear about whether Islam Said suffers from a learning disability, a psychiatric condition, or has simply been raised to be an aggressive predator against women with a deep hatred of America.

"It's all of the above," my interviewees say.

After Tissy left her daughters in Tulsa, she returned home to Dallas. And then Tissy called her daughters and begged them to come back to Dallas to accompany her to put flowers on their grandmothers' grave (the very grandmother who, a decade before, had turned their father in for child sexual abuse). Tissy told them that Yasser was contrite, that he only wanted to have tea with his daughters and to talk things through.

On television, Islam Said insisted that the boyfriends of Amina and Sarah were the ones who pulled the trigger. I think that Tissy's hand steadied that trigger far more fatefully.

I called Tissy. She answered immediately. I told her that I was interested in her side of this story. (I am.) She was indignant that I had called "so late" (it was 9pm), and ordered me to "never call again." She sounded very angry. Perhaps she was not alone, perhaps her every word was being monitored, both internally and externally. Maybe she was Yasser's victim too. Maybe mitigating circumstances exist that would diminish the charges that will—or should eventually be brought against her.

I asked my interviewees, four of Tissy's female relatives who represent both her maternal and paternal lines, whether they thought that Yasser beat her, whether Tissy was afraid of him. All four were adamant: Tissy loves him, he never battered her, they never saw any bruises on her.

By contrast, over the years, the Said girls were notoriously bruised, and had red welts visible on their bodies. In one instance, Yasser had embedded one of his daughter's braces in her lip. Tissy covered up each instance. And she never left him because he battered their daughters.

My four informants do not believe that Tissy is now being or was ever held hostage. Of course, if she kept herself apart, her relatives might not know such details. Even though they remember incidents in which Yasser did not let Tissy leave the house and an incident in which he once blocked her car–Tissy could have left at some other time.

Or could she?

I asked my interviewees if Tissy is simple-minded, mentally ill, or mentally retarded. They all said no—although they did view her as "very passive." One female relative thought that she might have been "jealous" of her ambitious, freedom-loving daughters but hastened to add that this was "only her opinion." All four interviewees did think that, after so many years of marriage to Yasser, that Tissy was probably brainwashed.

Brainwashing is often accomplished by isolating the target from others and immersing her in a culture of like-minded people. Both threats and rewards characterize a brainwashing campaign. This seems a likely possibility in Tissy's case—which, however, does not mean that she is morally or even legally innocent in the matter of her daughters' abuse and death.

At the beginning of this article, I asked how such a perversion of maternal behavior can be understood. At one level, it is quite simple to understand: Tissy behaves in the same way that any normal, uneducated Arab Muslim wife might behave. What makes such behavior unexpected, or culturally "abnormal," is that Tissy was born in America and raised in a Christian (although not in an especially religious) household.

However, like many girls in the Muslim world (and sadly, among the poor everywhere), Tissy dropped out of high school; she may only have completed the 8th grade. At fourteen or fifteen, she married Yasser, who apparently presented himself to her family as a wealthy Egyptian "prince"—someone who had property and other holdings back in Egypt. Unlike many American girls who cleave to their families of origin, Tissy's primary alliance is not with her own family but with her son, her husband, and with her husband's family. This is typical behavior for Arabs and Muslim women but is less typical of Europeans and Americans.

I am indebted to my colleague, the psychoanalyst and Arabist, Nancy H. Kobrin, for the following insight: What balances such family dynamics out and partially "protects" the women in a culture which otherwise despises and fears them are the practices of arranged marriage to one's first cousin and the relationship between brothers and sisters. If one's mother-in-law is also one's aunt, a daughter-in-law might be safer living with a family with whom she has probably grown up than among complete strangers.

Also, if Tissy had Arab Muslim brothers of her own, they might potentially have come to her aid against her husband or on behalf of her daughters, but they might also have helped her husband enforce the rules and customs of Islamic gender apartheid against her. These customs preserve a peaceful status quo partly by keeping the wealth within one's own family.

In the Arab and Muslim world—and in Tissy's world in Dallas—daughters are nothing but "trouble." Their chastity has to be guarded, their modesty ensured. Otherwise, they will bring shame to their entire family. Among other things, this means that no one will marry the family's sons or the other daughters. Disobedient daughters are dangerous and expendable.

But Tissy lives in Texas. Why does she behave as if she lived in the Middle East?

Some of Tissy's female relatives believe that she converted to Islam. However, they are not entirely sure since she has behaved in secretive ways. They have seen (or were told about) photos of Tissy and Yasser in Arab dress, posing with guns and knives in exaggerated "jihadic" poses. But they are unclear about whether Yasser and his family are religious or not. Or political. Or criminal. Violent—yes. Murderously "crazy" on the subject of women—yes. Gun-loving—yes.

But some non-Arabs and non-Muslims in America also engage in these behaviors, but not necessarily in all of these behaviors simultaneously: Some own guns and participate in a macho gun culture. Some batter and stalk their wives and some physically and sexually abuse their daughters. Non-Arab and non-Muslim mothers also stand by their batterers. Some have also been known to scapegoat their daughters for having "provoked" paternal lust.

But such non-Muslim, non-Arab, and non-tribal parents do not usually kill their daughters. Western culture has at least criminalized wife- and daughter-battering, incest, stalking, and femicide. While we may not always be successful in preventing or prosecuting such behaviors, we know that they constitute crimes.

What might we have to do to prevent honor killings in America? Can we eject all people whose cultural backgrounds value honor killings? Can we refuse to allow people from such cultures to become residents or citizens here? Can we "test" them on these issues? Or pre-educate them? If this approach became known public policy, some people might simply lie.

What if people who come from an honor killing culture desire asylum from it? What if the women of such cultures, transplanted to American shores, are relying upon American law to prevail and to save their lives? What is the "American" thing to do?

I do not have a simple answer. However, Sarah and Amina Said were American citizens. America was their culture. Their desire to live as Americans, and not as Arab Muslims in Egypt, is precisely what doomed them. They were each one of ours. We failed them. How can we do better?

I would like to acknowledge the brave and informed assistance of Gail Gartrell, Jill Owens, Joyce Boucher, and Connie Maggio.

Pajamas Media
3/16/08

- 13 -
The New York (Islamic) Times

How do we cut down on honor murders in the West? According to some people, you do whatever it takes to keep the girls from dishonoring their families so that their families do not have to honor-murder them.

According to *The New York Times*, "home schooling" the girls in America, re-creating a feudal, rural, parallel universe in California in which girls and women are kept hidden and apart, might be the sensible and merciful alternative to honor murders in The New World.

At a time when Islamists are at full jihadic throttle, *The New York Times* features a mild and lovely—a truly non-judgmental article about the proliferation of home schooling among Muslim communities in America.

How can anyone criticize home schooling? It's a venerable, Super-American Back-to-the-Land and Back-to-the-Bible custom. Well, according to the article, this folksy custom might be under serious advisement since we've learned that Osama Bin Laden's American mouthpiece, Adam Gadahn, was himself home schooled in rural California.

But really: How can I criticize the desire of immigrants to cling to their customs and their faiths? Isn't America's history one in which successive waves of immigrants retained their ethnic and religious identities—while their children and grandchildren became integrated into American culture? And don't we still allow religious communities to hold themselves apart and to train their women to be docile, modest, family-oriented servants of both men and God?

Well, yes, but I have always protested keeping women down in the name of religion, and have been quick to applaud the accomplishments of religious (and anti-religious) women who enter the modern professions, wage feminist battles against violence against women within their communities, and who also become both secular and religious leaders and authorities in their various faiths.

So, why is the New York Times making so subtle and so powerful an alliance with Islamists against women?

The way propaganda works is through persistence, subtlety, and images. Every week, sometimes every day, the *Times* has a Muslim- or rather, an Islamist-friendly article, usually with positive color photos. The Paper of Record knows how to cover its considerable derriere. Thus, it is careful to have comments from "both sides of the aisle" as long as the critical comments are buried-in-the-balance and do not deflect from the bottom line—propaganda having its way with us.

Ian Buruma writes an article that is so cleverly cobbled together than most readers do not understand that it is meant as a devastating attack on the heroic Ayaan Hirsi Ali. Tariq Ramadan, the genetic and intellectual heir to the man who founded the Muslim Brotherhood is, again and again, glowingly profiled, reviewed, published, and shown wearing trendy western dress. Noah Feldman continues to condemn Orthodox Judaism and to extol the virtues of Muslim religious (Sharia) law, not only for Turkey but for an unsuspecting West. Young, attractive women wearing headscarves are shown and they are quoted saying sophisticated, friendly things.

Steadily, slowly, inexorably, Western readers are being softened for the "kill," seasoned and habituated to accept the subordination of women as an inviolate cultural and religious reality.

Take a look at the March 26th edition of *The New York Times*. Titled "Resolute or Fearful, Many Muslims Turn to Home Schooling," the article was five columns wide and featured two sympathetic color photos. Both show female teenagers wearing head-and-shoulder hijab. The larger photo resonates for Westerners who may have seen similar images in great paintings of the Middle Ages; the photo somewhat resembles a particular Vermeer. The domestic intimacy, symmetry, harmony is all there. We are meant to "like" the young and smiling girl in hijab who, according to the caption, is reading the Koran.

The article explains that many Muslim families in California have opted for home schooling for their daughters; forty percent of Pakistani and southeast Asian families "in the district" have done so. Why? Many possible reasons are given: So that Muslim children will not be teased or mocked; exposed to pork; "corrupted" by American influences, but mainly, so that their girls do not engage in behaviors that would "dishonor" their families and require that they be honor murdered.

For example, Hajra Bibi stopped attending public school and began home schooling when she reached puberty. "Her family wanted her to clean and cook for her male relatives...'Some men don't like it when you wear American clothes–they don't think it is a good thing for girls... We don't want anyone to point a finger at us, to say that we are bad."

Because that might render them unmarriageable and as candidates to be honor murdered.

The smiling, Vermeer-like photo and the additional photo of three girls wearing heavy hijab and playing with their yo-yos, soften the blow that this information might otherwise elicit.

Why should American citizens or future American citizens, in California or elsewhere, be taught that girls must wear hijab or even niqab (face covering); that boys and men are entitled to boss girls around; that a minimal education and an arranged marriage to your cousin is all that an American female citizen needs? Why live in America if what you want to do is keep the girls culturally illiterate and down on the farm?

The Orthodox Judaism that Noah Feldman spurns does not practice honor murders. If a woman marries outside her fundamentalist faith, she may indeed be ostracized but then again, she may not. If a Christian woman marries outside her faith...but you get my point. The countless successive immigrant waves to America did not practice honor murders. Perhaps an ugly and agonizing ostracism as well as flat-out breaks took place; killing to enforce religious norms did not.

Can we just give it some time, wait and see, give the new-immigrant-on-the block a break? Well sure, but let's remember that some third generation immigrants in the UK have become radical Islamists. Given the "politically correct" way in which the British coddled Muslim immigrants (I view this as racist, others would view it as simply incompetent), and the rise of the radical, global mullahs, the expected integration did not "take."

There might be something different about contemporary Islam that does not lend itself to integration.

Why is *The New York Times* engaged in disinformation about such an important topic?

Pajamas Media
3/27/08

- 14 -

Still Dead in Dallas

Old News: The sisters, Sarah and Amina Said, are still dead; their father-murderer, Yasir Abdul Said, has not yet been found; the mainstream media continues its uncanny silence.

What's New: The reward for Said's capture has been doubled and Tissy Said, his wife and the mother of the two murdered girls, has been ejected from the home of her extended paternal Muslim family. Her beloved son, Islam (from whom she would not willingly part), has been sent away from her. The Said family presumably want him to be "around a man" (his paternal uncle in New York City) and not around his mother. According to Tissy's great-aunt, the brave, outspoken, Gail Gartrell:

> I feel Tissy is in grave danger from her own son. This is what I think his uncle is working through with Islam in New York. I fear his return. All the nieces and nephews in the Said family are accusing Tissy of this being her fault. They have turned on her. They blame her for allowing her daughters to see American boys. She has become the enemy. When I spoke to Tissy, she seemed more upset about this betrayal than about anything else. She told me she did not care if he (Islam? or Yasser?) killed her or not. Now, her spirit is broken since her Muslim family has walked away from her. Tissy told me that she wants to be buried next to her daughters.

Tissy is an American citizen who is about 36 years old. She was married to Yasser at fifteen.

Gartrell described being recently preyed upon by a local Texas reporter who said she was a private investigator—in an effort to gain access to Tissy. The ruse did not work but it sowed discord among family members. Gartrell and other great-aunts have, reportedly, been threatened online and warned not to write about this case. (One great-aunt was writing a book—she may no longer be doing so.)

Gartrell tells me that no one can save Tissy but Tissy herself. She has to "contact the police for help. A detective said the only way to protect her was if she would be willing to leave Islam and go into hiding!"

Why is the media so disinterested? Their disinterest makes it harder for the police to find Yasser and encourages the next honor murderer to strike. Chances are, he will not be successfully pursued. Chances are, the world will not much care. What about the young boys who tried to save Sarah and Amina and who remain in hiding? The media silence endangers them more each day.

Pajamas Media
5/18/08

CNN Newspeak in Atlanta: Honor Killing = Cultural Misunderstanding

This time, both the blogosphere and the mainstream media are covering this honor murder in Atlanta. Granted: CNN is based in Atlanta; but I still don't understand why they never covered the honor murder of the Said sisters in Dallas—which is only a 2 1/2 hour plane ride away.

In a mere matter of days, CNN not only wrote about the Atlanta femicide; they also turned to an alleged expert who says that honor murders are no different than domestic violence cases worldwide.

Columbia University Associate Dean of multicultural affairs, Ajay Nair, is quoted as saying:

> "My immediate reaction was that this is an anomaly in the South Asian community... Most South Asian-American families enjoy wonderful relationships within their families. I think there's ways that we can rationalize it and make sense of it, particularly in thinking about new immigrant communities in the U.S. and thinking about some of the struggles that they face and the generation gap and the cultural differences that children do face," he said. "I think there are some issues there, but by and large, this isn't a rampant problem within South Asian communities. What is a problem, I think, is domestic violence, and that cuts across all communities. I think more people need to recognize this as a global issue. It's not just a U.S. issue. I think it happens across the world, and

I think people need to recognize domestic violence and any kind of violence related to women as a serious, serious issue."

Nair said he believes a "significant human rights campaign" is needed to address such killings.

According to my study, which will be published in *Middle East Quarterly* next spring, most (non-Muslim/non-South Asian) batterers do not often or routinely kill their daughters or wives, and when and if they do, they are not seen as "heroes" or "martyrs," and they are not protected by their families and communities. However, the perpetrators of honor killings are rarely prosecuted in their home countries.

What is Nair doing at Columbia? Why is CNN turning to him as opposed to a Muslim or non-Muslim feminist, scholar, or activist?

Since Muslims come in all colors and hail from many geographical regions, how exactly is it "racist" to describe certain Muslim tribal practices accurately? How will it help the police and the judiciary in the West to defend society against what we view as crimes if newspapers describe crimes committed by Muslims—often in the name of Islam, including acts of torture and terrorism—as having been committed by "youths," "South Asians," "militants," "immigrants," and by "the oppressed?"

There is one exception.

FOX News was the only national media outlet that really covered the honor murder of Sarah and Amina Said in Dallas Texas early this year. Kudos to them for their interest in this subject. The crew told me that I was the only domestic violence expert willing to say that honor murders have something to do with....Islam and with Muslims.

The Fox team was utterly amazing: Friendly, professional, exceedingly well prepared. About six or seven serious men arrived with lights, cameras, and computers and they turned my home into a studio-quality locale. I was interviewed by the very beautiful and brainy Lauren Greene, but as I now understand it, the program will also be hosted by Megan Kelly. Let me thank Justin Laffer and Byron Garoufalis for providing excellent backup.

Pajamas Media
7/9/08

- 16 -

The Violent Continuation of the Dallas Honor Murders

Yasser Abdul Said, who honor murdered his two beautiful and brilliant daughters, Sarah and Amina, earlier this year in Dallas, is alive and well and has been using a calling card to allegedly threaten various Christian members of his formerly Christian wife Tissy's family. He did so as recently as three weeks ago.

When FOX-TV recently aired their documentary about honor murders in America, they showed a photo of the murdered girls' mother when she married Yasser. She was fifteen years old and Yasser was thirty. Tissy (Patricia) Said looked young enough to be Yasser's daughter. She now looks old enough to be Yasser's mother.

I can only wonder why.

I am told that Tissy has also sometimes been seen wearing hijab and has long ago been forgiven by her father-in-law, Yasser Said's father, whom Tissy lives near and whom she often visits. "Forgiven?" Yes, he has forgiven her for having run away with her daughters and their Christian, so-called boyfriends who were only trying to help the girls save their own lives.

Yasser and Tissy's son, Islam, has allegedly threatened to blow up Gail Gartrell's house.

Gail Gartrell, whom I have quoted many times, and who is Amina and Sarah's great-aunt, believes that Tissy's flight with the girls may have been a planned ruse since, after all, she then subsequently lured them to their deaths. According to Gail Gartrell, at least three to four Christian relatives now confirm that Tissy was neither tearful nor filled with grief

62

at the grave site of her two daughters.

These relatives also confirm that when they went over to help Tissy fix up her latest marital home in order to rent it out, they discovered the following: There were holes in the walls and doors punched there by both Yasser and Islam Said in fits of rage and to terrorize the girls. Their brother Islam, broke Sarah's desk in half with a hammer, yelling that "the whore bitch deserved what she got." These relatives confirm that Islam's rage is highly volatile and "at fever-pitch 95% of the time," and continues to this day.

Tissy took possession of Amina's two computers. One is now hidden, the other she destroyed. Again, I can only wonder why.

The reason this domestic tragedy is important to track is that this may be the first time that anyone involved in an honor murder in America is trying to re-create the family history and publicly share the unfolding details of how the parents, siblings, and extended family (uncles, etc.) behave both before and after an honor murder has been committed.

Gail Gartrell now believes that Tissy converted to Islam long ago and therefore does not mind "lying to infidels" or collaborating in the honor murder of her own daughters.

Pajamas Media
8/5/08

- 17 -
Honor Killings Are Gender-Based Hate Crimes

On October 4, 2008, ten months after this killing, but for the first time ever, the FBI described the double homicides of Sarah and Amina Said in Dallas as an "honor killing." This language accompanied the photo of Yasser Abdul Said on the FBI's Most Wanted List.

The Dallas representative of the Council on American-Islamic Relations, (CAIR—aka the Muslim Brotherhood in America), was outraged by the description of this crime as an "honor killing." He was quoted as saying: "Until motive is proven in a court of law, this is just a homicide." Great-aunt Gail Gartrell told me that an Imam also took to the airwaves in Dallas to express his outrage

By October 16, 2008, the FBI had deleted the phrase "honor killing" from their description of Yasser Abdul Said on their Most Wanted list.

I do not know why they have done so. Gartrell believes that "the Islamists are winning! I think it matters little who gets into the White House as the Islamists will do what they will and the law will back off due to legal threats! What country is this now....the USA OF Islamistan? They proved to me that the Islamists have much more power than I do! I've told the truth! They just deny truth! Even so, they were able to get this recanted...just like Amina and Sarah had to recant about the sexual abuse."

I have been told that the FBI was deluged by media requests. While categorizing an "honor killing" as such might be important in terms of preventing one, I am not sure how it might help in the capture of an honor killer. On the contrary: It might tempt Muslim civilians to shelter someone who has, arguably, been targeted as a Muslim murderer, and not just as a murderer.

I have no idea if the FBI yielded to any "legal threats." I would be surprised if they had. But I have a suggestion. Let's take a page from the "politically correct" handbook. Why not think about honor killings as "hate crimes" since, in the West, the victims are almost always girls and women? Or better yet, why not consider such crimes "Islamophobic" since the victims are most often Muslim? True, Sikhs and Hindus sometimes also perpetrate "honor killings" in the West but not as frequently as Muslims do. Why not view "honor killings" as Muslim-on-Muslim violence—which, after all, constitutes the greatest violence unleashed against Muslims in the world.

Sarah and Amina: Rest in Peace. The forces of American law are pursuing your murderer and your great-aunt is holding their feet to the fire.

Pajamas Media
10/17/08

- 18 -
Honor Killings: The Islamic Connection

S he knew.
     She told her friends that her father was going to kill her. She ran away twice, stayed at shelters, stayed with friends. Late last year, on December 10th, in Toronto, sixteen-year-old Aqsa Parvez's father. Mohammed, and her brother, Waqas, collaborated in her murder.

Aqsa's crime? She refused to wear hijab; she was becoming too assimilated; she had run away from home.

Her father and brother are currently in jail awaiting trial.

This seems to be an open-and-shut case of honor killing. However, Islamists in Canada disagree and have launched a protest against a popular Canadian magazine, *Toronto Life*, for daring to describe Aqsa's murder as an honor killing. An announcement, ostensibly penned by Michelle@urbanalliance.ca went out over Facebook calling for people to barrage the magazine's editor, Sarah Fulford, with email and telephone criticism; to attend a Speak Out and press conference which was to have taken place last night; and to write to a new pro-Muslim magazine titled *Aqsa-Zine*.

Ironically, the new zine is open to Muslim women only. No Christians, Jews, Sikhs, or Hindus need apply.

This is the problem: Islamic supremacism and separatism—aka Islamic gender and religious apartheid. It is practiced in Muslim countries and transported by global immigration. Tradition and religion have a stronghold, especially on immigrants in a strange, new land. However, many religious and cultural groups have managed to both integrate and to retain their own religious identities. Muslim immigrants (and their third generation descendants) seem to have a much harder time with this balancing act.

If we understand Islam as an all-encompassing political, military, religious, social, and cultural system entity (which it is), then things become clearer.

After Aqsa was honor killed, Mohammed Elmasry of the Canadian Islamic Congress, was quoted as saying: "I don't want the public to think that this is an Islamic issue or an immigrant issue. It is a teenager issue."

Islamists insist that honor killings have nothing to do with Islam. They say that it is a "cultural" but not an "Islamic" crime. Islamists also say that honor murders are the same as domestic violence. All men, all religions, engage in it. Wrong. Most honor killings in the West are committed by Muslims who believe that what they are doing is tribal- or community-required, or possibly a religious act. They may misunderstand the Qur'an but as yet, no mullah or imam has stood up in the global, public square to condemn such murders as dishonorable and anti-Islamic. No fatwa has ever been issued against a Muslim honor killer.

It is unfortunate, even shameful, but not surprising that Islamists seek to cover up this crime against Muslim girls and women by attacking those who would dare expose it as "Islamophobes."

We cannot afford to fall for this deception. A crime is a crime. The shame resides in the criminal, not in his victim. The shame will become ours if we justify the brutal sacrifice of Muslim girls and women in order to remain multi-culturally and politically correct.

FOX TV is presenting a fictionalized dramatic version of the Said double homicide.

I wonder: Will America's Most Wanted present Yasser Said as a "psychiatrically deranged" killer or will they present his daughter-killing as a culturally approved and heroized act? From a western point of view, those men who kill their wives or their children are, by definition, "sick" and might be diagnosed as "paranoid," or "sociopathic." But from a non-western point of view, such killers are often seen as "heroic" or as "defenders of the family."

FrontPage Magazine
11/13/08

- 19 -
The Case of the Missing Honor Killing

Psychologically, we tend to believe that what we see with our own eyes, especially if it is "acted out" for us, is the "truth." Our brains are wired so that visual images assume a permanent reality— even if that reality is a computer-generated or photo-shopped Big Lie. Mohammed al-Dura did not die in his fathers' arms even though that carefully staged image was seen round the world. Israel did not massacre anyone in Jenin even though that Big Lie has also taken on a life of its own.

I'm glad that *America's Most Wanted* chose to dramatize the honor killing of Sarah and Amina Said in Dallas. I hope the program helps aid in his capture. I applaud on-camera narrator John Walsh, who has turned his own grief at the loss of his kidnapped child into something positive for so many others.

However, the dramatization was oddly, perhaps even purposefully misleading. Key figures were either fatally mischaracterized or were entirely missing in action. Malevolent motives, which had no basis in fact, were attributed to the innocent girls and yet their mother, Tissy, was not presented as the collaborator in their murder which she surely was. Their older brother, Islam, a foul-mouthed man who bullied his mother, harassed and monitored his sisters, and ultimately justified their being honor murdered, was not in the TV picture.

Why would *America's Most Wanted* do this?

Tissy, the girls' mother, is and was a white, blonde, blue-eyed Texas-born Christian woman, a child really, when Yasser first married her. The dramatization chose to portray her as an Arab- or Hispanic-looking woman. Although the program has an on-camera interview with the

68

real Tissy, their choice of an Arab-looking actress to play Patricia accomplishes the following:

Viewers might think that the girls really were rebelling against their culture when, in fact, their mother and her extended family are Christian-Americans whose customs the girls were choosing. Second, by failing to show the real Tissy and how she enticed her daughters to come home, promised them that their father only wanted to make up, the program renders indistinct the fact that this was a classic honor killing, one which usually involves a family collaboration. That is probably why they did not include the girls' older brother, Islam. He would have also visually and verbally confirmed the concept that an honor killing is characterized by a family collaboration.

In other words, the producers did not want to inflame any white "racist" passion by showing an Arab Muslim male tyrant dominating a white, once- Christian American woman (his wife) and their daughters. The program wanted no part of the long, historical stench which has attended the usually false, but sometimes true allegations about "Indians" or "blacks" raping white women, and the terrible lynchings that have occurred thereafter.

But, even more: The producers did not want to be charged with "Islamophobia" by showing what a real, full-blown honor killing looks like. Further, they wanted to appear and present a "balanced" re-creation, even if they had to make things up in order to do so. Thus, they showed the two girls as plotting revenge or preemptive self-defense against their father. If only Sarah and Amina had followed through on this imaginary course of action, they might be alive today. But, knowing how American law works, they might also be in jail for life.

While the program tried to pack a lot of information into a limited amount of time, they did not show how brutally and continuously Yasser physically and verbally assaulted his daughters, tapped their phone lines, monitored their computers, watched them, and had them watched.

Finally, to be extra careful, the program chose an exceptionally soft-spoken Muslim boy, Zohair Zaid, the girls' friend, who said some strong, true things but who also presented such a peaceful face of Islam. It does exist and yet—what a perfect foil to Yasser Said's cold-blooded murderousness. One cancels the other out and we are left with...confusion. (I am not sure if Zohair really existed.)

Zohair advised the girls to take their fathers' threat to kill them seriously and go to the police. He also told them that "once you run away, you can never come back. He will become totally insane once he's lost control of you...His honor and dignity (will be) scarred."

What a shame they did not listen to Zohair but instead to their murderous mother. On camera, a subdued, soft-spoken Tissy actually defends Yasser. She says that when she would punish or ground the girls, Yasser would try to protect them. When she was asked whether Yasser was upset when he discovered that his daughters were dating Christian boyfriends, Tissy says: "I don't think so. He always said that we could work (everything) out as a family."

Either Tissy is dull-witted, exceptionally passive; was battered, brainwashed, primed to turn against her own daughters; is one hellava cunning criminal; or, long ago, converted to Yasser's brand of Arabian-Egyptian Islamism, and shares Yasser's view that disobedient daughters should be punished, even killed. A typical Islamist mother.

I want to know why the police have not arrested her and why *America's Most Wanted* has failed to portray her accurately.

I asked Gail Gartrell, the girls' great-aunt, what she thought of the program. Viewing it made her angry and broke her heart. Gartrell feels that the program failed to present this double homicide as a fully developed honor killing. She quotes John Walsh who said: "Some people say this was an honor killing. But, there's no honor in this."

"How dare he? I have worked hard to educate and get the word out about honor killings and he diminished what honor killings entail. You know, they are usually well planned in advance and others in the family involve themselves as well. How about this? Yasser shoots the girls, gets out of the cab without a single drop of blood on him, after 11 shots were fired at close range, and simply walks away. Who picked him up? He did not leave there on foot. Someone picked him up and fled with him."

Perhaps this is another face of jihad. Think about it. What if an American-despising Yasser was also interested in marrying Tissy in order to get a green card, become a citizen--and biologically produce American citizen jihadists? According to interviews with Tissy's relatives, Yasser is known to have owned many knives and guns, known to have taken his family to "Jihad military camps." At least, they are posed wearing keffiyehs and brandishing weapons. Maybe he was only joking. Maybe his annual visit back home to Egypt was only to visit another wife and family. Maybe Yasser is just a petty criminal and woman-hater.

But what if Yasser married as a form of jihad? What if his daughters were in turn expected to marry other Egyptian jihadists who would pay dowries for them?

I hope the FBI is considering all these questions.

FrontPage Magazine
11/24/08

- 20 -
Beheaded in Buffalo: The Honor Killing of Aasiya Z. Hassan

On February 12, 2009, in Orchard Park, a suburb of Buffalo, 44-year-old Muzzammil Hassan, a prominent Muslim business-man and pro-Muslim advocate, was arrested for having beheaded his wife, 37-year-old Aasiya Z. Hassan. Yes, he beheaded her. Aasiya's crime? She dared to obtain an order of protection which forced her extremely violent husband out of their home.

We are now sadly familiar with some high profile Muslim beheadings of infidels; Daniel Pearl and Nicholas Berg immediately come to mind. Sadly, we are also familiar with the practice of beheading, dismembering, burying alive, and stoning Muslim women to death in Muslim lands. But this latest atrocity took place in a suburb of Buffalo, New York—in America, Land of the Free and Home of the Brave. Why behead a wife who wanted a divorce and to live free from daily violence? Why didn't Hassan just agree to a divorce?

Because this foul murder is very probably a very unique kind of honor killing/femicide and not just another tragic example of Western-style domestic violence. Erie County District Attorney Frank A Sedita III has it all wrong. He commented: "Obviously, this is the worst form of domestic violence possible."

Although I do not, as yet, know all the details of this Buffalo case, let me say that one feature of at least half of all the honor killings that I have studied in the West involved the kind of barbaric cruelty that we associate either with Western serial killers or Muslim terrorists—and with ordinary honor-and-shame Muslim families globally.

In the November, 2008 Mumbai massacre, Muslim terrorists tortured and mutilated living beings and perhaps corpses as well. Perhaps they wanted to render their hated victims "deader than dead," as has been suggested in a recent Symposium in *Frontpage* in which I participated. Simple death was not enough to render their victims powerless. A beheading suggests that the murderer wants to separate his victim's mind from her body; he does not want to hear what she has to say, he wants her mute, beyond what duct tape can do, and he wants her consciousness of what is being done to her to be severed from her ability to flee.

This "cultural" honor killing in Buffalo is very important for another reason.

Often, it is argued that such barbarous acts are due to poverty, lack of education, lack of prospects, or to a history of being persecuted either by other Muslims or by "Islamophobic" infidels. Muslim-American groups and Muslim-Canadian groups strongly protest the idea that honor killings have anything to do with Islam, or with being a Muslim.

Some Muslim activists have attributed the crime to "teenager problems " or to "immigration" problems. Others have insisted that the practice is a pre-Islamic "cultural holdover." (As I will soon document, Hindus and, to a lesser extent, Sikhs, also perpetrate honor killing/femicides but they rarely do so in the West).

Muzzammil Hassan was neither poor nor uneducated. He was well-to-do, educated, powerful, creative, and living in freedom in the United States. In fact, he viewed himself as a spokesman and even a role model for other healthy, assimilated Muslims who also live here.

In 2004, Muzzammil Hassan founded Bridges TV, an English-language Islamic network to combat alleged anti-Muslim bias in the American media. Hassan, a former bank vice-president, teamed up with his primary investor, Omar S. Amanat, the founder of Tradescape, an internet brokerage company which Amanat had sold for 280 million dollars. Hassan and Amanat counted Nihad Awad and Ibrahim Hooper of the Council on American-Islamic Relations—a Muslim brotherhood front; Imam W. Deen Muhammad, president of the American Society of Muslims; Dr. Souheil Ghannouchi, President of the Muslim American Society; Aleem Rahman, President of IslamiCity; and Alex Kronemer, producer of PBS's movie about the prophet Muhammed as among their initial supporters and advisers.

At the time of the launch of Bridges TV, Awad emphasized the importance of North American Muslims having "our own media outlets, our own timing and our own kind of programming. Our channel is in English and about life in America. We want a Muslim child who grows up in America to be able to watch our channel and identify with the characters."

Hassan said: "American Muslims saw their entire faith hijacked as the perpetrators of these (9/11) murders claimed Islam as their religion," the fledgling company said. "The Muslim victims were not only the innocent souls that perished that day (on 9/11), but the entire 7 million American Muslims."

According to Joseph Farah's *World Net Daily*, at the time of the launch, Bridges TV said that "most of the programming will be original since very little exists that would be of interest to U.S. Muslims. The network plans to feature sitcoms that represent American Muslim family life, modeled after the "The Cosby Show," the hit program that portrayed an African-American family.

According to Daniel Pipes, Bridges had been failing. Perhaps Hassan and his supporters will argue that financial pressure drove him over the edge or led to temporary insanity. But, if so, why a beheading? When Hassan went to the police, he merely said that his wife was dead. He did not say that he had killed her. He did not express grief or remorse. In fact, some evidence exists to suggest that he first tried to cover up his role in the crime.

Brother Hassan might soon claim that Aasiya forced him to behead her, that she drove him to do so, that he had no other choice. And, from his own point of view, he might be telling the truth.

Pajamas Media
2/14/09

- 21 -
Cold, Premeditated, Ritual Murder

T he Buffalo beheader, a man who allegedly goes by many names, seems to have a history of domestic violence with other, previous wives.

Can a man who has a track record of serious domestic violence, in one marriage after the next, also, at the end of the day, suddenly commit an honor murder? Can a man who has had several wives who left him because of his violence, then "snap" and behead the last wife standing when she, too, leaves?

We are going to be wrestling with precisely these questions as the details of the case against Muzzammil Hassan or Syed Muzzammil Hassan or Steve Mo Hassan begins to emerge. Earlier today, I received an email from one Jordan Robinson who sent me to a blogsite which belongs to Zarqa Abid. First, Abid says that:

> It's been five days now that my family along with the rest of the community has been in shock. The fact that Muzzammil was married to my first cousin before marrying the victim still horrifies us. Ms. Zubair was his third wife. Both of his earlier wives filed divorce on the same grounds of severe domestic violence and abuses.

Is this true? So far, I could find no documented history of domestic violence (which does not mean it did not happen). There is only Zarqa's late-in-the-day word on this—and the February 6, 2009 order of protection obtained by Aasiya Z. Hassan.

Is Abid's account an attempt on the part of the Islamic community to cut Hassan loose? Perhaps, for Abid goes on to say that Hassan was not a religious Muslim, that he used and perhaps stole from the Muslim community to fund a fabulous lifestyle for himself, and that she, Abid, tried, unsuccessfully, to alert the Muslim community to Hassan's violent nature.

Most whistleblowers have a hard time alerting communities to the corruption and misogyny of their idealized leaders. But is it true? What interest in the matter might Abid have?

I Googled her. Abid is described as someone who wears a face veil and justifies doing so—even though she herself is a television media professional. Perhaps Abid is telling the God's honest truth. Perhaps this is a new form of *taqqiya*, purposeful, infidel-targeted disinformation, so that the Muslim community can back away, with some dignity intact, from this formerly prominent Muslim leader who has now been exposed as a wife beater and, allegedly, as a wife killer.

Perhaps approaching me was clever and deceitful. Maybe this is Abid's way of "defending the faith." Perhaps it was whole-hearted, or rather, brokenhearted.

According to Daniel Pipes, "One Salma Zubair posted at Blog-TalkRadio.com the following statement:

> I am sister of this brutally murdered woman. She lived her 8 years of married life with fear in heart. She never let it come to her eyes or lips she was this afraid of this man. He had already frightened her enough that she couldn't muster up her guts and leave him, and when she finally did gather that much strength he killed her so brutally. She lived to protect her children from this man and his family and she died doing so. Muzzammil Hassan's family including his parents and brothers never tried to help Aasiya. Even when he had hit her and bruised her body badly in front of them. Aasiya had always been a very loving person, not even one person in this world can say a small wrong word about her. ... And please make a special pray for her children and that they do not have to live with that family whose son killed their mother and they never helped her but rather supported their son.

Was Aasiya Z. Hassan the victim of an honor murder/femicide or was this simply a form of domestic violence? Did her husband kill her in an act of spontaneous passion or was her death carefully premeditated?

If we refuse to understand what an honor killing is and how it differs from western-style domestic violence, we will not be able to prosecute honor killers, grant asylum to those in flight from being honor murdered, nor will we be able to educate people against honor killing. Many Muslim-American organizations insist that honor killing is "Un-Islamic." Yet many scholars of Islam equally assert that both the Qur'an and custom permit grave punishment for "disobedient" women.

In one study of mine, nearly half the honor killings committed in the West are torture or overkill murders; they are gruesome and, for example, involve stabbing the woman 8-23 times, setting her on fire, raping her first, then immolating her, slashing her throat, decapitating her. The ferocity of the violence is equivalent to what serial killers do to prostituted women who are strangers to them or what Islamic terrorists do to targeted stranger-infidels.

In 1999, in St. Clairsville Ohio, an honor killing took place which somewhat resembles the one in Buffalo. The husbands in Ohio and New York are both Pakistani immigrants. In Ohio, Nawas Ahmed, an estranged Pakistani husband, outraged that his wife, Dr. Lubaina Bhatti Ahmed, 39 years old, had gotten an order of protection and was suing him for divorce, arrived at her home and slashed her throat—and for good measure, the throats of her father, sister, and her sister's child because they were there to support Dr. Lubaina in her attempt to flee a dangerously violent man.

Similarly, Aasiya Z. Hassan was 37 years old and reportedly either an architect or professionally involved in her husband's Muslim media venture.

I suggest that the murder of an adult spouse is another, somewhat less frequent kind of honor killing. Both Nawaz Ahmed and Muzzammil Hassan had wives who wanted to live violence-free lives. This is a Western concept, not a Muslim or Pakistani concept. From their point of view, the wives "knew what they were doing" and thus were viewed as having brought their deaths on themselves.

I know this is hard for us to believe, but in Muslim-majority countries and in many Muslim immigrant communities, an ownership/protector mentality normatively characterizes the relationship of fathers or parents and daughters, husbands and wives, brothers and sisters. Verbal abuse and physical violence are not criminalized. Ninety percent of the women in Pakistan are routinely and savagely beaten in childhood and when they are married wives and mothers. A recent study confirmed that "annually, one million Pakistani women are beaten while pregnant."

Given the fact that Aasiya called the police, hired a lawyer, and got an order of protection, we know she was being abused. We also know that she chose to resist the abuse. The fact that Muzzammil decapitated her (and did not shoot her from a distance), suggests that his violent rage was not necessarily spontaneous but was, rather, the kind of cold, calculating, and premeditated rage which precedes a classic honor murder.

My guess is that "Mo" Hassan feels he did the right thing, that Aasiya forced his hand. Joshua Rhett Miller, who has been doing some excellent reportage about this case and who recently interviewed me, told me that Erie County District Attorney Frank Sedita III said that, in custody, "Mo Hassan is vicious and without remorse."

What, really, was poor Aasiya's crime? In Muslim countries and communities in the West, women are not supposed to tell anyone that they are being beaten at home and if they do, they may be honor murdered because they've "told." In Aasiya's case, she not only told, she did so publicly and legally. From the Islamist and tribal point of view, Aasiya brazenly turned to an infidel/kuffir system of justice, one which is radically different than a Sharia system. Some Muslims might say that for this, she deserved to die.

One wonders: Does "Mo," who has lived here for thirty years, really believe that he is still living in Pakistan?

What does it mean to behead a woman? To behead a wife, not a stranger, not a despised prostitute, not a rival drug lord? To exert the same amount of force that several men had to exert in the Daniel Pearl and Nicholas Berg filmed beheadings?

"Mo" has, in a sense, created a public crime scene, very much like those created by serial killers or by terrorists. According to Arabist and psychoanalyst Dr. Nancy H. Kobrin, we associate our "identity with our faces, our heads. Our thoughts and speech are literally in our heads." "Mo" did not want to hear what his wife had to say. He wanted to stop her thoughts. Perhaps he also envied her the strength to break away from a tradition which he was duty-bound to uphold.

Indeed, in the only photo that we have of the couple, Aasiya seems to be high spirited and confident. "Mo" is harder to read, since he displays little affect. Did "Mo" envy his confident wife who had the strength and the courage to break free from abuse?

Decapitating and then having his wife's remains on display in the Bridges TV office is peculiar. Did "Mo" somehow want to "broadcast" his bloody deed? Since the TV venture was failing financially, perhaps

"Mo" was shamed on two counts: as a businessman/protector of a positive Muslim image and as a husband whose wife had just forced him out of their home and wanted a divorce.

Public Muslim beheadings have been seen on the internet and via satellite. Great public attention follows. Perhaps "Mo" wanted to make a public statement that, while his business-media venture might have been failing, that he was still in control of his wife who had ejected him from their home.

This was not a crime of passion or even of temporary insanity. This was a cold, cruel, premeditated act of ritual murder.

May Aasiya rest in peace. May her murderer rot in jail. (Capital punishment is not legal in New York State.) May Aasiya's children remain safe from any further harm and may they be spared the kind of life that their mother was forced to endure.

Even in America.

Pajamas Media
2/17/09

- 22 -
Beheadings and Honor Killings

She was an accomplished, professional woman in her late thirties, a wife and a mother. But her husband beat her—terribly, and for a long time. Finally, after much suffering, she worked up the courage to leave him. That's when, acting on his own, he killed her.

No, I am not talking about Aasiya Z. Hassan in Buffalo. I am talking about the 1999 St. Clairsville, Ohio case of Dr. Lubaina Bhatti Ahmed.

My study found that the majority of honor killings in the West are not of wives but of daughters—let's compare the 1999 Dr. Lubaina Bhatti Ahmed, Ohio case and the 2009 Aasiya Z. Hassan, Buffalo case.

Both families are Pakistanis, both husbands were "successful" in America. Both wives had professional training and careers. Both women were in their late thirties, both had two children, both marriages had a history of terrible domestic violence, and both wives, after much suffering, finally dared to leave and to sue for divorce. Indeed, this sounds like a Western-style domestic violence/femicide.

However, here is one sign that both femicides may also be Islamic-style honor killings. Both murders involved sensational overkill. Although Muzzammil Hassan will be pleading "not guilty," and did not confess his guilt to the police, after years of beating and threatening her, Hassan's wife was found beheaded in Hassan's office—after she had him ejected from his own home.

Barbarism describes what happened in St. Clairsville as well. Nawaz Ahmed, a former pilot in the Pakistani army, cut his physician-wife's throat—and, for good measure, cut the throats of her father, her sister, and her sister's child.

Although both men acted alone, I would nevertheless argue that both men acted with the full cultural entitlement of Pakistani male Muslim culture. Hence, the murderous overkill.

It's true: Beheadings sometimes occur in the West, but this occurs when serial killers murder prostituted women or once, when a student went on a berserk rampage. A beheading is an act committed against a stranger, not against a wife. Granted, many cases of Western-style domestic violence/femicide can also be gruesome; however, they do not involve beheading and do not routinely involve killing the wife and the wife's family members because they dared to support her decision to save her own life.

Let's consider two other cases in America which involved Muslim men who were domestically violent and who, seemingly, acted alone.

In 2000, in Chicago, Shapara Sayeed, aged 33, was burned alive by her Pakistani husband, Mohammed Haroon. They had allegedly been "fighting for a long time." It looks like another case of western-style domestic violence/femicide except for the method of murder: Immolation, which is associated with the Muslim honor killings both of intimate family women and of women who are seen as not "covered" enough or considered to be too "Western" by the Taliban, etc.

In 2002, in Jersey City, New Jersey, another victim, aged 29, was Marlyn Hassan, who refused to convert from Hinduism to Islam. Her husband, Alim Hassan, a Guyanese Muslim, stabbed her to death while she was late in pregnancy with his twin children—and he also stabbed her sister and her mother to death. Again, gruesome overkill.

In the St. Clairsville, Chicago, Jersey City, and Buffalo cases, we discern what may happen to a Muslim wife who lives in America and who acts as if she is entitled to certain rights. All died horrible deaths, the kinds of deaths these days, that are visited upon infidels and upon enemy Muslims who belong to the "wrong" Muslim sect.

In both the Ahmed and Hassan cases, from the husband's point of view: These wives took the kids away from their father (children who, in his view, literally belong to him, not her). Lubaina moved away, Aasiya had her husband ejected from "his" home (which, from the husband's point of view, belongs only to him, not to her). Both wives exposed their husband's violence instead of remaining to absorb it. From a Pakistani, Muslim, male point of view, both wives deserved to die.

FrontPage Magazine
2/20/09

- 23 -
A "Cultural" Offense/Defense

For the first time, in the wake of the Buffalo beheading, Muslim-American organizations which routinely claim that honor killings have nothing to do with Islam are now (finally!) saying that a classical honor killing involves the murder of a young girl or woman by multiple family members. It does. The Muslim organizations are not necessarily admitting that such a killing is related to Islam, but they are admitting that honor killings/femicides do exist, separate and apart from Western-style domestic violence/femicide. And, to be fair, many individuals and organization leaders are also condemning such murders in grave and heartbroken voices.

However, they are now doing so, loud and clear, in order to make the point that Muzzammil Hassan's "alleged" beheading of his wife, Aasiya Z. Hassan, does not fit the profile of a classical honor killing—and, of course, that Islam has nothing to do with it.

They may be right—or they may be wrong. As is often the case, the truth may turn out to be a complicated mix of criminal-legal, cultural, and psychological realities.

Even if the Buffalo case turns out to be the act of a "temporarily deranged" and violent man and not a classic honor killing—this does not discredit the importance of differentiating between a classic honor killing and domestic violence, and between the kind of tribal, cultural and/or religious ritual murders which are normalized in Muslim countries and communities versus the kind of domestic violence/femicides in the West which are viewed as crimes.

As I have argued, some violent Muslim men in America who eventually killed their wives after first beating them, all killed them in signature barbaric-Islamic kinds of ways. Daniel Pipes called my attention to an honor killing case that took place in India. Mohammed Suhaib Ilyasi "is a famous journalist who started the TV Show 'India's Most Wanted.' He also married a non-Muslim, Anju Singh, and converted her to Islam. She became Mrs. Anju Ilyasi. He took all her property, cash, and jewelry. She discovered his connections to a Muslim Mafia. So he murdered his wife by slitting her throat with a blade. He was caught by police and was in prison. But he managed to escape, as his father is leader of the All India Islamic Cleric Association."

Now, he has been released with the help of "politicians who are begging for Muslim community votes in elections. He is back in the media. Anju lost her life...and people forget."

American and European feminists, with a handful of exceptions, argue that domestic violence in the West and/or globally is far more en-demic than femicide—which, chillingly, it may be. All I'm saying is that domestic violence is not the same as femicide, that the two phenome-na are different and may require different analyses, different prevention strategies and different remedies.

This obfuscation or denial is similar to those Americans (pol-iticians, intellectuals, media) who absolutely refuse to "profile" Ar-ab-speaking men from the Middle East at airports or in terms of im-migration policies and who are more concerned with the civil rights of enemy combatants (some of whom, they believe may be innocent) than with America's right to defend herself from jihad.

Even though the Buffalo honor killing might strongly resemble Western-style domestic violence/femicide, the gruesome and ritually "signature" nature of the killing method strongly links it to Islam.

A *Middle East Quarterly* article, "Beheading in the Name of Islam" by Timothy R. Furnish in the spring 2005 issue, is enlightening. Furnish establishes that "ritual beheading has a long precedent in Islamic theol-ogy and history."

He begins with the Koranic verse 47:3: "When you encounter the unbelievers on the battlefield, strike off their heads until you have crushed them completely; then bind the prisoners tightly" and notes how both premodern (Tabari, Zamakhshari) and modern (Yusuf Ali, Khatib, Mawdudi) commentators of the Koran interpret this verse liter-ally. Furnish also notes a second Koranic verse, 8:12: "I will cast dread into the hearts of the unbelievers. Strike off their heads, then, and strike off all of their fingertips."

A quick survey of Muslim history, starting with Muhammad and continuing through the Almoravid Dynasty, the Almohad Caliphate, the Ottoman Empire, and various mahdist movements, shows that this verse was carried out in practice. In modern times, Furnish notes that decapitation is standard practice in the Saudi kingdom. He concludes with two points:

First, the practice has both Qur'anic and historical sanction. It is not the product of a fabricated tradition.

Second, in contradiction to the assertions of apologists, both Muslim and non-Muslim, these beheadings are not simply a brutal method of drawing attention to the Islamist political agenda and weakening opponents' will to fight. Al-Qaeda leader Abu Musab al-Zarqawi and other Islamists who practice decapitation "believe that God has ordained them to obliterate their enemies in this manner. Islam is, for this determined minority of Muslims, anything but a 'religion of peace.' It is, rather, a religion of the sword with the blade forever at the throat of the unbeliever."

I wonder if the prosecution can, for the first time ever, consider arguing a "cultural" offense/defense-like argument. Muzzammil Hassan has been charged with second-degree murder. In New York State, only the killers of police officers or those who torture their victims before they die are eligible for execution.

Surely, beheading is "torture." Surely, it is premeditated murder. Surely, it takes a while to saw off a woman's head. Surely, she is conscious for some time. Surely, he must be tried and, if convicted, sentenced to death. Yes, under American laws. But I do not want the defense to be allowed to claim that, according to Muzzammil's culture, Aasiya's departure normatively unhinged him and led to the beheading. Rather, Aasiya's departure unleashed in him a cultural-religious imperative to control the situation by killing his wife in a barbaric fashion.

Surely, Muzzammil beheaded poor, tragic Aasiya, not only because he was a Western-style domestically violent man, but also because he believed, psychologically, culturally, and religiously, that beheading is an accepted, even an approved way of executing a disobedient wife.

Pajamas Media
2/20/09

- 24 -
The Left and a Woman's Severed Head

Within hours of the news of Aasiya Z. Hassan's February 12th beheading by her husband, Muzzammil Hassan, in Buffalo, American-Muslim organizations and individuals began a dirge bemoaning the existence of domestic violence. But they affirmed that such violence exists among all faiths and ethnicities. Such family violence, they insisted, had nothing to do with Islam. Muslim leaders emphasized that honor killings were "anti-Islamic" or "un-Islamic," a holdover from "pre-Islamic times." They vowed to preach against it in the mosque. All well and good.

That Mr. Hassan beheaded his wife—well, that simply wasn't dwelled upon. Muslim religious feminists, Asra Nomani, and Irshad Manjie, both referred to the Buffalo beheading as an "honor killing" and despaired of the silence which still surrounded this form of domestic violence against Muslim girls and women. As Muslim women, they were not as squeamish about condemning violence against Muslim women by Muslim men and Islamic culture.

Zarqa Abid, a soulful-sounding religious Muslim woman, claimed that her cousin was once married to this same Hassan, and she denounced Hassan as a "monster." Abid also criticized the Islamic community for having refused to listen to her when she attempted to alert them to Hassan's criminal nature and deeds. Instead, they shunned her, continued to shower him with their money, and honor him.

Saleemah Abdul-Ghafur, a Muslim author and activist, bravely, sanely, said that "there is so much negativity about Muslims (this beheading) sort of perpetuates it. The right wing is going to run with it and misuse it. But we've got to shine a light on this issue so that we can transform it."

Imam Mohamed Hagmagid Ali, of Sterling, Virginia, vice-president of the Islamic Society of North America, said that "violence against women is real and cannot be ignored."

Nevertheless, Muslim organizations are relatively silent about this atrocity, given how vocal they usually are when Islam or Muslims are involved. A Google search of CAIR and beheadings only revealed that CAIR had given the alleged murderer an award.

Alright, some Muslims are calling it an honor killing, most are insisting that it is not an honor killing and that, however we wish to characterize the phenomenon, it has nothing to do with Islam. Some Muslims are admitting that, like other groups, Muslims also have a serious problem with violence against women.

What did American feminists have to say? Well, I'm certainly one, and I have been on record a long time opposing Islamic gender and religious apartheid, both in Muslim lands and in the West. Nonie Darwish, a Muslim-born Palestinian-Egyptian-American feminist (and an apostate), has condemned Sharia law as dangerous to women and other living beings. Now, for the first time, an American (non-Muslim) feminist has joined us.

On February 13, 2009, Marcia Pappas, the President of NOW-New York State, hit the ground running. She was quoted worldwide, even as far away as India. Pappas bravely asserted that the Buffalo beheading was a domestic violence murder that smacked of terrorism and jihad. The February 16, 2009 NOW-New York State press release quoted her as saying:

> And why is this horrendous story not all over the news? Is a Muslim woman's life not worth a five-minute report? This was, apparently, a terroristic version of "honor killing," a murder rooted in cultural notions about women's subordination to men. Are we now so respectful of the Muslim's religion that we soft-peddle atrocities committed in its name?... What is this deafening silence?

> And exactly what do orders of protection do? Was Aasiya desperately waving the order of protection in Muzzammil's face when he slashed at her throat? Was it still clutched in her hand when her head hit the floor? You of the press, please shine a light on this most dreadful of murders. In a bizarre

twist of fate it comes out that Muzzammil Hassan is founder of a television network called Bridges TV, whose purpose it was to portray Muslims in a positive light. This is a huge story. Please tell it!

Most feminist leaders either attacked Pappas or remained silent.

News of the beheading became public the evening of February 12, 2009. Eight days later, on February 20, 2009, more than a week after NOW-NY State President Pappas began talking to the media, and four days after Pappas released a press release, President of the National Organization for Women, Kim Gandy, published a column in which she stated that the beating of pop music star Rihanna is every bit as bad as the beheading of Aasiya Z. Hassan. Or the assassination of Benazir Bhutto.

Gandy joins many of the Muslim groups in failing to differentiate between a terrible, humiliating beating (Rihanna), and being stabbed many times and then beheaded while you are, quite possibly, still alive, perhaps even conscious.

I agree and share Gandy's concern: Domestic violence against women is an epidemic. Although we have laws against it, police officers and judges ready to arrest and prosecute, as well as (too few) shelters available for those intended victims who manage to escape—still, we have not managed to abolish the scourge of domestic violence. Gandy is, understandably, frustrated.

Many women, (the statistics vary), are killed by their intimate partners. Amy Siskind, at *The Daily Beast*, tells us that:

Sadly, this type of tragedy is hardly unusual in our country, where each and every day three or more women are murdered by their husband or boyfriend. In fact, statistics tell us that in the ten days since Aasiya died, 30 or more women in America have been murdered by their husband or boyfriend. The attention on this case comes as a result of the gruesome way in which Aasiya was murdered—torture and then decapitation—and what a beheading symbolically means.

However, Gandy and her supporters still refuse to consider that Muslim women and immigrant women in general probably face much greater danger, both in terms of being beaten and killed than do non-Muslim women; that Muslim women in Muslim countries are prey, targets, human sacrifices, every single day and in huge numbers; and that if we do not stop the forces of jihad that are headed our way that many more women will be beaten, veiled, and killed both at home and on the street.

Gandy rejects focusing on Aasiya Z. Hassan's beheading because it might play into the hands of conservative "racists;" it might lead to "profiling." Wait a minute. NOW has conducted a serious campaign against religion, mainly against Christianity and Judaism. Why the sudden respect for Islam, a religion which is not a race and today functions as a totalitarian political ideology which has undergone no evolution for 1,400 years and which is dangerous to women and other living beings?

Gandy fears that we might only focus on Aasiya's beheading or even on Rihanna's beating as entertainment, escape, lured by such sensational or celebrity cases. It's possible, but perhaps it is equally possible to learn from such cases precisely because they've grabbed our restless attention spans.

Muzzammil "Mo" Hassan's heart and mind remains in the East, in Pakistan. His body remains in custody in Buffalo, charged with second degree murder. Until or unless "torture" can be proved, he is eligible to be tried only for second-degree murder.

Hassan planned this beheading. He was not out of control when he stabbed and beheaded his wife. He was controlling the situation in a Pakistani male Muslim kind of way. Beating a wife is the "normal" way to relate to her. Killing her for being disobedient, in his mind, was what she deserved.

FrontPage Magazine
2/25/09

- 25 -

The Danger To the Prosecution of Calling an "Honor Killing" an Honor Killing

On February 17, 2009, a reporter quoted the Buffalo DA as saying that Muzzammil Hassan, in custody for the Buffalo beheading of his wife, is "a pretty vicious and remorseless bastard."

On February 18, 2009, the Buffalo DA wisely kept the media away from Muzzammil Hassan's hearing.

Nine years ago, on January 8, 1999, in Cleveland, Ohio, after attending mosque services with her parents, Methel Dayem was murdered in what prosecutors termed an "honor killing." Methel and her family were Arab Palestinians from the West Bank.

Methel's sister told the police that two of her cousins, Musa Saleh and Yezen Dayem, had been following Methel to school and to work. She was shot four times and died choking on her own blood. No money was taken nor was she sexually assaulted. The police arrested these two cousins.

The prosecution may not have understood that an honor killing is a family affair, an inside job. Sometimes, in Europe, the youngest (or the oldest) male family member may be designated to pull the trigger in the belief that a juvenile will receive a light sentence or that a grandfather will not mind sitting in jail for the sake of his family's "honor." Even in Cleveland, no family member would ever testify against another family member.

In the West, honor murderers do not always admit guilt, nor do they confess. They will say: "She is dead," as both Buffalo's "Mo" Hassan said of his decapitated wife or as Sandeela Kanwal's father said of the daughter he had just murdered. Or, they might say that the murder itself was an act of self-defense, that the girl's dishonoring of her family was an aggressive act against which the family had to defend itself. This, in effect, is what Palestina Isa's parents said after they murdered her in St. Louis, Missouri in 1989.

In the Methel Dayem case, the judge threw out an aggravated murder charge against one cousin, Musa Saleh, who still remained in jail because of pending burglary and witness intimidation charges. Perhaps the Cleveland prosecution had hoped that one cousin would turn on the other and provide an eyewitness account of the murder. Perhaps the prosecutors did not fully understand what they were up against. Thus, they granted Musa Saleh immunity on the pending charges in the mistaken hope that he would testify against Yezen Dayem.

When they were originally charged, prosecutor Carmen Marino had said: "What these two did was shoot a woman in the back of the head. They believe that their religious beliefs supersede our law." His comments led many of the thirty—yes thirty!—Arab Americans in the courtroom to simultaneously "clear their throats in an effort to try to drown him out." Sam Qasem, an Arab American activist, said: "The Muslim religion does not preach to kill a woman. If that's not racism, I don't know what is."

Thus, leaders of the Ohio Muslim and Arab communities denounced the prosecutors' "honor killing" theory as a "cultural slur based on an outmoded medieval custom." In my opinion, they engaged in what is known as *taqiyya* (dissimulation, disinformation), which is recommended Islamic practice when engaged in battle with the infidel. Once the prosecution described Methel's death as an "honor killing," the entire Muslim community organized in protest. They gave interviews to the media, they packed the courtroom. They and the defense lawyers insisted that the very concept of an "honor killing" was an "insult" to the Islamic faith.

The ruse (or tactic) worked. The fact that potential jurors had heard the phrase "honor killing" was deemed "prejudicial," "inflammatory," and "anti-Arab" to the defendant, Yezen Dayem, whose lawyer promptly requested and received a non-jury bench trial.

Circumstantial evidence pointed to Musah Saleh and Yezen Dayem's guilt: A video showed Dayem's car near the murder site; cell phone records revealed that whoever used his phone placed a call within minutes from a location not far from the murder site; the entire cultural context strongly suggests an honor killing. However, detectives found a pair of ski gloves covered with gunshot residue in the victim's car. Who placed it there, when, or why, remains unknown.

Nevertheless, because the DNA evidence retrieved from the gloves did not match the DNA of either of Methel's cousins, the second and presiding judge, Thomas Pokorny, found that this constituted "reasonable doubt." He therefore acquitted and freed Yezen Dayem. However, according to Amanda Garrett of the *Cleveland Plain Dealer*, Methel Dayem's mother, sister, and aunt were "devastated by the verdict. Methel's sister, Nebal Ali, shouted 'You will not get away from Allah. Allah will punish you.' Afterwards, both she and Methel's mother 'rushed' at Yezen Dayem's family...shouting 'Murderer' and a string of vulgarities."

In my view, the Arab, Muslim, and Palestinian community's immediate mobilization on behalf of the two accused killers was a mobilization which did not view the victim as an Arab, a Muslim, and a Palestinian. Had Methel been killed by Christian Americans or by Jewish Israelis the same community might have characterized the murder as a "racist" crime, as "Islamophobic," even "genocidal." But because Methel's own family believed that Muslim men were the most likely perpetrators, it did not matter that they had committed a Muslim-on-Muslim femicide.

Indeed, honor killings are mostly Muslim-on-Muslim (or Sikh-on-Sikh, or Hindu-on-Hindu crimes) crimes and, most often, male-on-female crimes. Sometimes Muslims or Sikhs and Hindus also murder a man for having married the "wrong" woman. Therefore, the activist Arab Muslim community in Cleveland viewed and defended the alleged murderers as the true "victims" and completely forgot that Methel Dayem was also an Arab Palestinian Muslim whose life had been cut fearfully short and for precisely the reasons that honor killings occur.

I hope that all future prosecutors who may handle honor killing cases take into account the aggressively organized nature of Muslim defenses in America. Based on their strategy in the Methel Dayem case, we see that an unproven or difficult-to-prove allegation about an honor killing/femicide may lead to the kind of activism which, when coupled with how Western law is practiced, might lead to the dismissal of a potentially "tainted" jury and to a bench trial.

The Cleveland defense lawyers claimed that the jury was already "tainted" merely because they'd heard the phrase "honor killing."

Sometimes, when a prosecutor tells certain truths (that an honor killing has been committed), people may be more outraged by the allegation than by the possibility of the dark deed itself.

Years later, when I was doing interviews for my book *The Death of Feminism. What's Next in the Struggle for Women's Freedom*, a Cleveland-based reporter wanted to interview me about the Dayem case. She was told she had to stay away from such material, that the newspaper had had enough trouble when they had covered the Methel Dayem case.

One wonders: What kind of trouble and how much of was the newspaper forced to endure?

Pajamas Media
2/26/09

- 26 -

A Civilized Dialogue Between Two Feminists
About Islam and Honor Killing—Part One

I t has been my privilege to know and to work with Dorchen Leithold, who is a fearless, tireless, and heroic champion of women's' rights. I remember Dorchen back in the days when we were both anti-pornography activists. She then became an anti-trafficking activist—which she still is. We have participated in many important demonstrations, conferences, and memorial services over the last forty-plus years. Dorchen went on to become a lawyer. She is now the director of legal services for battered women in New York City (Sanctuary for Families) and has, Sojourner-Truth style, literally rescued and saved the lives of many a woman.

We now have a genuine disagreement about whether or not Islam plays a role in domestic violence and honor killings, including in the recent horrific beheading of Aasiya Z. Hassan in Buffalo. Dorchen thinks not; I think there is a profound relationship that we deny at our own peril—and to the detriment of Muslim girls and women in the West.

With Dorchen's permission, I am now publishing our recent correspondence. This is how people, including feminists, might consider sounding when they disagree with each other. Instead of cutting or writing each other off, here is one example of how a civilized disagreement might sound.

Our exchange is rather long. Dorchen said I could publish it as long as I did not change or edit anything she wrote.

What matters is the exchange of such ideas and how Dorchen and I are modeling a civilized way of communicating.

In my *Middle East Quarterly* study, I recommend that we work with those mullahs, Islamic organizations, and individuals who are genuinely pro-woman, anti-domestic violence, and anti-honor killings–but that we must differentiate between such Muslims and those who will say the "right" thing on these subjects, (usually after an honor killing has taken place), but who have no intention of doing any of the hard and serious work against Muslim violence against Muslim women.

From her first letter, dated February 28, 2009, it is not clear whether Dorchen read my study or is aware that I mention one of her own cases in it. Without quoting her name, I wrote: "A number of feminist lawyers who work with battered women have credited pro-women sheikhs with helping them enormously. Sheikhs (mullahs, imams), should publicly identify, condemn, and shame honor killers. Those who resist doing so should be challenged."

From: Dorchen Leidholdt
Sent: Saturday, February 28, 2009

Dear Phyllis,

I cannot in good conscience not respond to the article that appeared on your blog, "The Left and a Woman's Severed Head." While I have had much respect for you and for the very important work you have produced over decades of writing, thinking, and activism, I believe that statements like this statement of yours—"Why the sudden respect for Islam, a religion which is, in reality, not a religion at all but is rather, a totalitarian political ideology which has undergone no evolution for 1,400 years and which is dangerous to women and other living beings?" —are misguided, divisive, and false.

First, like many in the movement against violence against women, I work with amazing, committed Muslim feminists. Statements like yours, which disparage Islam, tell them that they have no place in the feminist movement. As a feminist lawyer representing Muslim women victimized by male violence, I have seen over and over how their faith has provided them with an important source of support as they challenge male domination and abuse. I remember vividly how my courageous Pakistani client who survived domestic violence and threats of honor killing read her copy of the Koran in court to gather strength as her husband and his family members menaced her from across the waiting room. Now free from her husband's abuse, she is raising a vibrant, free-spirited daughter who is learning about Islam and feminism from a mother who sees no contradiction between the two.

I believe I told you the story of the time when my client, this same woman, learned that her older brother, who had threatened to kill her while in Pakistan, was now in New York City. When I learned of this, I realized that I needed to meet with him because he was a witness to threats my client's husband had made against her. I contacted him and told him that I wanted to meet with him at Davis Polk & Wardwell, the firm handling my client's asylum case. I set up a meeting with the brother and a male pro-bono attorney at the firm who had taken several of our most challenging gender-based asylum cases. Also from Pakistan, this attorney was a deeply observant Muslim married to a feminist doctoral student from Pakistan. We met with our client's brother, who, as you might imagine, had many questions of me. The pro-bono attorney challenged him about his treatment of his sister, and quoted many passages from the Koran about the obligations of an older brother to protect and support his sisters. At the end of the meeting, our client's brother agreed to testify on behalf of his sister, and two weeks later, to my astonishment, he did just that. I could clearly see that just as the Bible and the Torah can be used to support or prevent violence against women, so can the Koran.

Second, religious scholars point out that Judaism, Christianity, and Islam share many of the same roots, and I am struck over and over by the similarities of the three major monotheistic world religions. So many of the prophets and precepts are virtually identical. Sadly, all three in text, interpretation, and practice are pervaded with misogyny that can be used to justify violence against women. I'm not as familiar with the Torah as the Bible, but both contain passages like this one in Ephesians: "Be subject to your husbands as to the Lord: for the man is the head of the woman, just as Christ also is the head of the church... [women must be subject] "to their husbands in everything (Eph. 5:21-24)." Christian and Jewish feminist scholars, theologians, and practitioners have done much to transform the interpretation of the Bible and Torah. I have met Muslim feminists who are engaged in the same endeavor with the Koran. Your statement suggests that the Koran is inherently misogynist and their labors are futile. Surely you cannot be opposing their valiant and admirable work.

Finally, in some of your blogs you suggest that honor killing is peculiar to Islamic societies. That is absolutely false. Honor killing takes place all over the world, whenever a man, aided and abetted by others or not, kills a woman because he feels she has tarnished his honor. Almost always it's accompanied by usually spurious allegations of a sexual nature—of adultery, infidelity, or involvement in prostitution. Brazil was once considered the capital of honor-killing, and only recently eliminated the defense that a man was justified in killing an intimate partner because he believed his honor had been besmirched. Indeed, some scholars and activists have seen a connection between Catholicism and honor killing in Latin America. Similarly, beheadings and other gruesomely murderous forms of intimate partner violence are not peculiar to Muslims, whether we're talking about historical examples of femicide (Henry VIII's justification for the beheading of his wife Anne Boleyn was that she was an adulteress) or contemporaneous ones (remember that East Village man who beheaded and dismembered his girlfriend before making a soup of her remains, which he served to his neighbors).

Dr. Susan Wilt, Director of Epidemiology in NYC Dept. of Health's Injury and Prevention Program, published a study in March 1999 on female victims of homicide in New York City 16 and over killed between 1990 and 1994. She found that, like Aasiya Hassan, nearly half were killed by current or former husbands and boyfriends, more than half died in private homes, usually their own, and one third of the women killed by their husbands were trying to end the relationship when they were killed. Dr. Wilt was dismayed by the ferocity of the men's violence against the women they killed: "Where men are most likely to be killed by guns, the women's deaths were very different. We were surprised of the degree to which some of these murders just spoke of enormous rage. Some women were stabbed and also strangled. Some women were beaten, and they weren't dead yet, so they were thrown out of the window." The horrific nature of the deaths of these women were so disturbing to the research staff that they found it necessary to attend monthly support group sessions.

A few years later, Dr. Wilt conducted research into the femicide of immigrant women. She ultimately concluded that in New York City there was not a greater incidence of intimate partner homicides among immigrant women than among native born women.

Phyllis, I earnestly hope that you will reconsider the statements that you have made about Islam and honor killing and modify or disavow them. Not only are they false, for the reasons I explain above, but they fuel prejudice and discrimination and create divisions between non-Muslim and Muslim women at a time when we so desperately need to stand together.

In sisterhood,
Dorchen

Saturday, February 28, 2009 10:40 PM

Dear Dorchen:

I find it very surprising that you are now, here, revealing details of that particular case which you once brilliantly handled and which I have described in *The Death of Feminism*—a case which you forbade me from sharing any details about. I did not do so. Is this information (about the Pakistani case which you handled in the offices of Davis, Polk) now public? Are you doing so now in order to be able to prove that Muslims can also be good? Of course they can; like Jews, prick them, will they not bleed? Or do you wish to prove that in this instance the Qur'an was used for good, not for evil?

I don't doubt it. But how many other cases like this have you worked on?

In respect and sisterhood and with great affection,
Phyllis

From: Dorchen Leidholdt
Sent: Saturday, February 28, 2009 11:00 PM

Phyllis, this is not a public message and there is no one behind it but me. I wrote it in the space of an hour as I sat at my computer this evening. I must admit that I've been increasingly concerned about your messages about this case and have been hoping that they would take a different turn. I have such admiration and affection for you that reading them has been personally difficult for me. Finally, when I read this message tonight in my office, catching up on the deluge of e-mails that I get each week, I felt that I could stay silent no longer. By the way, I am very sympathetic to Israel and am much concerned about the resurgence of anti-Semitism in the world. At the same time, I see the discrimination, post 9-11, that our Muslim clients have experienced. Nonbeliever that I am, I believe that, like Christianity and Judaism, Islam is one of the great religions of the world and that it can be a force for peace and social justice but tragically has been hijacked by fundamentalists in the service of terrorism and misogyny.

In sisterhood, Dorchen

From: Phyllis Chesler
Sent: Saturday, February 28, 2009 11:15 PM
To: 'Dorchen Leidholdt'

Dorchen my friend:

Let me read your letter carefully and respond. Is it possible that we actually have a different point of view? Perhaps even based on different facts, different interpretations, with, perhaps, different concerns?

You are citing one 1999 study which studied immigrant women in New York City from 1990-1994, and found that there were no higher rates of domestic violence or femicide among them than among native-born women. I cite another state-wide study in Massachusetts, published in 2008, which examined the data in domestic violence deaths which took place between 1997-2006, and which found a higher-than-expected rate of such domestic violence femicides among immigrant women. We are comparing two small studies which looked at data in two different states and for different years. Unsurprisingly, the findings are different. Which is right? Which is true? And what about all those cases which go unreported and unrecorded and which may include honor killings which the police did not name appropriately?

Have you really read my article in *MEQ* which does differentiate a classical honor killing, (which the Buffalo case is not), from traditional Western-style domestic violence and from domestic violence femicide? This is important. Have you read that I've suggested working with pro-women's rights mullahs? And about the importance of making alliances with Muslim feminists, Muslim dissidents, ex-Muslim dissidents? Clearly, we both believe that this is a crucial alliance.

I would be very interested in some examples of helpful mullahs and Muslim lawyers because I really want to know. But I also know that "Islamophobia" is a false concept, one being widely used by scoundrels.

You may be right about Islam but only in the hands of those Muslims who risk their lives to take their religions back. Understandably, few actually do so. We must work with those who do. As I am. But I am not certain that Islam is a great and peaceful religion. Based on my information, it is not that. Many scholars tell me that individual Muslims may be peaceful, but Islam, as it is written and unrevised, is not. They insist that Islam is a political ideology, a totalitarian ideology, not the kind of "religion" that we are used to in the West.

Western non-Muslims do not routinely kill a teenage daughter; nor do multiple family members conspire in her murder. Muslim reasons are very diverse but often include a girl's refusal to face-veil, marry her cousin, or because she wants an education. Wives are another matter and only here is where Muslim-perpetrated honor killings may resemble a Western-style domestic femicide.

I look forward to our dialogue.

With warmth,
Phyllis

Pajamas Media
3/2/09

A Civilized Dialogue Between Two Feminists About Islam and Honor Killing—Part Two

L ast night I posted the first part of a dialogue between myself and my esteemed colleague. From Dorchen's point of view, she has seen "racism" in action against Muslims in America, and among Muslim victims of domestic violence with whom she works. She might view what happens when a Muslim approaches the criminal justice system as similar to what happens when an African American does so. I agree that this is a real concern. However, focusing only, or even mainly on this injustice, may also blind feminists to the fact that the majority of Muslim and/or African-American domestic violence victims are women whether they are Muslim and/or African-American.

In *The Death of Feminism*, I write about how Islamic gender apartheid has penetrated the West. At issue, is the relationship between multi-cultural relativism and universal human rights, including women's rights. Secular feminists either lump all religions together as either dangerous or inconsequential or they theoretically view all religions as equally capable of doing either good or evil on earth. In doing so, they fail to contemplate the ways in which Islam may be—and may function differently from other religions in the West. They genuinely, unbelievably, do not want to understand the ways in which Islam is different.

Last evening, another feminist joined this debate: Artemis March, in the pages of *The New Agenda* in a piece titled: "The New Feminism: Breaking the Multicultural Relativism Taboo." In her wonderful article, March discusses the ways in which such multi-cultural relativism is harmful to women, Muslim women especially. She writes:

Despite commonalities among all forms of male violence against women, we ought not simply disappear honor killings into the general Violence Against Women (VAW) category by dismissing the importance of making distinctions that derive from their cultural or religious context... If we lump honor killings in with all VAW, we beg the question of the exportation of Sharia Law to non-Muslim countries... Not only are honor killings migrating to many parts of the world, but so also are demands for a dual legal system that accepts and glorifies rather than punishes the perpetrators. As we observe this process in Europe, we can be sure that these demands for a double standard in our laws are coming to a neighborhood near you.

And now: For the conclusion of my dialogue with Dorchen.

From: Phyllis Chesler
Sent: Sunday, March 01, 2009

Hi dear Dorchen.

First: May I now write about the case that you handled which emanated from Pakistan and which involved helpful men, and which used the Qur'an in a helpful way? Please recall that I DID write about this case in *The Death Of Feminism* but only in part, and in a disguised way at your request. I was not allowed to include it in my study because you would not tell me the country of origin. I DO recommend seeking or being open to just such interventions and have written as much in my study. This Pakistani story does set a good example and I will be happy to say so again, this time with more details. May I do so? If you say no, it will be no.

Second: We may only seemingly disagree right now because your priority may be working to save battered women and mine right now concerns working to save Western civilization. I see the two goals as joined. You may not. We may both be "right." The Muslim Chechen leader has just had seven women murdered for "immorality" and threatens to kill others for the same reason. Is he Muslim? Is what he is doing based on the Qur'an? Must we, can we, draw any conclusions from acts such as these which are taking place ALL over the Islamic world and which have also penetrated the West?

Third: Do you realize that based on a handful of cases (the Pakistani case, others like it), you have concluded that Islam is good, and that Muslims are also good. In my view: Some are, some aren't, the good guys have not yet begun to fight within their own religion—and those who ARE fighting are just killing each other and murdering their own and each others' women—in the name of Islam.

Show me ten more examples like the Pakistani case. Show me eight more. I will study them and write about them as a model to follow.

Do you want to keep our dialogue private or might you want me to publish it? In part? I will not do so if you wish to remain private.

All best,
Phyllis

(Dorchen gives me permission to do so.) She adds:

Phyllis, coincidentally this client called me last night about another matter. She said that I could discuss her case with you. I should mention that after this, the young Muslim male lawyer and I together gave a presentation on domestic violence, with one of Sanctuary's lawyers, a Muslim feminist, at the Islamic Cultural Center on domestic violence. Since then the Imams have referred domestic violence victims to our organization for shelter and other services.

My priority is working to create a world in which women enjoy fundamental human rights. I think that there are few things more dangerous to all of the civilizations of the world, Eastern and Western, Northern and Southern, than religious intolerance. Brutal, murderous violence against women in the name of men's honor is not an Islamic creation that has penetrated the West. It has deep roots in patriarchies all over the world and has been justified in the name of Christianity (punishing the "whore") as well as in the name of Islam. By the way, if we really want to hold a major religion accountable for atrocities I'd start with my own religious tradition, Christianity, which carried out some of the world's most horrific, murderous genocidal campaigns, in the form of the Crusades and pogroms, not to mention the Holocaust and the recent genocide in Rwanda, which, of course, involved major complicity on the part of the Church.

I think that each of these religions (Christianity, Judaism, and Islam) can be forces for good or evil, depending on who's doing the interpreting. I don't base my conclusions on a single case. As a lawyer representing domestic violence victims, I have worked with hundreds of Muslim women from the Middle East, Africa, Asia, and Europe. I also have long (for decades) worked with Muslim feminists through the Coalition Against Trafficking in Women.

I am right now with a devout Bengali mother. We have just reunited her with her nine-year-old son after a separation of six months—her husband battered and abandoned her and abducted him. I wish I could say that this kind of abusive behavior involving the separation of mothers from children is peculiar to Muslims, but we see it carried out by men of all faiths. Like my other client, this mother, a pillar of strength and courage, has turned to the Koran. I respect her doing so and am grateful that she can draw on her faith for strength. When we parted, she hugged me and said that God is working through me. She sees Sanctuary for Families, a feminist organization, as an instrument of God, her God, who is part of her Muslim faith. I took it as the highest compliment. Phyllis, you may publish it if you wish. If you choose to do so, please publish it in its entirety.

Warm regards, Dorchen

Dear Dorchen:

I appreciate your willingness to allow me to publish this dialogue. This is rather exciting. We are agreeing and disagreeing without cutting each other off and without condemning each other either.

Happy Times.

I must comment upon your focus on Christianity. As you know, I am a somewhat religious Jew and have been writing about the epidemic return of anti-Semitism, which is primarily now coming at us from the Muslim, not the Christian world. True, the Catholic Church has a bad record on women in terms of the alleged witch-burnings and I have written about this at length. And true, the Catholic and Protestant Churches indoctrinated their followers into Jew-hatred which, arguably, paved the way for a national socialist and pagan Nazism which conducted the genocide of six million Jews and of five million other human beings during World War II. However, Church doctrines have evolved. The attitude towards "whores" in our world, while reprehensible, is not quite the same as the Church's former mass, public torture and immolation of women as "witches." And, by the way, Jesus stood by

Mary Magdalene, who was a prostitute. Perhaps the problem also lies in some men's inability to practice the very doctrine they preach and which they insist that only women follow.

But, contrary to myth, the Crusades were actually a very belated response to the vicious, widespread imperialism of Arab Peninsula Muslims who were converting Christians by the swords, building mosques where once proud churches stood, and committing genocide against the Jews, the Buddhists, the animists, and against Christians. Yes, genocide. Muhammed the Prophet began this awful Islamic practice which, to this day, has not been rescinded. Please read some books on this subject. Please read Ayaan Hirsi Ali, Zeyno Baran, Andrew Bostom, Nonie Darwish, Steve Emerson, Irshad Manji, Asra Nomani, Ibn Warraq, Daniel Pipes, Robert Spencer, and Bat Ye'or for starters.

Christianity has evolved. So has Judaism. Islam has not. At least, not yet. I welcome the feminist wrestling with Islamic doctrine towards this end. Christianity and Judaism have, in large part, become more tolerant, more user-friendly. Islam, which once, in certain places, may indeed have been gentler, has become more intolerant, and even more barbaric. Ask Algerian, Iranian, Afghan, Pakistani, Somali, Egyptian, Gaza/West Bank, Muslims who live in exile in the West.

Also please realize that what the holy text actually says may be less important than what people believe it says. Many Muslims interpret the Qur'an as commanding wife-beating, the beheading of infidels, the forced conversion of infidels, a death sentence for apostates, i.e., for Muslims who leave the faith, the importance of lying to non-Muslims, and the command to commit military Jihad, not as an inner, spiritual struggle but an outer, external, military onslaught.

According to my friend and colleague, Ibn Warraq, who is also from India/Pakistan:

> The root cause of Islamic fundamentalism is Islam. American foreign policy has nothing to do with the stoning to death of a woman for adultery in Nigeria. It has everything to do with Islam, and Islamic Law. The theory and practice of Jihad - Bin Laden's foreign policy - was not concocted in the Pentagon, it is directly derived from the Koran and Hadith, Islamic Tradition. But Western Liberals and Humanists find it hard to admit or accept or believe this. They simply lack the imagination to do so....The fact is Christianity has absorbed many principles of the Enlightenment, and Islam

has not. Then there are the crimes of Western imperialism
- some undoubtedly true and a disgrace to Western ideals,
but which must be seen in comparison to Islamic Imperialism to put it all in perspective. Islamic Imperialism virtually
destroyed several cultures - Eastern Christianity and the culture of Pre-Islamic Iran."

Dorchen: I hope that we continue this conversation. As we both
know: Women's lives depend upon what we come to understand. Men's
lives too.

In loving sisterhood,
Phyllis

Pajamas Media
3/3/09

- 28 -

Islam on Trial: That's What the Buffalo Beheading Is All About

Maryam Namazie, the Muslim feminist founder of "One Law for All," a group which opposes Sharia law, has just posted a report and images of her rally in London.

I especially loved her placards: "End Racism and Cultural Relativism," "Sharia Law Discriminates Against Women," "Equal Rights for All," and "No to Sexual Apartheid." Judging by the images, the rally and the conference were attended by both men and women, and by Muslims, ex-Muslims, and non-Muslims. I love the fact that Namazie described the rally as an "anti-racist rally against Sharia and religious-based laws in Britain and elsewhere." An inspired touch.

Even more, I love the fact that there was no violence, no threatened violence, and no signs demonizing either America or Israel; absolutely no scapegoats or diversions from the issue at hand.

Namazie's rally and public meeting featured speakers from the Southall Black Sisters and Women Against Fundamentalism; the Central Council of Equal Rights Now–Organization against Women's Discrimination in Iran; Democratic Muslims; British Muslims for Secular Democracy; One Law For All; and many other groups and speakers including Kenan Malik, Naser Khader, A.C. Grayling, Terry Sanderson, Sohaila Sharifi, Yasmin Alibhai-Brown, etc.

Imagine: Many Muslim-American organizations, many feminists, and some domestic violence activists are now all insisting that "domestic violence" is the same as "honor killing femicide," that a beating is the same as a beheading, and that there is no advantage, only a disadvantage, in looking at the special needs of different victims-of-violence.

A shelter for battered Muslim women who have escaped potential femicide might require a different staff with different skills than one for Orthodox Jewish, Catholic, and Protestant women. For example, they might require a halal kitchen, social workers who can speak Arabic, Farsi, Pashto, Hindi, Urdu, and Kurdish for starters; mullahs and imams who have already begun the work of campaigning against domestic violence and against femicide/honor killing to counsel the women; law enforcement ties that understand that such victims, as opposed to victims of other cultures and other faiths, may require the equivalent of a federal witness protection program; and "adoptive" family networks—something I believe tribal women may require.

Let me end by quoting Namazie:

We won't stand idly by whilst the British government relegates a huge segment of our society to sham courts and regressive rules and appeases the Islamists here or elsewhere. We will bring the political Islamist movement to its knees in Britain.

Pajamas Media
3/11/09

- 29 -
Vindicated by Muslims Against Sharia Law

O ccasionally, if a thinker-activist lives long enough and keeps in the fight, she might just experience a moment of vindication. For me, last evening was one of those moments.

Yesterday, I completed a Q&A with the *National Review* about honor killings/"honorcides" which appears there today. I also did a long interview with a major news service on the subject which is slated to appear tomorrow. Like many other wire services and like the mainstream media, ideas such as mine are usually sidelined, marginalized, attacked, or simply "disappeared." I do not think this will happen tomorrow.

And now, I have a number of honorable allies. One surely is NOW-New York State President, Marcia Pappas who is now also being attacked for her having linked the Buffalo beheading with "honor killings," with "Islam," and even with "Islamic terrorism." Indeed, she was attacked yesterday by a coalition of eight domestic violence victim advocacy providers in Erie County where the Buffalo beheading took place. I quickly posted a blog which dealt with this (it deserves a longer piece), but I mainly praised the recent rally in London which was sponsored by One Law For All.

Lo and Behold: A second honorable ally wrote to me. I want to share what he said. His name is Khalim Massoud, and he is the President of Muslims Against Sharia Law, an international organization. After reading my most recent blog post, he wrote me as follows:

> There is absolutely no doubt in my mind that (the) Buffalo beheading is a honorcide. We, Muslims Against Sharia, prefer this term to honor murder. Beheading is not just a murder, it's a ritual. It's a form of control and humiliating a family member who 'stepped over the line,' in this case, wife taking out a TRO (order of protection) and planning to divorce her husband.
>
> Ms. Pappas must be commended for her courage to call a spade a spade. (The) PC-climate presents considerable danger for future honorcide victims. Trying to sweep cultural/religious aspects of honorcide under the rug keeps the problem from being addressed. While most of the media wouldn't touch the issue with a ten-foot pole, (for) fear they would be portrayed as Islamophobic, a few brave women, the true feminists, like Marcia Pappas and Phyllis Chesler are speaking out on the subject just to be slammed by so-called victim advocacy groups because they dare to expose Islamism's dirty laundry. Muslim women in America are at great risk because Muslim establishment, with help of the media, wants to portray honorcide as fiction.
>
> Honorcide has no place in the modern world, but especially in the West. It must be forcefully confronted; not written off as domestic violence. Almost a year ago, MASH started STOP HONORCIDE! initiative. The goal is to have honorcide classified as a hate crime. The Buffalo case is a perfect example why honorcide should be a hate crime. The suspect is being charged with the 2nd degree murder. If honorcide were classified as a hate crime, he'd be charged with the 1st degree murder.
>
> Khalim Massoud
> President

Muslims Against Sharia

Pajamas Media
3/12/09

- 30 -
Brother on Trial for Killing Sister in Ottawa

I n the fall of 2006, in Ottawa, Canada, an Afghan-Canadian brother, Hasibullah Sadiqi, shot his 20-year-old sister, Khatera Sadiqi, and her fiancé, Feroz Mangal, while they sat in a parked car. Both victims died.

Now, three years later, Sadiqi is on trial. According to the Ottawa Citizen, "The defence is expected to advance the argument of provocation, which could reduce a murder charge to manslaughter...The Crown, meanwhile, intends to prove that Sadiqi's actions were planned and deliberate."

In other words: Sadiqi will argue that the alleged "dishonor" his sister brought upon her family by choosing her own husband was a "provocation."

Tellingly, Hasibullah shot his sister Khatera "in the head and torso" while he shot her fiancée, Feroz, "in the neck and chest." True, Hasibullah did not behead Khatera, but he did shoot her—and only her—in the head. This suggests that he wanted to assassinate her way of thinking; it also suggests that this was a political execution.

In 2006, another news source, CBC, quoted Khatera's boss at a clothing store in a Mall. "Her manager, Jenny Jeffrey, said the young woman was gorgeous, both in looks and personality. She was fun. She was bubbly. She was pleasant. It was a real shock that something could happen to somebody that's so young," she said.

Khatera was not cowering, she was not cowed, nor was she obedient and subordinate. She grasped her happiness with both hands. For this, her brother (and perhaps her family), decided she deserved to die.

And, as I watch documentaries and videos in which Arab and

111

Muslim women argue in favor of women's subordinate status, I can't help but note how very angry and aggressive these women in head and shoulder scarves are—how filled with hate they are for those women who seek women's elevation within the mosque. But also, their affect, even their rage, seems dead, flat, as if they are following a script that has been brutally drummed into them all their lives.

In the spring of 2008, in Henrietta, New York, another Afghan brother, Waheed Allah Mohammed, goaded by his mother, stabbed his sister Fauzia many times. Her crime? She was too "western" in her clothing choice, and she planned to leave the family home in upstate New York to attend college in New York City. Waheed described her as a "bad Muslim girl." Luckily, Fauzia lived. Her brother will stand trial and, in my opinion, her mother should be indicted as well as a co-conspirator.

One honor murder, one attempted honor murder: Both perpetrated in the West by Afghan Muslims. Yet, some of my former, Westernized Afghan relatives assure me that honor killings are foreign to Afghanistan. Perhaps they are right. Many Muslims, including Afghans, do not often acknowledge that the traditional indignities visited upon Afghan and Muslim women in which women are sacrificed, bit by bit, all throughout their lives, are tantamount to a long, drawn out human sacrifice.

Thus, such Afghans rarely view the burqa, polygamy, arranged marriage, or wife-battering as necessarily related to femicide, which an honor killing surely is.

Perhaps the Arab/Al-Qaeda influence in Afghanistan and living in an era of global jihad have endangered Afghan and Muslim women even further. Will someone argue that the stress of immigration made these men murder? Even when the new country is far safer and filled with many more opportunities than the old country ever was? Or, will someone argue that alleged racism in the New World "provokes" bestial, barbaric behavior among Muslim (and sometimes, more rarely, Sikh) families? Even when the New World potentially frees people from the caste, class, and tribal rivalries that would mean constant warfare in the Old Country?

Where can these young Muslim women go in the New World that will keep them safe from their own families? How can we successfully educate domestic jihadists here?

Pajamas Media
5/8/09

- 31 -

The Montreal Massacrist and Hasibullah Sadiqi Have the Same Kind of Father

I am close to an Afghan brother and sister who are in their thirties and are very dear to me. They are both thoroughly westernized, sophisticated, charming—and yet, in many ways, they remain "Afghans." They are devoted to their parents, socialize inter-generationally
with Afghan relatives—but they also go "clubbing" with non-Muslims
who are closer to them in age. Although they view themselves primarily
as citizens of the world, they are always very upset when Muslims are
blamed, hated, or feared—justifiably or not.

This brother-sister couple grew up in the West from the time they
were five and six years old. Hasibullah Sadiqi, who murdered his sister
Khatera and her fiancée in cold blood, came to Canada when he was
five months old. Why didn't Hasibullah assimilate? Why did he need to
destroy two of his own children—merely to punish the woman who had
fled from his violence?

In reading all the newspaper coverage, there is one fact that towers above all others. Mr. Sadiqi, Hasibullah's father, was a domestic tyrant, an abuser, a wife-beater—and a daughter-abuser as well. This man
(whose name I've not yet found), was so bad that his wife, Nasima Fayez,
had to flee for her life.

In court, she described herself as "more open minded" than her
husband.

But the close-minded monster held onto his "property," his children. He did not allow them to see their mother for six long years. The (unspecified) paternal abuse "worsened." In poor Khatera's case, her father drove her to at least one suicide attempt and ultimately caused her to flee to her mother in Vancouver. Fayez sent tickets to all three children to join her. Her two daughters came. Hasibullah did not do so. In fact, Hasibullah tried to have Khatera return to their abusive father.

One can only speculate as to why Hasibullah did not break with his father. Perhaps his father treated him differently, better, because he was a son, not a mere daughter. Perhaps Mr. Sadiqi humiliated and beat Hasibullah as well, turned him into his personal servant too-—but nevertheless, he became Hasibullah's male role model.

Hasibullah became his father's eventual enforcer and avenger. He rejected his mothers' version of reality: "Don't talk to me about my dad like that." His mother wept.

Please remember that, in 1989, Marc Lepine, who mass-murdered fourteen female engineering students in the Ecole Polytechnic in Montreal, also had a wife-beating Muslim father. This fact, which I found crucial, was completely ignored by the police and by all those who wrote about this tragedy. The police saw this as the isolated act of a madman.

Lepine was born Gamile Rodrigue Gharbi to an Algerian Muslim father and a French Canadian mother who had formerly been a nun. Lepine's father, Liess Gharbi, physically and psychologically brutalized his wife and son. He probably taught his son that women are chattel property who deserve to be beaten even when they are obedient—perhaps murdered when they are not. Perhaps Gharbi/Lepine scapegoated women for the considerable crimes of his father.

If we allow violent men to live with and rear children, we will inherit that old whirlwind. The daughters of violent, domestic tyrants will marry violent men, thus condemning their children to a similar fate; they have been "seasoned," prepped to do so. The sons of violent men—father humiliated sons—will become violent men themselves: wife-beaters and child abusers, both verbally, physically, and perhaps sexually.

This is true for any family in the world. We certainly have violent fathers in the West. And yet, Arab, North African, and Muslim fathers have not, traditionally, been viewed as "sick" or treated as "criminals" if they routinely beat or rape their wives or cruelly tyrannize their children.

Somehow, this must change. If not—nothing else will.

Pajamas Media
5/11/09

- 32 -

Two Muslim Brothers, Two Honor Killed Sisters, Two Very Different Systems of Justice

Her brother was outraged. How could his sister—his own sister!—conduct herself like a whore? How dare she choose her own husband and worse yet, how dare she carry on a relationship with him prior to the marriage that should never have taken place? Both he and his family felt as if she had deliberately attacked them. Killing her—killing them both—was only an act of self-defense.

No, I am not talking about the Afghan-Canadian brother, Hasibullah Sadiqi, who has just been found guilty in Ottawa, Canada for having killed his sister and her fiancée and who has just been sentenced to 25 years to life. Rather, I am talking about the Pakistani-Dane Akhtar Abbas, who in 2006 shot his sister Ghazala Khan to death and also shot her husband, Emal Khan, who survived the deadly shooting.

There are many similarities between these two cases, and one very important difference. First, the similarities:

– Both cases involved Muslim brothers who shot and killed their younger Muslim sisters, aged 18 and 20, and who shot their Muslim brother-in-laws as well; only one brother-in-law died of his wounds.

– Both sisters were deemed guilty, not only of marrying men of their own choosing but of being intimate with them before marriage.

– Both victims were lured to their deaths by promises of false reconciliation or understanding.

– Both victims did not want to "believe" that their brothers or their families would really kill them.

– Both brothers and their sister-victims had essentially grown up in the West.

– The fathers of both victims had lived either in Canada or in Denmark for thirty to forty years.

– The prosecution in both cases recognized the murders as "honor killings" and prosecuted them as such.

Here's the crucial difference between these two cases. In Denmark, the designated shooter was tried—but so were eight other family members who decided that Ghazala must die. Ghazala's father, a taxi driver who had lived in Denmark since 1970 and who had ordered the "hit," received life in prison. Ghazala's brother, who was 30 years old when he pulled the trigger, (he was also a taxi-driver), received 16 years in prison.

Here is where it gets interesting. Perveen Khan, Ghazala's aunt-by-marriage who kept in contact with Gazala, and who arranged a "fake" reconciliation meeting, received fourteen years to be followed by permanent banishment from Denmark. Other Ghazala relatives and contacts—a maternal uncle, two paternal uncles, and three family friends—were also convicted of facilitating and collaborating in the murder and were sentenced to terms ranging from ten to sixteen years to be followed by permanent banishment from Denmark.

No doubt, Ghulam Abbas, the Pakistani-Danish father, sees himself as a noble martyr who sacrificed his own freedom for the sake of family honor so that his daughters and granddaughters and other relatives would remain eminently "marriageable."

However, in Canada, only the brother, who was 23 years old at the time of the murder, was tried, convicted, and sentenced. But it is clear to me that Hasibullah Sadiqi's father, whose name has not been released in the media, was behind this murder and responsible for it.

Even though this father had abused both his wife and children, Hasibullah, who may once have functioned as Khatera's protector, now wanted Khatera to ask their abusive father for permission to marry and wanted her to invite him to the wedding. Perhaps Hasibullah had been directly ordered to do so by his father—in which case the father should also stand trial. Perhaps Hasibullah had incorporated his father's way of thinking and needed to avenge his father's honor even more than his own. Perhaps Hasibullah was also abused by this father and sought, finally, to win his respect and even love.

Honor killing families are a lot like Mafia or crime families. They plan and collaborate on assassinations, they intimidate juries and witnesses (this happened in the Danish case and in other cases in North America), they commit cold-blooded murders without guilt, but rather, with pride. Their potential victims, if saved, require federal witness protection programs just as those who testify against organized crime often require.

Going forward, the West will have to start trying all the conspirators and collaborators involved in Islamist crimes committed on our soil.

Pajamas Media
6/2/09

- 33 -
A Frenzy of Honor Killings: Neda, Soraya, Bursa – and Me

The world has just watched the cold-blooded murder of Neda in Tehran. The last sentence she uttered was: "Death to the Dictator."

The blood of Muslim women, murdered either by the state or by their families, continues to cry out—not only in the Middle East, Asia, and Africa—but also in the West.

Two days ago, on June 24, 2009, in Germany, a Turkish father, Mehmet O, a kebab shop owner, repeatedly knifed his fifteen-year-old daughter, Bursa, while she was sleeping. Despite the fact that Bursa, her mother, and her sister all wore hijab, Mehmet O. still felt Bursa was too "westernized," because she did not want her "strict Muslim father to control her life."

Bursa's friends described her as a "fun-loving girl, (who) loved hip hop music....But that is no reason to kill someone."

This is certainly not the first honor killing (or honorcide) in Germany or in Europe—and by a Muslim father or brother.

This June, in Norway, an Iraqi woman, Vian Bakir Fatah, who had divorced her violent husband, converted to Christianity, and was dating a Norwegian man, was stabbed to death by her ex-husband and by her violent 16-year-old son.

Earlier this year, on March 4, 2009, a Turkish brother strangled his 20-year-old twin-sister, Gulsum Semin, because she allegedly had an abortion. Her father has been arrested as an accessory to this murder.

On May 15, 2008, Ahmad-Sobair Obeidi, a twenty-four-year-old

Afghan, brutalized his 16-year-old sister, Morsal for months—then stabbed her twenty three times in a parking lot. He was ashamed of his sister for wearing "inappropriate clothing" and felt that she had "disconnected from her family." Ahmad himself had a long history of criminal behavior. Obeidi was sentenced to life in prison.

In June, of 2005, a Turkish 25-year-old brother, Ali Karabey, repeatedly shot his 20-year-old sister, Gonul Karabey, in a garden shed to prevent her from marrying her German boyfriend. In 2006, this brother received a life sentence. As in so many other honor killings, Ali promised his sister that he would help with the marriage if they met.

What can be done to prevent such honor killings in the West? Perhaps nothing. The tribal, cultural, and/or religious imperative might prove too strong even for those who are living in the West. However, some people believe that life sentences, and serious jail time for family accessories will serve as a disincentive.

Some people think that all Muslim fundamentalists or the families of Muslims who commit an honor killing should be deported from the West. Some people believe that Muslim immigrants must be educated about our laws and must sign an agreement to follow them. The Dutch government is now trying this idea out.

Some people believe that shelters specifically for battered Muslim girls and women who may be honor killing targets should be funded and staffed by experts skilled in this area.

And, some people believe that violence against girls and women is both overwhelming and universal and that it is "racist" or "persecutory" to single out only Muslim violence. Doing so, allows us to forget how much bigger violence against women, including femicide, really is.

I agree with all these points. I also believe that honor killings are not the same as Western-style domestic violence.

Pajamas Media
6/26/09

- 34 -
Are Honor Killings Simply Domestic Violence?

When a husband murders a wife or a father murders a daughter in the United States and Canada, too often law enforcement considers the matter a case domestic violence. Murder is murder; religion and culture are irrelevant. Honor killings are, however, distinct from Western-style wife battering and child abuse—and even from Western-style domestic femicide.

An analysis of more than fifty reported honor killings shows they differ significantly from more common domestic violence.[1] The fre-

---

1 Citation for honor murders drawn from Ellen Francis Harris, *Guarding the Secret: Palestinian Terrorism and a Father's Murder of his Too-American Daughter* (New York: Scribner, 1995); James Brandon and Salam Hafez, *Crimes of the Community: Honor-Based Violence in the U.K.* (London: The Centre for Social Cohesion, Jan. 2008), p. 13, 44; *The Cleveland Plain Dealer*, July 22, 26, 2000; *Pittsburgh Post-Gazette*, Sept. 13, 1999; *CBC News*, Apr. 22, 2004, Mar. 1, 2005; *The Indian Express* (New Delhi), Jan. 30, 2005; *The Asian Pacific Post* (Vancouver, B.C.), July 24, 2003; Soundvision.com, Sound Vision Foundation, Bridgeview, Ill., May 6, 2002; *The New York Daily News*, July 31, 2002; *Stabroek News* (Georgetown, Guyana), Dec. 3, 2003; Canwest News Service (Don Mills, Ont.), July 8, 2008; *The Rochester Chronicle and Democrat*, Apr. 25, 2004, July 17, 2008; *The Washington Times*, Jan. 3, 2008; *The Dallas Morning News*, Jan. 6, 9, 2008; *The Chicago Tribune*, July 8, 2008; CNN, July 7, 2008; *The Daily Mail* (London), May 2, June 12, 2007, Jan. 8, 2008; *The Observer* (London), Oct. 8, 2000, Nov. 21, 2004, June 20, 2006; *The Daily Telegraph* (London), Jan. 28, 2002, Feb. 27, 2005; CNN.com, Oct. 2, 2003; BBC News, Sept. 30, 2003, May 4, Nov. 19, 2004, Apr. 8, 2006, Jan. 8, 2008; *Tech-CentralStation* (TCS Daily), Feb. 2, 2005; *Time* (European ed.), Oct. 11, 2004; CUL-COM: Cultural Complexity in the New Norway, Feb. 17, 2006; *Expatica* (Amsterdam), Dec. 1, 2003, Apr. 27, 2005; *The Times* (London), Nov. 18, Dec. 4, 2004, Jan. 21, 2007, Feb. 3, Mar. 29, 2008; HiA Report, Humanity in Action Foundation, Washington, D.C.,

121

quent argument made by Muslim advocacy organizations, that honor killings have nothing to do with Islam and that it is discriminatory to differentiate between honor killings and domestic violence and femicide, is wrong.

Background and Denial

Families that kill for honor will threaten girls and women if they refuse to cover their hair, mask their faces, or their bodies or act as their family's domestic servant; wear makeup or Western clothing; choose friends from another religion; date anyone at all; seek to obtain an advanced education; refuse an arranged marriage; seek a divorce from a violent husband; marry against their parents' wishes; or behave in ways that are considered too independent, which might mean anything from driving a car to spending time or living away from home or family. Fundamentalists of many religions may expect their women to meet some but not all of these expectations. But when women refuse to do so, Jews, Christians, and Buddhists are far more likely to shun rather than murder them. Muslims, however, do kill for honor (both in the West and in Muslim lands), as do, to a lesser extent, Hindus and Sikhs. (In a later study I will document that Hindus honor kill but mainly in India and only for caste violations.)

The United Nations Population Fund estimates that 5,000 women are killed each year for dishonoring their families.[2] This may be an underestimate. Aamir Latif, a correspondent for the Islamist website *Islam Online* who writes frequently on the issue, reported that in 2007 in the Punjab province of Pakistan alone, there were 1,261 honor murders.[3] The Aurat Foundation, a Pakistani nongovernmental organization focusing on women's empowerment, found that the rate of honor killings was on track to be in the hundreds in 2008.[4]

June 29, 2006; *Deutsche Welle Radio* (Bonn), May 1, 2005; *The Guardian* (London), May 8, 2003, July 15, 2006, May 24, 2008; *Stern Magazine* (Hamburg), Oct. 4, 2007; Associated Press, June 27, 2006; *The Independent* (London), May 7, 2003, Feb. 21, 2007; *The New York Times*, Dec. 19, 2004, Dec. 4, 2005, Aug. 26, 2006; *The Evening Standard* (London), May 14, 2007; United Press International, July 3, 2003; *The Sun* (London), Jan. 23, 2008; *FOX News*, Jan. 5, 2007; *International Herald Tribune* (Paris), Dec. 1, 2005; *The Daily Times* (Lahore), July 3, 2004.

2 Chapter 3: "Ending Violence against Women and Girls: 'Honor' Killings," *The State of World Population, 2000*, United Nations Population Fund.

3 *IslamOnline.net*, Jan. 11, 2007.

4 *The Daily Times*, Sept. 20, 2008.

There are very few studies of honor killing, however, as the motivation for such killings is cleansing alleged dishonor and the families do not wish to bring further attention to their shame, they do not cooperate with researchers. Often, they deny honor crimes completely and say the victim simply went missing or committed suicide. Nevertheless, honor crimes are increasingly visible in the media. Police, politicians, and feminist activists in Europe and in some Muslim countries are beginning to treat them as a serious social problem.[5]

Willingness to address the problem of honor killing, however, does not extend to many Muslim advocacy groups in North America. The well-publicized denials of U.S.-based advocacy groups are ironic given the debate in the Middle East. While the religious establishment in Jordan, for example, says that honor killing is a relic of pre-Islamic Arab culture, Muslim Brotherhood groups in Jordan have publicly disagreed to argue an Islamic religious imperative to protect honor.[6]

Yotam Feldner, a researcher at the Middle East Media Research Institute, quotes a psychiatrist in Gaza who describes the honor killing culture as one in which a man who refrains from "washing shame with blood" is a "coward who is not worthy of living ... (is) less than a man." Therefore, it is no surprise that the Jordanian penal code is quite lenient towards honor killers. While honor killing may be a custom that originated in the pagan, pre-Islamic tribal past, contemporary Islamist interpretations of religious law resist denouncing it as "anti-Islamic." As Feldner puts it: "Some important Islamic scholars in Jordan have even gone further by declaring honor crimes an Islamic imperative that derives from the 'values of virility advocated by Islam.'"[7]

Islamist advocacy organizations, however, argue that such killings have nothing to do with Islam or Muslims, that domestic violence cuts across all faiths, and that the phrase "honor killing" stigmatizes Muslims whose behavior is no different than that of non-Muslims. For example, in response to a well-publicized 2000 honor killing, *SoundVision.com*, an Islamic information and products site, published an article that argued that:

Four other women were killed in Chicago in the same month ... They were white, African-American, Hispanic, and Asian

---

5 Brandon and Hafez, *Crimes of the Community*, pp. 143-6.
6 Yotam Feldner, "'Honor' Murders—Why the Perps Get off Easy," *Middle East Quarterly*, Dec. 2000, pp. 41-50.
7 Ibid.

... Islam is not responsible for [the Muslim woman's] death. Nor is Christianity responsible for the deaths of the other women.[8]

In 2007, after Aqsa Parvez was murdered by her father in Toronto for not wearing hijab (a head covering), Sheila Musaji wrote in the *American Muslim*, "Although this certainly is a case of domestic violence ... 'honor' killings are not only a Muslim problem, and there is no 'honor' involved."[9] Mohammed Elmasry, of the Canadian Islamic Congress, also dismissed the problem. "I don't want the public to think that this is an Islamic issue or an immigrant issue. It is a teenager issue," he said.[10]

Indeed, denial is rife. In 2008, after Kandeela Sandal was murdered for honor by her father in Atlanta because she wanted a divorce, Ajay Nair, associate dean of multicultural affairs at Columbia University, told the media that "most South Asian communities in the United States" enjoy "wonderful" relationships within their families and said, "This isn't a rampant problem within South Asian communities. What is a problem, I think, is domestic violence, and that cuts across all communities."[11] In October 2008, Mustafaa Carroll, executive director of the Dallas branch of the Council of American-Islamic Relations (CAIR), dismissed any Islamic connection to a prominent Dallas honor killing, labeled as such by the FBI, arguing, "As far as we're concerned, until the motive is proven in a court of law, this is [just] a homicide." He continued, "We [Muslims] don't have the market on jealous husbands ... or domestic violence ... This is not Islamic culture."[12]

Case studies suggest otherwise.

Domestic Violence versus Honor Killing

Domestic violence is a significant problem in the United States. Between 1989 and 2004, 21,124 women died at the hands of an intimate; 8,997 men died in domestic violence during the same time period.[13] Because the U.S. Department of Justice does not catalogue the victim's or

8 *SoundVision.com*, Aug. 24, 2000.

9 Sheila Musaji, "The Death of Aqsa Parvez Should Be an Interfaith Call to Action," *The American Muslim*, Dec. 14, 2007.

10 *Fox News.com*, Dec. 12, 2007.

11 *CNN.com*, July 9, 2008.

12 *FoxNews.com*, Oct. 14, 2008.

13 "Homicide Trends in the U.S.: Intimate Homicide, 1976 -2005," U.S. Department of

murderer's age, religion, ethnic background, or immigration status, it is not possible to know what proportion of these killings are honor-related.

Unni Wikan, a social anthropologist and professor at the University of Oslo, defines an honor killing as "a murder carried out as a commission from the extended family, to restore honor after the family has been dishonored. As a rule, the basic cause is a rumor that any female family member has behaved in an immoral way."[14] While honor killings are just a minority of total domestic violence recorded in the United States and Canada, they constitute a distinct phenomenon. (See Table 1 below.) A 2008 Massachusetts-based study found that "although immigrants make up an estimated 14 percent of the state's population, [they, nevertheless,] accounted for 26 percent of the 180 domestic violence deaths from 1997-2006."[15]

Lenore Walker, author of *The Battered Woman Syndrome*,[16] agreed that fundamentalist immigrants control and patrol their women very closely. "Given the strict rules, there are a lot of things to kill them for," she said. Walker confirmed the difference between the victim-perpetrator in honor killings and ordinary domestic violence.

In ordinary domestic violence involving Westerners, it is rare for brothers to kill sisters or for male cousins to kill female cousins. And while child abuse occurs in which fathers may kill infants and children, it is very rare for Western fathers and/or families to kill teenage daughters.[17]

Other discrepancies exist. Walker observed that Western men are more apt to kill little boys than girls in their family. "Women with post-partum depression (may) kill their babies, and men may kill babies by shaken baby syndrome," she explained. She did not "know of any batterers who are helped to commit the murders by their brothers or cousins or other family members. Occasionally, the man's relatives may be in the house when the murder goes down, but that is quite rare in my experi-

---

Justice, Office of Justice Programs, Bureau of Justice Statistics, July 11, 2007, accessed Oct. 2, 2008.

14 Unni Wikan, "The Honor Culture," Karl-Olov Arnstberg and Phil Holmes, trans., accessed Sept. 23, 2008, originally published as En Fraga Om Hedre (A question of honor), Cajsa Mitchell, trans. (Stockholm: Ordfront Forlag AB, 2005), accessed Dec. 12, 2008.

15 *The Boston Globe*, Sept. 12, 2008.

16 New York: Springer, 1984.

17 Author e-mail interview with Lenore Walker, Sept. 27, 2008.

ence."[18]

The press has reported a number of honor killings in the United States, Canada, and Europe. These cases show the killings to be primarily a Muslim-on-Muslim crime. (See Table 2 and Table 3 below.) The victims are largely teenage daughters or young women. Wives are victims but to a lesser extent. And, unlike most Western domestic violence, honor killings are carefully planned. The perpetrator's family may warn the victim repeatedly over a period of many years that she will be killed if she dishonors her family by refusing to veil, rebuffing an arranged marriage, or becoming too Westernized. Most important, only honor killings involve multiple family members. Fathers, mothers, brothers, male cousins, uncles, and sometimes even grandfathers conspire in or commit the murder, but mothers and sisters may lobby for the killing. Some mothers collaborate in the murder in a hands-on way and may assist in the getaway. In some cases, taxi drivers, neighbors, and mosque members may prevent the targeted woman from fleeing, report her whereabouts to her family, and subsequently conspire to thwart police investigations.[19] Very old relatives or minors may be chosen to carry out the murder in order to limit jail time if caught.

Seldom is domestic violence celebrated in the West, not even by its perpetrators. Western wife batterers and wife killers are ostracized. On the contrary, Muslims (and others) who commit or assist in the commission of honor killings view these killings as heroic and even view the murder as the fulfillment of a tribal, religious, and/or family obligation. A Turkish study of prisoners found no social stigma attached to honor murderers.[20] While advocacy organizations such as CAIR denounce any link between honor killings and Islam, many sheikhs still preach that disobedient women should be punished; and few sheikhs condemn honor killings as anti-Islamic. Honor killings are not stigmatized.

---

18 Ibid.

19 Brandon and Hafez, *Crimes of the Community*, p. 94.

20 *Today's Zaman*, July 12, 2008.

Table 1: Differing Characteristics of Honor Killings and Domestic Violence

Honor Killings	Domestic Violence
Committed mainly by Muslims against Muslim girls/young adult women.	Committed by men of all faiths usually against adult women only.
Committed mainly by fathers or male relatives against their teenage daughters or sisters and daughters in their early twenties. Wives and older-age daughters may also be victims, but to a lesser extent.	Committed by an adult male spouse against an adult female spouse or intimate partner.
Carefully planned. Death threats are often used as a means of control.	The murder is often unplanned and spontaneous and may be in reaction to a woman's attempt to flee.
The planning and execution involve multiple family members and can include mothers, sisters, brothers, male cousins, uncles, grandfathers, etc. If the girl escapes, the extended family will continue to search for her to kill her.	The murder is carried out by one man without the complicity of his family or the victim's family of origin.
The reason given for the honor killing is that the girl or young woman has "dishonored" the family.	The batterer-murderer does not claim any family concept of "honor." The reasons may range from a poorly cooked meal to suspected infidelity to the woman's trying to protect the children from his abuse or turning to the authorities for help.
At least half the time, the killings in the West are carried out with barbaric ferocity. The female victim is often raped, burned alive, stoned or beaten to death, cut at the throat, decapitated, stabbed numerous times, suffocated slowly, etc.	While some men do beat a spouse to death, they often simply shoot or stab them.
The extended family and community valorize the honor killing. They do not condemn the perpetrators in the name of Islam. Mainly, honor killings are seen as normative.	Sometimes, remorse or regret is exhibited.

Table 2: North American Honor Killings, Successful and Attempted

Victim Name (age)	Year, Location	Perpetrators' Name, Origin	Motive	Method
Palestina Isa (16)	1989 St. Louis, MO	Maria & Zein Isa, parents, sisters also encouraged it / West Bank. (M)	"Too American," refused to travel with her father, a member of the Abu Nidal Palestinian terrorist group, as "cover."	Stabbed 13 times by father as her mother held her down.
Methal Dayem (22)	1999 Cleveland, OH	Yezen Dayem, Musa Saleh, cousins / West Bank. (M)	Refused to marry her cousin; attended college; sought independent career as elementary school teacher; drove her own car; too independent; turned back on her culture.	Two cousins allegedly shot her, choked on own blood.
Dr. Lubaina Bhatti Ahmed (39)	1999 St. Clairsville, OH	Nawaz Ahmed, estranged husband / Pakistan (M) Former pilot.	Filed for divorce.	Throat cut; her father, sister and sister's young child's throats also cut.
Farah Khan (5)	1999 Toronto, Canada	Muhammed Khan, father, and Kaneez Fatma, stepmother / unknown region. (M)	Suspected child was not his biologically.	Father and step-mother cut her throat, dismembered her body.

Jawinder "Jassi" Kaur (25)	2000 Pakistan	Gang of men hired by Malkiat Kaur, mother, and Surjit Sing Badesha, uncle / Canada/Pakistan(S)	Against her wealthy, farming parents' wishes, married a man who was of inferior financial status, a Pakistani rickshaw driver.	Kidnapped, throat slashed
Shahpara Sayeed (33)	2000 Chicago, IL	Mohammad Harroon, husband / Pakistan(M)	Motive is unclear. But they had been fighting for months.	Burned alive
Marlyn Hassan (29)	2002 Jersey City, NJ	Alim Hassan, husband / Guyana (Hindu wife) (M)	His wife refused to convert from Hinduism to Islam.	Husband, an auto mechanic, stabbed wife (and the twins in her womb), the wife's sister, and the wife's mother.
Amandeep Singh Atwal (17)	2003 British Columbia, Canada	Rajinder Singh Atwal, father / East Indies (S)	Wanted daughter to end relationship with non-Sikh classmate, Todd McIsaac	Father stabbed daughter 11 times.
Hatice Peltek (39)	2004 Scottsville, NY	Ismail Peltek, husband / Turkey(M)	Had been molested by brother-in-law	Stabbed, bludgeoned with hammer along with daughters.
Aqsa Parvez (16)	2007 Toronto, Canada	Muhammad Parvez. father, Waqas Parvez, brother (M) / Pakistan	Refusing to wear hijab; ran to shelters.	Strangled
Amina Said (17)	2008 Irving, TX	Yasser Said, father; mother assisted / Egypt (M)	Upset by her "Western" ways; rejected arranged marriage.	Shot

Sarah Said (18)	2008 Irving, TX	Yasser Said, father; mother assisted / Egypt (M)	Upset by her "Western" ways; rejected arranged marriage.	Shot
Fauzia Mohammed (19)	2008 Henriettta, NY	Goaded by mother, Waheed Allah Mohammed, brother / Afghanistan (M)	Too "Western," immodest clothing, planned to attend college in New York City	Stabbed
Sandeela Kanwal (25)	2008 Atlanta, GA	Chaudry Rashid, father / Pakistan (M)	Filed for divorce after arranged marriage	Strangled

Legend: M = Muslim; S = Sikh

In these cases, the average age of the victims was 21.5, and 10 of the 14 were daughters. Importantly, more than half the cases involved multiple perpetrators. Nor is there a significant difference between honor killings in North America and Europe. Neither the average age (20) nor the percentage of daughters as victims in the European cases is significantly different from those in the North American cases. (See Table 3.)

Table 3: European Honor Killings

Victim Name	Year, Location	Perpetrators' Name, Origin	Motive	Method
Surjit Athwal (27)	1998 lured to India from England	Bachan Athwal, grandmother-in-law, her son and another relative / India (S)	Having an affair, planning to divorce.	Lured to India for 'family wedding' and strangled.
Rukhsana Naz (19)	1999 England	Brother and mother / Pakistan (M)	Refused arranged marriage; pregnant with boyfriend's baby.	Strangled by brother while held down by mother
Fadime Sahindal (32)	2002 Sweden	Father and brother / Kurds from Turkey(M)	Rejected arranged marriage; dated non-Muslim; sought higher education; sought legal remedy against father and brother.	Shot
Heshu Yones (16)	2002 England	Abdalla Yones, father / Iraq (M)	Dating a Christian; too Western.	Stabbed, throat cut
Sohane Benziane (17)	2002 France	Jamal Derrar, ex-boyfriend and schoolmates / Algeria (M)	Too Western	Raped, tortured, and burned alive
Anooshe Sediq Ghulam (22)	2002 Norway	Nasruddin Shamsi, husband / Afghanistan (M)	Failure to listen to her husband, divorce.	Shot
Maja Bradaric (16)	2003 The Netherlands	Nephew and 3 others / Bosnia (M)	Using Internet to find a boyfriend	Burned to death

131

Sahjda Bibi (21)	2003 England	Rafaqat Hussain, cousin / Pakistan(M)	Refused arranged marriage	Stabbed 22 times
Anita Gindha (22)	2003 Scotland	Relative suspected / Pakistan (S)	Married non-Sikh.	Strangled
Shafilea Ahmed (16)	2003 England	Parents suspected / Pakistan (M)	Opposed her parents' plans for an arranged marriage	Strangled or smothered
"Gul" (32)	2004 The Netherlands	Husband /Afghanistan(M)	Sought divorce	Shot
Hatin Surucu (23)	2005 Germany	Three brothers / Turkey (M)	Fled forced marriage; did not wear scarf.	Shot
Rudina Qinami (16)	2005 Albania	Father / Albania (M)	Accepted ride by male, non-relative.	Shot
Banaz Mahmod (20)	2006 England	Mahmod Mahmod, father, her uncle Ari Mahmod / Kurds from Iraq (M)	Having an "affair."	Raped, strangled
Samaira Nazir (25)	2006 England	Azhar Nazir, brother and cousin / Pakistan (M)	Fell in love with Afghan refugee; refused to consider arranged marriage in Pakistan	Stabbed, throat cut
Sazan Bajez-Abdullah (24)	2006 Germany	Kazim Mahmud, husband / Iraq (M)	Acting in an "immodest way."	Stabbed, set on fire
Sabia Rani (19)	2006 England	Shazad Khan, husband and in-laws / Pakistan (M)	Wanted divorce	Beaten
Ghazala Khan (18)	2006 Denmark	Brother, father and other family members / Pakistan(M)	Family did not approve of husband	Shot

Caneze Riaz (39)	2006 England	Mohammed Riaz, husband / Pakistan(M)	Too western-ized	Immolated
Sayrah Riaz (16)	2006 England	Mohammed Riaz, father / Pakistan(M)	Too western-ized	Immolated
Sophia Riaz (15)	2006 England	Mohammed Riaz, father / Pakistan(M)	Too western-ized	Immolated
Alicia Riaz (10)	2006 England	Mohammed Riaz, father / Pakistan(M)	Too western-ized	Immolated
Hannah Riaz (3)	2006 England	Mohammed Riaz, father / Pakistan(M)	Too western-ized	Immolated
Hina Saleem (21)	2006 Italy	Father and brother-in-law / Pakistan (M)	Did not respect Paki-stani culture, divorced, wore clothing that showed her midriff	Stabbed
Sana Ali (17)	2007 England	Husband / Pakistan (M)	Not known, but detectives consider hon-or motive	Stabbed
Morsal Obeidi (16)	2008 Germany	Ahmad Obei-di, brother, and cousin / Afghanistan (M)	Wanted too much freedom; did not appreciate Muslim values	Stabbed

Legend: M = Muslim; S = Sikh

In more than half the cases, in both North America (to some extent) and Europe (to a greater extent), family members conducted honor killings with excessive violence—repeatedly stabbing, raping, setting aflame, and bludgeoning. Only in serial-killing-type scenarios are Western women targeted with similar violence; in these cases, the perpetrators are seldom family members, and their victims are often strangers. Despite the obfuscation of Muslim advocacy groups, these case studies show that honor killings are quite distinct from domestic violence. Not all honor killings in the West are perpetrated by Muslims, but the overwhelming majority are. Ninety percent of the honor killers shown in Tables 2 and 3 were Muslim. In every case, perpetrators view their victims as violating rules of proper conduct and act without remorse.

While the sample size is small, this study suggests that honor killing may be accelerating in North America and may correlate with the numbers of first generation immigrants. The problem is diverse but originates with immigration from Muslim-majority countries and regions—the Palestinian territories, the Kurdish regions of Turkey and Iraq, majority Muslim countries in the Balkans, Bangladesh, Egypt, and Afghanistan. Pakistanis accounts for the plurality.

Conflict of Cultural Moralities

The problem the West faces is complex. Muslims, Sikhs, and Hindus view honor and morality as a collective family matter. Rights and responsibilities are collective, not individual. Family, clan, and tribal rights supplant individual human rights.[21]

There are legal interventions underway in Europe, home to between twenty and thirty million Muslim immigrants and their descendents, as opposed to perhaps four million in the United States and Canada.[22] Honor-based violence is, therefore, more visible in Europe than in North America. In 2004, Sweden held an international conference on honor killing, calling for "international cooperation" on the issue. Conference participants concluded:

> Violence in the name of honor must be combated as an obstacle to women's enjoyment of human rights. Interpretations of honor as strongly connected with female chastity must be

---

21 Wikan, "The Honor Culture."

22 Daniel Pipes, "Which Has More Islamist Terrorism, Europe or America?" *The Jerusalem Post*, July 3, 2008.

challenged. It can never be accepted that customs, traditions, or religious considerations are invoked to avoid obligations to eradicate violence against women and girls, including violence in the name of honor. Violence against women must be addressed from a rights-based perspective. ... Measures should be taken in the areas of legislation, employment, education, and sexual and reproductive health and rights. Respect for women's enjoyment of human rights is intrinsically linked to democracy. International conventions must be incorporated into national legislation.[23]

There have since been local conferences in England, France, and Germany. British law enforcement has begun to hide women in a program equivalent to the U.S. Federal witness protection program.[24] Great Britain has passed legislation to empower police to rescue British female citizens whose families have kidnapped and forcibly married them against their will, usually in Pakistan; the police will return them to Britain if they can find them and if the brides request it. There is a special police unit that deals with the forced, arranged marriages of children.[25] A new movement has also arisen in England, "One Law for All. A Campaign against Sharia Law in Britain," launched by Maryam Namazie, an advocate opposed to honor killing and other honor-related violence. She has launched this movement to oppose the use of Sharia courts because they discriminate against women.[26] Additionally, schools in the Netherlands have been asked to be "more alert to honor violence,"[27] following research conducted for the Ministry of Integration.

U.S. law enforcement has made tremendous progress over the last forty years on issues related to violence against women. However, there are not yet any shelters for battered Muslim, Hindu, or Sikh girls or women who fear that they will be murdered by their own families-of-origin. A regular shelter for battered women does not specialize

23 "Combating Patriarchal Violence against Women—Focusing on Violence in the Name of Honor," The Swedish Ministry of Justice and The Swedish Ministry for Foreign Affairs, Stockholm, Dec. 7-8, 2004, p. 51.

24 *International Herald Tribune*, Hong Kong ed., Oct. 20, 1997; *The Observer*, Nov. 21, 2004; "So-called Honor Crimes," Committee on Equal Opportunities for Women and Men, Council of Europe, Paris and Brussels, Mar. 7, 2003.

25 Brandon and Hafez, *Crimes of the Community*, pp. 13, 44.

26 Author e-mail with Maryam Namazie, Dec. 1, 2008.

27 *Nederlands Dagblad* (Barneveld), Nov. 19, 2008; *Islam in Europe*, Nov. 19, 2008.

in honor killings, nor are there any provisions for foster families—Muslim or otherwise—who can protect girls targeted for murder by their own families-of-origin. Many people might view such rescues as a form of cultural oppression; victims would have to forfeit their communal ties and perhaps their very identities in order to remain alive.

It will be more difficult to save adult Muslim women from honor killing because an adult immigrant may not have any regular contact with people outside her immediate family. Only if she survives injuries that require medical attention (and is she is allowed to seek that intervention), will she have contact with strangers who may try to help her rescue herself.

Religious education may also be necessary. According to this study, 90 percent of honor murders in the West are committed by Muslims against Muslims. The perpetrators may interpret the Qur'an and Islam incorrectly, either for malicious reasons or simply because they are ignorant of more tolerant Muslim exegesis or conflate local customs with religion.

Here, Muslim-American and Muslim-Canadian associations might play a role so long as they cease obfuscation and recognize the religious cover given to as well as tribal roots of the problem. Now is the time for sheikhs in the United States and Canada to state without qualification that killing daughters, sisters, wives, and cousins is against Islam. A number of feminist lawyers who work with battered women have credited pro-women sheikhs with helping them enormously. Sheikhs should publicly identify, condemn, and shame honor killers. Those sheikhs who resist doing so should be challenged.

As with issues relating to terrorism, law enforcement and civil servants must be mindful of which Muslim community activists they seek to engage. Many self-described civil rights organizations—CAIR or the Islamic Society of North America, for example—lean towards more radical interpretations of Islam. Groups such as the American Islamic Congress and the American Islamic Forum for Democracy advocate for gender equality and human rights,[28] but because their efforts against radicalism may displease Saudi Arabia and other sources of funding, they often lack resources. Given alternative funding, they might be willing to assist in an effort to educate Muslims against honor murder.

U.S. and Canadian immigration authorities should also be aware

---

28 "Milestones," American Islamic Congress website, accessed Dec. 10, 2008; "Founding Principles and Resolutions," American Islamic Forum for Democracy website, accessed Dec. 10, 2008.

of the issue. They should inform potential Muslim immigrants and new Muslim citizens that it is against the law to beat girls and women, that honor killings are crimes, and that both the murderers and their accomplices can and will be charged. However, as long as Islamist advocacy groups continue to obfuscate the problem, and government and police officials accept their inaccurate versions of reality, women will continue to be killed for honor in the West; such murders may even accelerate. Unchecked by Western law, their blood will be on society's hands.

Middle East Quarterly
Spring 2009

- 35 -
Kingston Police Call it A Muslim Honor Killing

At 2pm EST today, on a CFRA radio press conference, it was announced that the deaths of four Afghan-Canadian girls and a woman was a "Muslim honor killing." If so, this is the fifth known honor killing in Canada since 1999 and it brings the death toll to nine victims. According to statisticians, this is a very high number given that the Muslim population in Canada is no more than 750,000.

The Canadian police have just charged the Shafia family with four counts of first-degree murder and four counts of conspiracy to commit murder in this case. In other words, they understand that both classic honor murders are planned and performed by families, not only by individuals.

Kingston police chief, Stephen Tanner said "It was a needless and senseless loss of human life...They had their lives cut short by members of their own family."

This is also the second (known) Afghan-Canadian honor killing. The first one took place in 2006, and was a father-directed, brother-on-sister murder. The brother, Hasibullah Sadiqi, shot his sister and her fiancée in a shopping mall in Ottawa. Sadiqi stood trial in 2009.

Here is the background to this latest developing story in Canada.

Mohammed Shafia and Rona Amir Mohammed married in Kabul in 1979, the year the Soviets invaded the country. Rona was Mohammed Shafia's first and only wife—that is, until it was clear she could have no children. At some point, he married a second wife, Tooba Mohammed Yahya, with whom he had seven children: both daughters and sons.

The daughters were all born in Kabul, the son might have been born in Dubai. They all moved to Canada in 2007.

No one in St. Leonard, a suburb of Montreal, knew that Shafia was living with two wives. Rona, his first wife, was an intimate member of the family, variously introduced as a "relative," an "aunt," or a "cousin." From a Muslim point of view, Shafia behaved honorably because he did not divorce or banish his first wife even though she was infertile. (Such infertile first wives may become as servants to a fertile second wife.) How polygamy may psychologically affect an entire family is another matter entirely. And, while Shafia may have appeared westernized, that was far from the truth.

Last month, 50-year-old Rona, 19-year-old-Zainab, 17-year-old Sahar, and 13-year-old Geeti were mysteriously all found dead in a car submerged in the Rideau Canal.

Shafia, a polygamist, considered his eldest daughter Zainab, to be a "rebel." He accused her of having a boyfriend. He also told the police that Zainab had taken the car "on a joyride." Shafia mocked Zainab's driving ability.

The fact that his first wife was found dead along with the second wife's "rebellious" older daughter suggests that Rona might have argued for Zainab or might, herself, have longed for a more westernized life. I am not sure why the two younger girls also had to die. Perhaps they were seen as already too influenced by their older sister. Maybe they were in the wrong place at the wrong time.

Yesterday, the police arrested Mohammed Shafia, his second wife, Tooba, and their eldest son on their way to Montreal's Trudeau's International airport. Why would they be leaving at this point? Where were they going?

Rona's sister, Diba Massomi, contacted the police. It was she who first suggested that this was an honor killing. Massomi emailed the Kingston police and said that "for some time, my sister and the Shafia couple's oldest daughter Zainab, had been receiving death threats for social, cultural, and family reasons."

Pajamas Media
7/23/09

- 36 -
Dishonorable Muslim Mass Murder in Canada

The information is so overwhelming and so awful that even the mainstream media has increasingly been forced to describe the plight of women in Muslim lands. Over the weekend, Nicholas D. Kristof tells the story of a new Pakistani hero: Sixteen-year-old, Assiya Rafiq, who was kidnapped, sold, beaten and raped for a solid year—and then raped again when she went to the police to press charges. She, her supportive parents and siblings now live in hiding as she prepares to prosecute both the gang-members and the police.

Today, the *New York Times* and the *Wall Street Journal* both have articles about the return of the Taliban to the Swat Valley in Pakistan and about what that means: The increased kidnapping and indoctrination of children into becoming jihadic warriors and the parallel brutalization of women, infidels, and civilians through beheadings, acid attacks, forced, harsh veiling, and bans on women shopping.

Islam Watch has just reported an increase in the caning of women in Bangladesh (a dangerous and crippling punishment). The same article also discusses the nightmare of one battered Afghan wife whose husband and in-laws kept trying to kill her—and whose own brothers are now trying to kill her because she dared flee and divorce the human monster. This one particular woman has lost custody of her nine children and lives in hiding with the help of an American charitable NGO.

This brings me to the Afghan-Canadian family which has just been charged with the mass murder of four of its female members. We in the West had better start factoring in the international and cultural realities that govern the histories and psychologies of immigrants from Muslim countries.

For example, the Canadian Kingston police did not describe the cold-blooded murder of the Shafia girls and woman as a "Muslim honor killing." Journalists did so but the police were very careful, and rightly so, to refrain from explicitly saying this.

The police are on record as saying that they have evidence that the submerged car, in which all four victims were found drowned, had been driven or tampered with by the three Shafia family members now under arrest; and that a female relative of Rona's who lives in France told the media and the police about credible "death threats" that were leveled against Rona, who was Mohammed Shafia's first wife, (a fact that Mohammed did not disclose to the police or to his neighbors). Implied, but not yet clear, were possible death threats against Zainab Shafia, the oldest of the three murdered daughters, who was becoming too "western."

Shafia and his second wife have seven children. Three are now in state care and one, Hamid Mohammed, is now in police custody.

Initially, the family members put on quite a performance. Mohammed Shafia and Tooba Mohammed Yahya, the biological mother of the three murdered girls, went to the police to report that their family members and second car were missing. They wept, appeared distraught, seemed in shock, carried on like mourners. But it was all an act.

Where else have we seen such behavior? Ah yes: The iconic Arab Palestinian, Mohammed al-Dura's father, was also distraught about his son's death—presumably at Israeli hands. That death turns out to have most probably been staged by Palestinians. The world was sold a bill of Pallywood goods. Read Philippe Karsenty, Richard Landes, Nidra Poller, and Pierre Rehov on the al-Dura case and on other instances in which Muslim propagandists and terrorists have tricked the world media into believing that Israel was the "Nazi" aggressor—all the while diverting attention from Palestinian crimes against their own people, as well as from their considerable aggression towards Israelis, Jews, and Christians.

A number of Canadian newspapers from Vancouver and Montreal to Toronto have cited my study on honor killings which appeared in the spring issue of *Middle East Quarterly*. The media also found people who said that this may not be an honor killing; that dishonorable honor killings are rare and certainly not as epidemic as Western-style domestic violence (not true—not all domestic violence ends in femicide); that honor killings have nothing to do with Islam (alright, but if so, why are so many—mainly–Muslims in the West murdering their daughters, sisters, and wives?).

Pajamas Media
7/27/09

- 37 -

Was Mandana Shojaeifard Honor Murdered in Roslyn, New York?

On Friday, August 7, 2009, Mohamed Shojaeifard, a 49-year-old Iranian scientist, shot his estranged 40-year-old Bangladeshi physician wife, Haleh Mohseni, in the abdomen. Shojaeifard did not stop there. He also shot and killed Mohseni's 65-year-old mother, Batool Biraman—and his own 17-year-old daughter, Mandana, who had just graduated from Roslyn High School and was planning to attend SUNY at New Paltz.

Then he shot and killed himself.

Not a single media account has mentioned this crime as potentially related in any way to culture, ethnicity, religion, immigration, or assimilation. No one raised the possibility that we might be looking at an honor killing.

In some ways, it is a classic honor killing. Shojaiefard was known to have "stalked" his daughter Mandana. According to a neighbor, Shojaiefard "was really violent and kept the mother and daughter as prisoners. The daughter was scared to go to school sometimes because she came covered in bruises. He moved four blocks away, but he drove by all the time, stalking them. It was creepy."

Shojaeifard was a successful professional, a scientist, an educated man. (Oddly, the list of his academic publications have gone missing in the last 24 hours. From my notes: He is/was listed as a faculty member of Iran University, Science and Technology, and published many academic papers in the area of automotive engineering such as "Thermal Contact Analysis Using Identification Method.")

Poverty, starvation, or having to drive a bus or a taxi for the rest of their days did not drive Shojaeifard or other Muslim men to kill their wives, mothers-in-law or daughters.

True, men who honor killed might also have suffered from a psychiatric disorder, refused to take medication, or were driven to violence by medication. However, these men may all have been culturally programmed to torment, beat, and even kill any close female relative who flouted their authority, even in a minor way. The wives in three recent cases (Mohseni, Bhatti-Ahmed, and Hassan) had all moved for divorce; they had moved out of the home (Bhatti and Mohseni) or had their husband evicted (Aasiya Z. Hassan). Mandana Shojaeifard attended a mixed-gender public High School and was leaving, not only her father, but her mother too, to live alone and independently at college.

Assuming Ahmed, Hassan, and Shojaeifard all grew up in a country and culture in which men are taught to feel "unmanned" and dishonored when they lose their grip on their women, they wouldn't need a psychiatric disability to explain their familicidal actions.

Interestingly, all the wives involved were also professional, educated women. Ahmed's wife, Lubaina Bhatti, was a physician—as is Shojaeifard's wife, Haleh Mohseni. Aasiya Z. Hassan worked alongside her husband in an ambitious media enterprise: Bridges, TV.

What may have killed the teenage Mandana Shojaeifard was her mother's perceived westernization. Haleh got out from under the control of her most important male relative. And she took her daughter along with her.

Muslim women may be at special risk when they come to the West. They have major incentives to assimilate and, of course, major incentives not to. When Muslim women assimilate, they either risk being honor murdered—or they risk losing their whole community because they cannot marry within it. They may never have children, and may never exactly "fit" into any other community.

The price of freedom for them may be very high indeed.

Haleh Mohseni, a beloved Bronx family physician, survived the attack. She has lost the two people she loved most: Her daughter, bright with promise, and her emotionally supportive mother. If she has the strength and courage, she might consider founding a shelter for battered Muslim girls and women, as well as talking to medical, law enforcement, and school officials about what happened to her.

Every young girl she saves will never replace Mandana—but they will all call her "mother."

Pajamas Media
8/9/09

- 38 -

Honor Killing Averted: Muslim Convert to Christianity Flees for Her Life

Yesterday afternoon, my living room was filled with lights, cameras, and two very friendly ABC crew men. We were taping an interview for *Good Morning America* which appeared today and which is preserved at their website. We talked about honor killings and the plight of Fathima Rifqa Bary, the Muslim teenager from Ohio who converted to Christianity and who ran away from home because she knows her father will kill her.

Seventeen-year-old Rifqa's plight is heartbreaking. She knows that if a Muslim leaves Islam, converts to another religion, becomes is an "apostate," that they are supposed to be killed by any other Muslim; this includes members of her own family.

If someone from a Jewish or Christian fundamentalist home converts out, they may be ostracized, they may be treated as if they had died, but they are not physically killed.

Weeping, the very frightened teenager from Sri Lanka knows that most western journalists (and the police who turned her over to the state and forced her into a public trial), do not believe this can be true. How quickly they forget Salman Rushdie's situation. How easily everyone is lulled into viewing fundamentalist Islam as a religion just like any other, as if Islam-on-the-march today is still the "soft," cosmopolitan, hospitable culture it has occasionally been in the past, in certain cities and for certain monied people.

Rifqa is the seventeen-year-old teenager who secretly converted to Christianity and who fled her family's home in 2009. Not only did she claim serious childhood abuse, she also insisted that her family would honor murder her now that her conversion was known.

At the time, as a psychologist and the author of studies about honor killings in the West, I was asked by Florida's Attorney General to submit an affadavit on Rifqa's behalf. I did so, as did my friend and colleague, Ibn Warraq, the author of *Leaving Islam: Apostates Speak Out*.

We both explained that Rifqa's fears were utterly realistic; that apostasy is considered a capital crime in Islam; and that Muslim women had already been honor murdered in the West for this alleged "crime" and for refusing to convert to Islam. Some had been forced into hiding to save their lives.

In addition, I focused on the fact that Muslim girls and women have been honor murdered in the West for having Christian or non-Muslim friends, including boyfriends; for wanting to marry Christian men. Imagine how much more of a sin it is for a Muslim to choose a Christian God!

Rifqa did not get her day in court in Florida. She was returned to state custody in Ohio where she has been living with a foster family.

She is in real danger. On camera, Rifqa keeps saying: "You guys don't understand, my life is at stake, this is reality, this is the truth, they have to kill me if they love God more than they love me."

Here is what can happen to her. Rifqa may be "forced" to return to Islam. Her family may place her under house arrest, and bring in the mullahs to reason with or brainwash her; her mother may beg her to relent so that the family may remain together as before. If all else fails, Rifqa may be sent back to Sri Lanka either to be killed or to be confined to a lunatic asylum. She may be killed here. What absolutely cannot happen is for her religious Muslim family to remain close to her as she follows another religious path very publicly.

I do not have all the facts at my disposal. Thus, it is possible that Rifqa's father may genuinely view her as mentally ill (because only a "crazy" girl would do such a blasphemous thing) and, because he loves her, has decided not to abandon her, but to try and reach her, help her... return to her senses and therefore to Islam.

By the way: the weeping and terrified Rifqa has probably been coached for the interview, she is slightly "hysterical," she seems somewhat auto-hypnotized. And yet, she also makes perfect sense. She is quite in touch with reality.

What can we offer someone like Rifqa in America? There is, as yet, no shelter in America for the intended victims of an honor killing. So far, no prosecutor has accused any murderer of committing an honor killing in America. I hope and pray that Rifqa Bary is not returned to her parents. Even so, her life will be very hard. She is a young immigrant with, as yet, no marketable skills, who will never again be able to claim the protection of an extended family of origin. She may have to live in hiding for the rest of her life. But, she will have her religion, and to the extent to which she remains fervently religious, she may also have a faith-based community.

And, she will remain alive. Nothing more but at least that.

Pajamas Media
8/13/09

- 39 -

Muslims Don't Kill Apostates—and 9/11 Has
Nothing to Do with Islam

Fathima Rifqa Bary, the Muslim teenager who converted to Christianity at least four years ago but who only recently ran away, has been taken away from the two good Samaritan Christian pastors who took her in and is now in state custody in Florida. On Friday, a judge will decide whether her case should be heard in Florida or Ohio. Her parents have "lawyered" up, her father, Mohamed Bary, a jeweler, insists that he never threatened to kill her, that he wants her to come home. The mainstream media is getting nervous. What if they believe what Rifqa says and they end up sued? Or worse?

After all, the Columbus police have challenged the girl's claim that she is in danger. Sgt Jerry Cupp, chief of the Columbus police missing person's bureau, has said that "Mohamed Bary comes across to me as a loving, caring, worried father about the whereabouts and the health of his daughter."

So much for Ohio. But allow me to point out that for weeks, Afghan-Canadian Mohammed Shafia and his second wife, Rona Amir Mohammed, wept, mourned, and generally carried on about the deaths of their three daughters and of Mohammed's first wife—until the police arrested both Mohammed and Rona, along with one of their sons, for having been behind these heinous, heartless, murders.

Now, Florida Imam Hatim Hamidullah, with the Islamic Society of Central Florida, has informed us that the Muslim faith does not call for a father to hurt his child, should she convert to another religion.

"It is not Islam for the father to bring harm upon his blood daugh-

149

ter or any other human being because of anger," he said. "Our position is to exhaust all measures that would bring peace and harmony back to the family...Being angry and threatening the life of someone is not one of those methods."

Someone has got to explain the technique of *taqiyya* (the high Islamic Art of disinformation) to the Ohio police, to the judiciary in both Ohio and Florida, and to the mainstream media.

A Muslim is a human being who, like all other human beings, will probably lie to save his life. In addition, a Muslim, (or another tribally-identified person), might also lie to save his...honor. No Muslim (or Hindu or Sikh) is going to tell the world that: "Oh yes, by the way, some of us, might actually kill one of our own."

Thus, the attacks on 9/11 were really not Muslim or even Saudi "operations." True, most of the hijackers were Arab Sunni Muslims from Saudi Arabia but that is entirely beside the point. These attacks were, rather, undertaken by a) Muslims who hijacked an otherwise "peaceful" religion; b) the attacks were an "anti-Islamic" operation undertaken specifically to give "peaceful" Islam a bad name; c) everyone knows that 9/11 was an inside CIA and Zionist plot meant to justify America's attack on Iraq/al-Qaeda/Afghanistan.

This is *taqiyya* in action.

Therefore, when an honor killing of a daughter, wife, or female cousin occurs in the West, Muslim leaders insist that the crime has absolutely nothing to do with Islam or with the Qur'an; that the murderer is just one more domestically violent man, just like the violent men who exist everywhere, even in the West.

The usual teenage "crimes" of "Westernization" are not as important as converting to another religion, away from Islam. A boyfriend is bad enough. Another God? Unthinkable. Shameful. Christianity and Judaism are seen, at best, as lesser, earlier, failed religions which should have embraced Islam as the more perfected religion but which refused to do so. The serious persecution of Christians and Jews in Muslim lands for this precise reason is well-known.

Fathima Rifqa Bary apparently converted to Christianity more than four years ago. If so, it is impossible for the Pastors, Beverly and Blake Lorenz to have "kidnapped" or "influenced" her. According to one media report:

> Rifqa, a high school junior in well-off suburban New Albany, had been questioning her faith for several months, her father

said. She attended church with friends from school and later attended services at another church, Xenos Christian Fellowship, a megachurch that emphasizes small groups meeting at home....After Rifqa proselytized with a Bible at school, Mohamed Bary said, the family asked her to stop because it wasn't an appropriate activity in school. They also told her she had an obligation to study her original faith first, before choosing another.

One wonders whether or not such an obligation to study Islam might not be considered a lifelong obligation. All Muslims, even parents, have an obligation to kill any Muslim who converts to another religion. This is why some Muslim apostates write under pseudonyms.

Now, if Rifqa's family were an assimilated, anti-religious or non-religious Muslim family with many non-Muslim friends, relatives, and business colleagues—perhaps with family members who themselves had converted to an other religion—it might be a different matter. That does not seem to be the case here.

Religious freedom and religious tolerance are Western values. Such tolerance does not exist in Muslim countries, certainly not today. Also, no matter where a Muslim might have grown up, Islamic identity today, even among second-and-third-generation immigrants, but especially among many first-generation and recent immigrants (which the Barys are), is increasingly a globalized identity, and one which is an increasingly radicalized one.

One hopes that the Florida judge will seriously consider the information about how Muslims utilize *taqiyya*, treat apostates, as well as Christians in the Middle East and Asia, and why Muslims honor murder their daughters and female relatives. Based on such information, perhaps the judge will not return Rifqa to Ohio. If she or he does, one hopes that the Ohio judge will never return Rifqa to the custody of her parents.

Pajamas Media
8/18/09

- 40 -

Freedom of Religion: A Precious American Right, an Islamic Capital Crime

G iven the anti-Christian views of many Muslims and those of Western atheists and secularists, I wonder if Rifqa Bary, the teenage convert from Islam to Christianity, is seen as a hero who is fighting for her freedom of religion—or, more likely, as someone who has taken a forbidden or reactionary path. Perhaps if Rifqa had launched a lawsuit for the right to wear hijab or a burqa in Ohio she might immediately have gotten mainstream media sympathy.

The mainstream American media simply refuses to cover the Islamification of the West. Publishers run scared when I mention this as a possible next book title of mine. Newspapers are reluctant to cover honor killings or attempted honor killings in America at all, or in an accurate and informed way.

As yet, I cannot find Rifqa's amazing and important story anywhere in the national mainstream media. I know that Fox is working on a story because they've talked to me about the issues this case raises. Am I surprised? Not really. There was either no or very little coverage of the honor killings that took place in the last decade in North America in Cleveland, St. Clairsville, Toronto, Chicago, Jersey City, British Columbia, Scottsville, Ottawa, Toronto, Dallas, Atlanta, Oak Forest, Alexandria, Buffalo, Kingston, Canada, Roslyn.

What is really going on?

The guiding template is Israel versus the Palestinians. The actual aggressors are seen as innocent, misunderstood, and noble, their real victims are seen as provocative, rebellious, evil or mentally ill—especially if they dare to fight back, run away, or expose the truth of the matter.

The Israelis are "Nazis" perpetrating a new "Holocaust" against the Palestinians. In the case of the incredibly brave Rifqa Bary, we now have a victim of a potential honor killing trying to save her own life—and she is being portrayed as "mentally ill" or as a liar. I am told that she is being characterized in the local Ohio media as unstable while her father is being portrayed as loving and caring.

Twenty years ago, two honor killings took place in Ohio. I have written about them in my most recent book, *The Death of Feminism*, which discusses how Islamic gender apartheid has penetrated the West and how Western progressives have failed to take a stand against it. A decade ago, the Ohio media covered one of the trials very carefully and comprehensively.

Guess what? In 2005, when my book first came out, a number of reporters from Ohio contacted me. They were interested in talking to me about my views on those very Ohio cases. I agreed to talk to them. The interviews never appeared. And why? Because "higher ups" would not allow the journalists to do the story. By now, Islamists have put down roots in Ohio while other Islamists have intimidated the Hell out of the West through a series of non-stop, highly co-ordinated suicide bombings, airplane hijackings, acid attacks, stonings, riots, video-ed beheadings, and lawsuits.

We are engaged in a new kind of war in which civilians are prized military targets and in which truth tellers may be forced to self-censor, stop publishing altogether (except in cyberspace), publish and embrace poverty, publish and face being demonized, kidnapped, murdered—or sued.

When anyone tries to tell the truth about fundamentalist Islam or about Muslim terrorists; when they try to talk about the overt subordination of Muslim women both in their home countries and in the West, the truth-tellers are inevitably described as racist, Islamophobic, reactionary, and hopelessly conservative. (This last is meant as an insult and is not a mere descriptor.)

America: We have got to do better than this. We have got to understand that many of our most prominent and influential professors, intellectuals, and journalists have fallen under an evil spell.

They believe every piece of *taqiyya* (disinformation) which comes their way; fall for Big Lies and Blood Libels; do not check whether what they are being told in English is the same thing that is being said in Arabic or Persian; fail to understand that the same sentence may mean one thing to a western non-Muslim audience but something else entirely to a Muslim audience.

Finally, our "best and our brightest" stubbornly, even suicidally, refuse to learn from experience. No matter how many Big Lies have been exposed as devilish ruses—(the Israelis murdered Mohammed al-Dura, perpetrated a massacre in Jenin, and are harvesting organs from Palestinians to sell for huge profits)—Western journalists continue to believe the new Big Lies, one after the other.

As the song asks: When will they learn, when will they ever learn?

Pajamas Media
8/20/09

- 41 -

Mother of Dead Dallas Girls Calls
Their Murder An Honor Killing

The mother who lured her two young daughters, Sarah and Amina, to their tragic deaths at the hand of their father, Yasser Said, now regrets what she did. Downplaying her own role, or rather, insisting that she is innocent, Tissy Owens Said calls the murder of her daughters an "honor killing" by an "evil man." Despite years of paternal child abuse at home, Tissy now insists that she had no idea that Yasser was actually going to kill the girls whom he had sexually and physically abused and whose "too Western" ways had enraged him.

Sarah and Amina refused to marry older, unknown men from Egypt in arranged marriages. They had American ways, academic ambitions, and Christian friends, including Christian boyfriends. Unthinkable! And, like Rifqa Bary, they knew they were in danger and so they ran away. Their mother sweet talked them back home. They were dead within hours. Their father has never been found.

My guess? Tissy is angry that Yasser never sent for her—and that she has also lost her son, Islam, who has been living with his paternal uncles or perhaps with his father. She is alone. She has no one. Perhaps she wants some attention—and the media is only too ready to provide Tissy with that for another fifteen minutes of infamy.

Are female collaborators guilty, morally if not criminally, in the crimes committed by their husbands, boyfriends, or by their male business associates toward even more vulnerable women and children? Was the battered Hedda Nussbaum guilty in the death of Lisa Steinberg, the five-year-old non-adopted daughter who was tragically and repeatedly abused and then finally beaten to death by Joel Steinberg?

Is Tissy likewise responsible? Are the wives who don't ask and don't tell anyone, including themselves, about their husbands' sex slaves, also morally and criminally liable? If not, why not?

At the G8 conference in Rome about Violence Against Women, Isoke Aikpitanyi, a most dignified and beautiful young woman, spoke about how she was trafficked into Italy from Nigeria and exposed the fact that other women were the ones who trapped her and kept her trapped. This brave soul has now set up a shelter for other victims of trafficking in Italy.

Although Tissy may be slow-witted and may also have been controlled by her husband, whom she married when she herself was only a child—in my opinion, Tissy should have been arrested a long time ago as an accomplice in this honor murder.

I hope the Florida Rifqa Bary Court takes note that teenage Muslim girls have been honor killed in North America by their fathers and that prior to their deaths, even if there is a record of child abuse (as exists in the Said case), that ultimately, the state does not necessarily remove the children from the household, the state does not always protect children from their own families.

Pajamas Media
9/18/09

- 42 -
Western Justice for Honor Killers

W hen girls or women suddenly disappear, we tend to assume that they've been kidnapped by pedophiles or traffickers. Some of us think they were probably prostitutes and either deserved to die or were, tragically, lured to their deaths by a serial killer.

We do not think they might have been killed by their own families. And we always assume that the kidnappers and slavers are men. Both beliefs are wrong.

For example, in 1999, in a suburb north of London, a fifteen year old Kurdish Turk, Tulay Goren, suddenly disappeared. The family insisted that she had simply run away. Now, a decade later, her father, Mehmet Goren and her paternal uncles, Cuma Goren and Ali Goren, are on trial at the Old Bailey for her murder and for having conspired to kill her boyfriend, Halil Unal.

This case may be the first honor killing which the British police have re-opened after a decade and which they are trying as an "honor killing." I do not usually praise the British, but I must do so here. They are leading the European pack in terms of dealing with honor killings.

What was this poor child Tulay's crime? She fell in love with a Sunni Muslim; Tulay was from the Alevi branch of the Muslim faith. Her father demanded that she take a "virginity test." Her father felt "dishonored, humiliated." He punched and kicked Tulay. Wisely, Tulay ran away from home twice and asked to be put in a children's home. Tulay wanted to marry Halil (he had asked for her hand in marriage), but she had already been "promised" to her first cousin.

Tulay's mother, Hanim, sweet-talked her into returning home. Meanwhile, Tulay's father consulted with his older and younger brothers on the matter, and with their approval and encouragement, killed his daughter. At least one of the brothers helped dispose of Tulay's body, which has never been found. At least fifteen family members attended a meeting which led to the decision to murder Tulay. Tulay was viewed as a "worthless commodity" who had shamed her entire family.

Now, her mother is testifying for the prosecution. Although she was sent away the night Tulay was murdered, Hanim has now recanted what she formerly told the police, namely that Tulay had run away. Hanim admits that she noticed the "earth being disturbed in the garden, knives and bin-bags disappearing and her husband washing his shirt." She has also testified to seeing a "deep injury" to her husband's palm and her daughter's clothes missing.

Tulay tried to escape and was even able to warn her boyfriend—which saved his life.

Mehmet Goren apparently had a hard time assimilating. He could not master the English language, had a gambling problem, and was never regularly employed. Thus, while Mehmet may or may not have been a religious fundamentalist, he and his family certainly upheld the cultural traditions of Kurdish Turks who are Muslims.

Tulay's case is a classic honor killing, one in which a fairly young girl—a female child, really—is killed by multiple perpetrators, all members of her family of origin, especially her father, with her mother's complicity. Her crime? She refused to marry her first cousin and dared to choose her own husband-to-be.

Tulay was assimilating, she was becoming "too westernized." This alone is a capital crime. She imagined a future of her own, one not entirely chosen for her by her family. Tulay had to be stopped, an example had to be set, so that other immigrant girls would not take this path and would continue consenting to arranged marriages to their first cousins so that they may "breed" acceptably inbred babies.

I wonder what influenced Tulay's mother to now break with her entire family. What will the consequences of doing so be?

Pajamas Media
10/12/09

- 43 -
Spinning Out of Control: Honor Killings and Media Bias

W e are entering an all-spin zone, a wild, weird and spooky season and I am not talking about Halloween.

With a few exceptions, the mainstream media continue to kill stories about honor killings and attempted honor killings in North America. How often did you read stories about the honor killings that took place in Toronto (07), Dallas (08), Atlanta (08), Oak Forest, Illinois (08), Alexandria (08), Buffalo (09), and Kingston, Canada (09)—on and on, until the most recent attempted honor killing in Phoenix?

There are two killers still on the loose: Yasser Said, the Dallas monster out of Egypt who abused, stalked, and murdered his two daughters with the help of his wife, their mother, and his son, their brother—and Iraqi-born Faleh Hassan Almaleki, who is also on the lam.

Just last week, Almaleki ran over his 20-year-old daughter, Noor, with a car because she was "too western." He mowed her down with a two-ton Jeep Grand Cherokee. Faleh also tried to kill the older woman who was with her, Amal Edan Khalef, with whom Noor was living. Amal had rescued Noor, but she was also the mother of Noor's boyfriend. Both women are now in the hospital; Noor remains unconscious and is barely clinging to life.

Noor had been fighting with her father for years. She did not want to agree to or to remain in her arranged marriage (in Iraq!) and had left the Middle East and dared to choose a boyfriend of her own. Yes, Noor also had pages on Facebook and MySpace. Noor knew she was living in the United States and not in the Middle East. Apparently, her father did

159

not accept this reality.

With the exception of brief, one-time reportage, the mainstream national media have not covered this murder. Only *True Crime Reports* has updated the story. The local Arizona media have covered it and they've said things as strange as the local Dallas media did in the Said case (it was not an honor killing, honor killings have nothing to do with Islam or with Muslims), and as strange as the Florida media did in the case of Rifqa Bary, the teenage apostate runaway whom a Florida judge has just sent back to Ohio.

Although the matter was decided narrowly, as a strictly jurisdictional decision, the local media downplayed the danger that former Muslims face after they leave Islam. Hopefully, the Ohio judge will not do so. And by the way: In custody cases (and Bary's case is just that), judges usually have the discretion to listen to the wishes of minor children as young as 12. Bary is 17 years old and old enough to know where danger lies.

Now, back to the 4,000-pound raging Iraqi father.

The *Arizona Republic* quotes Tom Keil, a professor at Arizona State University who said that honor killings exist "deep in the isolated hills of Appalachian Kentucky... (and is) prevalent in clannish societies."

With all due respect to the scholar of Appalachia, I have just completed a study of honor killings on five continents that will be published in *Middle East Quarterly*. Although some Sikhs and Hindus do commit honor murders in the West, this is primarily a Muslim-on-Muslim crime.

But I'm going up against the most incredibly smooth and seamless spin, one that is constant, omnipresent. Really big.

Allow me to suggest that Obama's White House, (and the politicians and media it influences), is engaged in micro-managing the news about Islam.

For example: A network (which shall remain nameless) approached me for a comment on a story they were doing about President Obama's faith advisor, Dalia Mogahed. Let us say that the subject concerned Sharia law, Muslim women, and gender justice. But before the network could publish their story (which challenged some of Mogahed's views and acts), guess what? A major interview with Mogahed suddenly appeared in the pages of *US News and World Report*. The interview allowed Mogahed to backtrack, explain, put a slightly different spin on what she'd previously said about Muslim women's view of Sharia law as the vehicle which provides gender justice.

I mean minutes, perhaps no more than an hour, before the first story was slated to appear. That story is now cancelled.

And oh yes: Here's what Jordanian journalist, Rania Husseini, recently said on Amy Goodman's program *Democracy Now* about honor killings in Jordan. According to my source, Martin Rosenthal, "Husseini claimed that honor killings have nothing to do with any particular religion." He sent me a small excerpt of what Ms. Husseini said in the interview:

> So it's [honor killings are] really not restricted to any religion. I have covered cases of Christian women who were killed in Jordan for tarnishing their families' honor, same in other parts of the Middle East. So really it has nothing to do with any religion. I think it's mostly a tribal—I'm sorry, it's a traditional practice more than a religious. For example, in India, Sikh families kill their daughters. In Iraq, a woman from a Yazidi faith was stoned to death recently. So, really, it has nothing to do with any religion, as much as it has to do with peoples' wrongful cultural and traditional beliefs.

It is never, ever about Islam and tribalism, *and* when Muslims do something truly ghastly (like mow down their own daughter with a car or fly planes into the World Trade Center and the Pentagon), it is always someone else's fault: The Zionists, the Americans, the Western colonialists, the daughter herself who, after all, forced her father into having to defend his honor.

Pajamas Media
10/26/09

- 44 -
Honor Killings All Over America

Last week, the Iraqi father who drove a two ton jeep into and over his daughter in Arizona for being "too westernized" high-tailed it out of town, drove down to Mexico where he abandoned his vehicle and caught a flight to London. UK Port of Entry authorities denied him entry, contacted US authorities and placed him back on a plane to the US. Almaleki was arrested when his plane landed in Atlanta, then returned to Arizona where he now sits in jail.

"Agencies involved included the US Marshalls Office, Immigration and Customs Enforcement, the FBI, Arizona Department of Public Safety, officials in the United Kingdom, and officials from the Nogales and Sonora, Mexico Police."

Hurrah for the combined law enforcement heroes in action.

What's missing from the coverage (at least so far) is the usual Islamist spin. No hard-line representative of the Islamic community is insisting that this was not an "honor killing" or that if it was, it has nothing to do with Islam or with Muslims; that's it's a typical 'teenage" thing or a typical case of domestic violence.

Which brings us to the second attempted honor killing story which might be a first of its kind. A woman, defending the honor of Islam, tried to kill her easygoing husband. He lived—but the attempted murder was serious. Will Islamists defend and support her, embrace her as a good Muslim? Or shun her as a psychiatrically troubled woman?

Rabia Sarwar, a religious Muslim wife living on Staten Island in New York, attempted to murder her husband because he "enjoyed booze and pork and wanted her to dress in revealing clothing." She claims he tried to force her to drink alcohol and eat pork too. Rabia piously tried to slit his throat. So far, the experts quoted on this case in the *New York Post* (Ayaan Hirsi Ali, Amil Imani) are actually talking about honor killings, mentioning the case of Rifqa Bary, Almaleki, and Sarwar in the same breath and relating them all to Islam. Imani is quoted as saying: "In the privacy of their home, Muslim parents will call every American woman a prostitute, every man corrupt."

However, a more complex picture emerges in the *True Crime Report* version of this case, one which explains that Rabia and her family feel utterly deceived by Rabia's husband, who was no "Sheikh Naseem" but was really "Eddie," a man who was married twice before, is a Norwegian-Pakistani, and actually a Unitarian!

> But after they married, she found that he'd mostly dated white women, had been married before and liked to drink. He'd also said he was a devout Muslim, but she later discovered he was Unitarian. She further wrote that his favorite writer was Salman Rushdie, author of *The Satanic Verses*, which caused such a stir in the fundamentalist Muslim world that Iran officially put a hit on Rushdie.

My guess: Islamists will portray Rabia Sarwar as mentally ill, not as an honorable enforcer of the tribal custom of slaughtering those who stray from the straight-and-narrow. (Eddie certainly thinks she's crazy too and claims that's she's done time in a loony bin.) Indeed, Muzzammil Hassan (the Buffalo man who beheaded his long-battered wife, Aasiya), is already jockeying for a mental health expert who can describe his state of mind as "extremely emotionally distressed."

Pajamas Media
11/1/09

- 45 -
Canada to Immigrants: No Tolerance for "Honor Killing"

The Canadian government has just revamped its citizenship guide for immigrants. The document is titled "The Rights and Responsibilities of Canadian Citizenship." According to Canada's *National Post*,

> "In Canada, men and women are equal under the law," the document says. "Canada's openness and generosity do not extend to barbaric cultural practices that tolerate spousal abuse, 'honour killings,' female genital mutilation or other gender-based violence. Those guilty of these crimes are severely punished under Canada's criminal laws."

Western governments are beginning to wake up to criminal and barbaric practices among immigrants—especially among Muslim immigrants in the West. Whether such practices are pre-Islamic, non-Islamic, even anti-Islamic (and people have argued all of the above), the truth is that such practices are most often committed by Muslims against Muslims. Sikhs and Hindus, to a much lesser extent, also commit Sikh-on-Sikh and Hindu-on-Hindu honor murders in the West.

Canada has just sentenced a man to a year in jail for threatening—just threatening—violence against his daughter. In 2007, the town council in Herouxville, Quebec passed a motion "governing the behavior of immigrants, including provisions against stoning women and genital mutilation."

Canada is not the only country moving in this direction. For example, Britain has opened a special police section to deal with honor-based crimes, including honor-related violence and honor killings. They have the power to find and return a girl or woman who has been kidnapped, sent to her country of origin and married against her will—if she signals for help, can be found, and states a desire to return to the UK. Scotland Yard has also reopened cases that they now believe were honor killings but were not classified as such a decade ago.

If a family collaborates in the honor murder of one of its members, and some remain bystanders to the crime, what might serve as a possible disincentive? Why not make it clear that western governments will not only jail, try, and sentence the murderer and all his accomplices but will also deport even the presumably innocent ("bystander") members of the extended family? For immigrants who care deeply about their extended families, something like this might serve as the only disincentive.

Pajamas Media
11/13/09

- 46 -

In Three Separate Honor Killing Cases:
A Father Convicted in London,
A Husband Convicted in Holland—
An Entire Clan Convicted in Denmark

A decade ago in London, Tulay Goren's father terrorized then plotted to honor-murder his 15-year-old daughter. And then the girl simply...disappeared. Nevertheless, due to a British police decision to revisit and reclassify old cases, the father has just now been convicted of her honor murder.

Although her body has never been discovered, first-person testimony by the girl's mother, Hanim, by her sister, Hatice (in a video, taken before her death), and by the victim's fiancé, Halil Unal, led to this verdict.

In an amazing break with tradition, a mother sided with her daughter, not with the husband who fed, clothed, battered, and terrorized her. She exposed the kind of murderous, at-home tyranny with which women are expected to collaborate. Bravely, she broke with the normalization of woman's inhumanity to woman.

Mehmet Goren, the convicted honor murderer, now 49 years old, immigrated from the Kurdish region of Turkey. His daughter Tulay's crime? She dared fall in love—and with a man who was not only twice her age but who was a Sunni, not a Shiia Muslim. Her father and his brothers strongly disapproved of this match. Tulay then "sinned" again—she ran away from home twice, a home in which both she and her mother were routinely battered and terrorized. Mehmet's brothers were not found guilty of conspiring in Tulay's murder.

Mehmet also tried to murder Tulay's boyfriend, Halil Unal, who survived the attack. Tulay herself reported being attacked twice by her father.

According to the Telegraph, it was ten years before Tulay's mother Hanim agreed to tell the truth about her violent husband. In emotional scenes in court a sobbing Mrs. Goren said:

> In the children's bedroom I saw Tulay lying on the floor face down. Her hands and her feet were tied. Her hands and her feet were all a purple black colour.

> Hatice cried and screamed and jumped on her and the two of us tried to untie her, and Tulay said: "Mum don't untie me, I want to die." In the meantime Mehmet had come from downstairs and said "don't untie, don't touch," he said.

Mrs. Goren continued: "After that Mehmet said: 'So that she doesn't run away again I have tied her up.'"

She also gave key evidence about the aftermath of the murder, in which she found knives missing from the kitchen, bin bags used up, and the back garden of her home in Glastonbury Avenue, Woodford Green, dug over.

Hanim said she was "suspicious" when she saw Mehmet's freshly laundered shirt, as he had never done the washing in more than 20 years of marriage. She also noticed injuries to her husband's hands, including a large gash to one of his palms.

This conviction is due to an increased incidence and exposure of honor killings in the UK and in the West; to resources dedicated to prevent or prosecute such cases; and, as I've suggested, to the ultimate bravery of family members who finally chose to testify for the victim.

In 2007, a conviction was also obtained in another other honor-killing case, which took place in the UK long ago. Banaz Mahmod was stripped naked, raped, and then strangled on the orders of her father, Mahmod Mahmod. Her father, uncle, and a third man, Mohammed Hama, were convicted and given life sentences.

Meanwhile, this same week, a Dutch court in Amsterdam sentenced Younis K. (39) to nine years for having brutally murdered his wife Aisha K. (36). The court called the murder "horrible" and said that Aisha must have suffered "terrible pain." Aisha, the mother of four children, wanted to divorce her husband. He responded by "beating her many times with cricket bats." His cousin, Tariq S., who presumably helped him, was acquitted. The prosecution had asked for 14 years in prison for both men.

However, in terms of understanding and successfully prosecuting an honor murder as a family conspiracy, Denmark leads the pack. As I've previously noted, last week, a Danish court convicted an entire clan in the murder of 18-year-old Ghazala Khan, a Danish-born woman of Pakistani origin. Her thirty-year-old brother, Akhtar Abbas, had been delegated to shoot her to death two days after she married an Afghan man; her Pakistani family had not arranged this marriage. This was Ghazala's capital offense.

Her aunt betrayed her when she lured the newlyweds to a promised reconciliation. Ghazala was shot dead, her husband survived the attack.

The Danish verdict is historic, not only because the entire clan was punished, but also because the head of the family, who ordered the killing, was given a heavier sentence than the actual murderer.

I still fear for the brave mother who testified against her husband in London. Since Mehmet Goren's brothers were not found guilty, I would hope that the brave Hanim is already in a witness protection program. They will surely come after her.

Pajamas Media
12/17/09

- 47 -
Honor Killers: Prosecuted in Europe, Seen as Psychiatric Victims in America

On October 20, 2009, near Phoenix, Arizona, Noor Al-Maleki's father, Iraqi-born Faleh Hassan Al-Maleki, ran over his 20-year-old daughter with a two-ton Jeep. The case has been described, correctly, as an "honor killing." According to Arizona Central, Arizona lawyer Billie Little, who represented Faleh Hassan Al-Maleki, insisted that since Andrew Thomas, the prosecutor in the case, is a Christian, that: "(We need) some level of assurance that there is no appearance that a Christian is seeking to execute a Muslim for racial, political, religious or cultural beliefs."

This statement does not belong in a courtroom.

Perhaps Islam is not and should not be on trial here, but Muslim customs, Muslim behavior, surely is. It is the proverbial elephant in the room. How can the prosecutor not mention it? And, once mentioned, how easy it will be to gain pity for the poor, allegedly "racially profiled" murderer?

In addition, Mr. Little is demanding that his client be psychiatrically evaluated because "he does not understand basic court proceedings." I wonder: Is Mr. Little consulting with Muzzammil Hassan's lawyer in Buffalo? He's the Pakistani-born charmer who severely battered and then beheaded his lovely wife Aasiya. Hassan's lawyer is arguing "extreme emotional disturbance." This is rather ironic since this kind of defense has been used, often unsuccessfully, on behalf of battered women.

Then, there is the case of Nidal Malik Hasan, the Fort Hood massacrist. The Fort Hood Hasan is now also being seen as suffering from a psychiatric disorder, a secondary or even pre-post traumatic syndrome. As I pointed out right away, he is an Islamic Islamic jihadist; a jihadist should not be viewed as having a psychiatric disorder because he perpetrates jihad in the West.

In yet another recent and precedent-setting European decision, a Turkish-Muslim family who live in Graz, Austria, were sentenced to probation for threatening to kill a female member because she wanted to marry an Austrian man who was not of Turkish origin and who was not a Muslim.

Here is part of the story in *Kleine Zeitung*:

"In our cultural circle," says (the sister), a 19 year old with a Graz dialect, "it's not common to marry an Austrian."

"You are also Austrian," prosecutor Hansjörg Bacher reminds her.

Her older sister (20) fell in love with an Austrian, a Christian. "We couldn't envision our daughter marrying an Austrian," says the father.—"You are also Austrian!"

The mother and father are accused of threatening the daughter and her friend, mentioning "death" and a "killing spree." They then agreed that the two would get married, but the father had to leave the country for losing face. And they couldn't vouch for their relatives.

The father was sentenced to twelve months probation, the mother to ten months probation, and a sister was fined. Please note: Legal action was taken because verbal threats were made. The Austrian Court understood that such threats are to be taken quite seriously. The girl (the intended honor killing target) has gone into hiding.

Pajamas Media
1/14/10

- 48 -

Can Counseling Prevent a Potential Honor Killing?

The lawyers in the Rifqa Bary case have negotiated a reasonable and potentially life-saving settlement which will allow Rifqa to remain in state custody until she becomes 18 in August, at which time she herself will decide whether or not she wishes to be reunited with her family.

According to the Columbus-Dispatch, Rifqa admitted that she'd been "unruly" when she'd fled her home, and that the "family will try to resolve their issues with counseling." In a statement read by Rifqa's attorneys, "both she and her parents said they loved each other and believe counseling is the best route."

The family's honor has now been slightly salvaged by Rifqa's open admission (clearly, an admission that had been required) that she'd been…"unruly."

Is it "unruly" to choose one's own God, or to try and save one's own life? In grand American tradition, "counseling" is seen as an all-purpose, face-saving panacea, a way of avoiding a more superficial or harsher rule of law—a way of dealing with problems that are far beyond (or beneath) a judge's purview. Thus, "The case plan for Rifqa and her parents says they should talk about their respective religions and visit and communicate regularly."

And so, the Bary family (the teenager and her parents) will now enter counseling—always a dicey proposition, in my opinion: Girls and women are especially vulnerable to false promises of happy endings. Many grown, battered Western women report how well their sociopath-

171

ic batterers bond with their counselors, and how their own anxieties and justified paranoia are minimized, scorned. Ultimately, these women may not only be diagnosed as "crazy," they may also lose their children, their homes, even their lives—right under their counselor's nose.

One can only hope that the counselor in the Bary case will know a great deal about the nature of honor killings and the fate of apostates in Islam.

However, according to one source, the Bary parents want a Muslim-only counselor; do not want her to receive Christmas cards; and are asking the court to hold Rifqa in contempt for refusing to meet with a Muslim counselor.

Update: The magistrate did allow Rifqa to live apart from her parents.

Pajamas Media
1/20/10

- 49 -
Honor Killings in Finland

I'm not at all surprised by the "surprising" news coming out of Finland concerning a potentially new kind of honor-based victim.

Native Finnish women who marry "immigrant" men (the article simply will not use the word "Muslim") have begun to flee for their lives to avoid being honor-killed—not only by their husbands, but also by their husbands' family, even by his entire clan. One Finnish woman who married into an "immigrant" family says:

> "They've threatened to kidnap my children, and my husband has repeatedly threatened to kill me. He says nobody can stop them, that horrible things happen, and he doesn't even have to do them himself, that revenge will come from the clan…." The Multicultural Women's Association, Monika, which runs a safe house for immigrant women and their children, says that more and more Finnish women are turning to them when Finnish authorities fail to understand the threat of honour violence.

According to Nasima Razmyar, Monika's Project Manager:

> You can have 200 people involved in honour-related violence, that is, the entire extended family. And not just the family in Finland, but relatives abroad and back in the home country. In general, our laws need to understand much better this type of group threat…One problem is that Finnish authorities in

social services and on the police force treat honour violence just like any other case of domestic violence. They don't take into account the fact that instead of a dispute between two individuals, honour violence pits a single woman against the wrath of a large group of people.

Tundra Tabloids reports that Finnish state news had pulled the article about honor-related violence in Finland but restored it recently in a more sanitized form. Here's what was deleted from the original article:

Among immigrants honor violence has occurred in Finland for many years.

She said that her marriage was hell, but no one believed her.

The woman is the man's property and thus he can assault the woman however he pleases, if the woman refuses to obey the rules.

Honor violence has been increasing in recent years in Finland, when unmarried young women immigrants from a foreign culture struggle under the pressure. They may be forced to marry and be prohibited from socializing with Finns.

We're currently unable to secure and protect the lives of people in the way that the authorities should do, Hukkanen says.

The Phyllis Chesler Organization
1/20/10

- 50 -
Major Israeli Palestinian Arab Demonstration
Against Palestinian Honor Killings

While Vice President Joe Biden played the part of a dishonored diplomat in Jerusalem, his wife, Jill Biden, was visiting the Bedouin Women's Empowerment Project in the Negev.

I hope she understood just how "empowered" these women really are. Sixty of these Israeli Arab Bedouin women recently came in busloads from the Negev to Nazareth to join a total of 500 Israeli Arabs in a protest against honor killings in their communities. They constituted the largest contingent of women, "thanks to the work of Hind el Sana, a lobbyist in Shatil's Bedouin Women's Leadership Project. The Project, which is funded by the American State Department in conjunction with The New Israel Fund, is run in collaboration with Ma'an, the Forum of Arab Women's Organizations in the Negev, where el Sana is based."

The anti-honor killing demonstration was attended by Israeli MKs (Members of Parliament), the mayor of Nazareth, (a city in northern Israel and protected by Israel), and other prominent figures. Many demonstrators were young, many were not; most wore Western clothing, many wore hijab. They carried amazing signs and banners in Arabic: "Your Silence Equals Permission to Kill"; "A Civilized Society Does Not Kill Women"; "The Hands are the Killers, but Silence and Understanding are a Society's Crime"; and signs which bore the name of Palestinian Arab honor murder victims such as Reem Abu Ghanem (murdered in 2006), Halima Ahmed (murdered in 2009), and Abeer Abu Damous (murdered in 2010).

The demonstrators called for an "end to the murder of women who are thought to sully the honor of their families by violating traditional, patriarchal restrictions on relationships between men and women. A young woman who dates a young man without her parents' consent falls into this category."

"There is no honor in this crime," declared MK Masoud Ghanayem.

MK Muhammad Baraka added: "Whenever someone kills his sister, his daughter, his wife, he does not become more honorable, but he becomes a murderer and villain."

The demonstration was organized by Women against Violence in Nazareth. This kind of demonstration has never taken place in Gaza City or in West Bank cities under the control of the Palestinian Authority.

This demonstration is wonderful news. Arab men and women, young and old, modern and traditional—all marching for Palestinian women's' lives.

In April 2008, two American college graduates, Emma Hansson and Elizabeth Freed, did a study, "Women Under Siege," which was supported by Dorot, a Jewish group which provides grants for students to study in Israel.

They found that in "Palestine, the integration of traditional tribal laws and the establishment of official laws through the PA result in an unstable and inconsistent application of law. Being based on patriarchal and tribal structures this legal fusion [creates] a system [which] is highly discriminatory against women. Domestic violence is considered a 'minor' offense, 'honor' killings are regarded as a family matter, and if a rapist marries his victim, he escapes punishment."

They suggest that violence against women, honor-related violence, and honor killings in Palestine "serve to uphold the male dominated structures, instilling fear in women."

Hansson and Freed mention the Intifada at least twice—but only as one of many factors which may exacerbate violence against Palestinian women. Violence may have increased since the Palestinian warlords declared yet another jihad against the Jews—but the authors quote Palestinian feminist Nadera Shalhoub-Kevorkian, who "declares that the Intifada has led to an increased politicization of Islam and a failing respect for human rights."

Hamas has cracked down against women and against women's clothing; more Palestinian women are wearing the Islamic Veil than ever before. Palestinian-on-Palestinian violence (both male-on-male and male-on-female) is generally, routinely quite high; it may now be even higher.

The Nazareth protesters, both male and female, did not blame the alleged Israeli "occupation" for an increase in Palestinian male violence towards Palestinian women. These demonstrators are all Israeli citizens which is precisely why they could launch such a spirited defense of women's human rights.

On January 23, 2010, the British medical journal *The Lancet* published a piece which did just that—blamed the Israelis for an increase in wife-battering among Gazans. I challenged that article.

At the time, I had not yet read the Hansson and Freed article—which the *Lancet* researchers do not cite. They do not have to cite it because they chose to omit honor killing as a form of domestic violence against Palestinian women. And why? Because that is a tribal, cultural, patriarchal, Arab, perhaps Muslim custom for which the Israelis cannot be blamed. Hence, the *Lancet* authors dropped the most extreme form of violence against Palestinian women—femicide.

The good news? According to Hansson and Freed, a shelter for women (a *Mehawar*) has finally opened its doors in Israel/Palestine for the victims of incest, rape, childhood sexual harassment and domestic violence.

Hansson and Freed address their remarks and make their suggestions to the Palestinian Authority—not to the Israeli authorities.

The Western mainstream media did not cover this marvelous demonstration against honor killing in Nazareth. However, it appeared in the Arabic media.

Pajamas Media
3/18/10

Is Being "Americanized" a Capital Crime in America for Muslim Women?

Her mother was in on the honor/horror killing; her brother and a paternal relative knew about it—if not in advance then immediately afterward. Her brother, Ali, had begun to call his sister "vile" names. Ali also believed that she had "dishonored" the family. Her own mother, Seham, viewed her daughter as "dirty," as someone who was living with a "dirty" woman, a "liar." She even told her daughter that she was no longer her mother—that the "dirty" woman was now her mother.

My main question: Will the Arizona police haul in Seham and Ali as accomplices to this honor/horror killing? European courts have begun to do just this. Will America follow suit or not?

Kudos to Paul Rubin, who has written a long and excellent journalistic account of the Noor Al-Maleki case in a suburb of Phoenix, Arizona. Rubin obtained access to unreleased police records. I also tip my hat to Jeffrey Imm of R.E.A.L., who brought Rubin's article to my attention.

Allow me to draw some important conclusions from Rubin's detailed account.

The honor/horror killing family will never tell the police the truth. It will have to be dragged out of them. Evidence will have to face them down. Even then, they will keep "spinning" the story. This was the case with the Kingston, Canada mass honor femicides, and it is the case here.

Thus, at first, Noor's mother, Seham, said she knew nothing, did not know where her husband Faleh was, had no idea how he had gotten away, did not know if he had tried to kill their daughter or not. However, according to cell-tower records, the police found out that "within minutes of Faleh's fleeing the bloody scene, he spoke by cellphone to his wife, to their son Ali, and to at least two other members of his extended family." At first, Seham Almaleki, who had been in California at a job, claimed that "all she knew was that there was a family problem of an unspecified nature." When the police told her that her husband had "intentionally slammed into Noor and Amal (the older woman with whom Noor was living), this is all Seham said: "This woman is a liar. This woman is dirty. Her family is dirty."

Not a word of concern about her daughter. The police "got it." Therefore, when Seham said that she wanted to see her daughter immediately, they did not allow Seham to visit the hospitalized and unconscious Noor. Seham's response? "I'm a danger?" Seham shouted. "I'm a Muslim. We can't kill our daughter."

The police learned that a young man of Middle Eastern origin and a "veiled" woman had picked up a prescription for diabetes in Faleh's name. Ali finally admitted that his father had called him before the murder to tell him to "man up" because his father would not be around any longer. And, Seham finally admitted that yes, she and her son had picked up the medicine for Faleh—but that subsequently, "she'd thrown the pill bottles out of her car window, though she couldn't come up with a reason for having done so." (Faleh had his medicine with him when he was apprehended in the UK).

Seham continued to adamantly blame Amal, another woman, for what her husband had done. As the author of *Woman's Inhumanity to Woman* (which I was recently interviewed about), I am not at all surprised by a mother betraying her own daughter and blaming another woman for her husband's crimes.

Faleh is also a practiced liar. First, he claimed that it had all been a "freakish accident." Then, he asked, why would he kill his daughter with a car? "I have no problem with my daughter...If I want to kill her, I go buy a gun, I know where they live. I just lost control of the car."

Eventually, he said that he had also lost control of his "brain," that it was not a premeditated crime. But then he said that his daughter "should not have become so Americanized—that it was wrong." And then he justified the murder. "If your house has got a fire in just part of the house, do we let the house burn or do we try to stop the fire?" Noor was the "small fire" that had to be extinguished.

Ali managed to contradict himself as well when he told the police that the "slaying was unplanned." And then he warned the media. "You guys be careful what you say. That's my father you're talking about. And my father is a loving man. He loved Noor…Why would he do this if he loved her?"

Ali's explanation: "He lost his mind."

Muzzammil Hassan in Buffalo who savagely battered and then beheaded his wife Aasiya is also arguing "extreme emotional distress" and portraying himself as a battered husband and victim. The other Hasan, Dr. Malik, the Fort Hood shooter, has also been presented (mainly by the media) as having suffered from "secondary post-traumatic stress"—allegedly caused by all that listening to soldiers who suffered in Iraq or Afghanistan.

In other words: Just as many Islamists are demanding the right to practice Islamic gender and religious apartheid in the West, using Western concepts of religious pluralism and tolerance—just so, are Islamists beginning to describe what their culture may view as a "righteous kill" as motivated by and proof of emotional suffering and mental distress.

And, Faleh, like Muzzammil, is crafty, aggressive, and persistent. Muzzammil writes letters to the newspapers from his jail cell describing himself as a wounded, long-suffering victim; he signs the letters with his mother's name. And Faleh has asked his cousin to get the Iraqi Consulate to intervene, to explain that an "Iraqi is worth nothing without his honor." Faleh has also suggested that Jamal (his cousin who fled to Iraq) do the following:

> Have friends sit across from the U.S. Embassy in Iraq and hold signs saying 'The Iraqi honor is precious.' Signs that say I'm not a criminal, that I didn't break into someone's house, that I didn't steal…for an Iraqi, honor is the most valuable thing…we are a tribal society that can't change, I didn't kill someone off the street.

Faleh asked his wife and son to find a good lawyer—preferably not a Jew—to find a "loophole in this subject—you know, clans, tribalism, something like that." And then, he contradicts himself. "The Jews know of it (loopholes)."

Does this sound like a contrite father? Or like a mentally unbalanced man?

For those new to this case, here are Noor's presumed "crimes." Raised in America, Noor ran away from a marriage that her father had arranged for her in Iraq. She came back to America. She wore American clothes, used American-youth expressions (like "Dude,") had pages at

Facebook and Myspace. She dressed glamorously, attractively—and she had a boyfriend. After seeking refuge with another Iraqi woman, Amal, a former friend of her family, Noor developed some kind of relationship with Amal's son. (It is unclear what kind of relationship this was, exactly).

As the oldest girl in the family, with three younger sisters, Noor was setting a bad example for her younger siblings. Who would marry them? Worse: They might all follow Noor's example.

I am giving the last word to beautiful Noor herself: In an email exchange with a friend just before she was murdered, Noor typed "Dude, I am so scared....I'm so shaky...My dad is a manipulative asshole. I've honestly never met anyone...so evil."

Pajamas Media
4/1/10

- 52 -
Worldwide Trends in Honor Killings

To combat the epidemic of honor killings requires understanding what makes these murders unique. They differ from plain and psychopathic homicides, serial killings, crimes of passion, revenge killings, and domestic violence. Their motivation is different and based on codes of morality and behavior that typify some cultures, often reinforced by fundamentalist religious dictates. In 2000, the United Nations estimated that there are 5,000 honor killings every year.[1] That number might be reasonable for Pakistan alone, but worldwide the numbers are much greater. In 2002 and again in 2004, the U.N. brought a resolution to end honor killings and other honor-related crimes. In 2004, at a meeting in The Hague about the rising tide of honor killings in Europe, law enforcement officers from the U.K. announced plans to begin reopening old cases to see if certain murders were, indeed, honor murders.[2] The number of honor killings is routinely underestimated and most estimates are little more than guesses that vary widely. Definitive or reliable worldwide estimates of honor killing incidence do not exist.

Most honor killings are not classified as such, are rarely prosecuted, or when prosecuted in the Muslim world, result in relatively light sentences.[3] When an honor killing occurs in the West, many people, including the police, still shy away from calling it an honor killing. In the West, both Islamist and feminist groups, including domestic vio-

---

1 "Ending Violence against Women and Girls," *State of the World Population 2000* (New York: United Nations Population Fund, 2000), chap. 3.

2 *BBC News*, June 22, 2004.

3 Yotam Feldner, "'Honor' Murders–Why the Perps Get off Easy," *Middle East Quarterly*, Dec. 2000, pp. 41-50.

lence activists, continue to insist that honor killings are a form of West-ern-style domestic violence.[4] They are not.[5] This study documents that there are at least two types of honor killings and two victim populations. Both types differ significantly from each other, just as they differ from Western domestic femicide (or women-slaughter). One group has an average age of seventeen; the other group's average age is thirty-six. The age difference is a statistically significant one.

Methodology

This study analyzes 172 incidents and 230 honor-killing victims. The information was obtained from the English-language media around the world with one exception. There were 100 victims murdered for honor in the West, including 33 in North America and 67 in Europe. There were 130 additional victims in the Muslim world. Most of the per-petrators were Muslims, as were their victims, and most of the victims were women.

The perpetrators and victims in this study lived in the following twenty-nine countries or territories: Afghanistan, Albania, Bangladesh, Belgium, Canada, Denmark, Egypt, France, Gaza Strip, Germany, In-dia, Iran, Iraq, Israel, Italy, Jordan, Netherlands, Norway, Pakistan, Rus-sia, Saudi Arabia, Scotland, Sweden, Switzerland, Syria, Turkey, United Kingdom, United States, and the West Bank.

In general, statistically significant interactions were found for age, geographical region, the participation of multiple perpetrators (mainly members of the victim's family of origin, including the victim's father), family position, multiple victims, the use of torture, and the stated mo-tive for the murder. Between 1989 and 2009, reported honor killings may have also escalated over time in a statistically significant way. (It is always possible that media coverage and police involvement have in-creased rather than the actual number of honor killings).

Worldwide, the majority of victims were women; a mere 7 percent were men. Only five men were killed by their families of origin whereas

---

4 See, for example, *SoundVision.com*, Islamic information and products site, Aug. 24, 2000; Sheila Musaji, "The Death of Aqsa Parvez Should Be an Interfaith Call to Action," *The American Muslim*, Dec. 14, 2007; Mohammed Elmasry, Canadian Islamic Congress, *Fox News.com*, Dec. 12, 2007; Mustafaa Carroll, Dallas branch of the Coun-cil of American-Islamic Relations, *FoxNews.com*, Oct. 14, 2008.
5 See Chapter 34. Phyllis Chesler, "Are Honor Killings Simply Domestic Vio-lence?" *Middle East Quarterly*, Spring 2009, pp. 61-9.

the rest of the male victims were killed by the families of the women with whom they were allegedly consorting or planning to consort with either within or outside of marriage. The murdered male victims were usually perceived as men who were unacceptable due to lower class or caste status, because the marriage had not been arranged by the woman's family of origin, because they were not the woman's first cousin, or because the men had allegedly engaged in pre- or extramarital sex. Men were rarely killed when they were alone; 81 percent were killed when the couple in question was together.

Although Sikhs and Hindus do commit such murders, these sampled honor killings, worldwide and in the West, are mainly Muslim-on-Muslim crimes. In this study, worldwide, 91 percent of perpetrators were Muslims. In North America, most killers (84 percent) were Muslims, with only a few Sikhs and even fewer Hindus perpetrating honor killings; in Europe, Muslims comprised an even larger majority at 96 percent while Sikhs were a tiny percentage. In Muslim-majority countries, obviously almost all the perpetrators were Muslims. With only two exceptions, the victims were all members of the same religious group as their murderers.

In the West, 76 individuals or groups of multiple perpetrators killed one hundred people. Of these perpetrators, 37 percent came from Pakistan; 17 percent were of Iraqi origin while Turks and Afghans made up 12 and 11 percent, respectively. The remainder, just under a quarter in all, came from Albania, Algeria, Bosnia, Egypt, Ethiopia, Guyana, India, Iran, Morocco, and the West Bank.

Families Killing Their Young Women

The study's findings indicate that reported honor killings accelerated significantly in a 20-year period between 1989 and 2009.[6] This may mean that honor killings are genuinely escalating, perhaps as a function of jihadist extremism and Islamic fundamentalism, or, more likely, that honor killings are being more often reported and prosecuted, especially in the West, but also in the East. The expansion of the Internet may account for wider reporting of these incidents.

The worldwide average age of victims for the entire population is twenty-three (see Table 1 below). This is true for all geographical regions. Thus, wherever an honor killing is committed, it is primarily a

---

6 According to the Pearson product-moment correlation coefficient, the most widely used measure of correlation or association.

crime against young people. Just over half of these victims were daughters and sisters; about a quarter were wives and girlfriends of the perpetrators. The remainder included mothers, aunts, nieces, cousins, uncles, or non-relatives.

Honor killings are a family collaboration. Worldwide, two-thirds of the victims were killed by their families of origin. (See Table 1). Murder by the family of origin was at its highest (72 percent) in the Muslim world and at its lowest in North America (49 percent); European families of origin were involved almost as often as those in the Muslim world, possibly because so many are first- or second-generation immigrants and, therefore, still tightly bound to their native cultures. Alternatively, this might be due to the Islamist radicalization of third or even fourth generations. Internationally, fathers played an active role in over one-third of the honor murders. Fathers were most involved in North America (52 percent) and least involved in the Muslim world; in Europe, fathers were involved in more than one-third of the murders.

Worldwide, 42 percent of these murders were carried out by multiple perpetrators, a characteristic which distinguishes them considerably from Western domestic femicide. A small number of the murders worldwide involved more than one victim. Multiple murders were at their highest in North America and at their lowest in Europe. In the Muslim world, just under a quarter of the murders involved more than one victim. Additional victims included the dead woman's children, boyfriend, fiancé, husband, sister, brother, or parents.

Worldwide, more than half the victims were tortured; i.e., they did not die instantly but in agony. In North America, over one-third of the victims were tortured; in Europe, two-thirds were tortured; in the Muslim world, half were tortured. Torturous deaths include: being raped or gang-raped before being killed; being strangled or bludgeoned to death; being stabbed many times (10 to 40 times); being stoned or burned to death; being beheaded, inexpertly suffocated, or having one's throat slashed.

Finally, worldwide, 58 percent of the victims were murdered for being "too Western" and/or for resisting or disobeying cultural and religious expectations (see Table 1). The accusation of being "too Western" was the exact language used by the perpetrator or perpetrators. Being "too Western" meant being seen as too independent, not subservient enough, refusing to wear varieties of Islamic clothing (including forms of the veil), wanting an advanced education and a career, having non-Muslim (or non-Sikh or non-Hindu) friends or boyfriends, refusing to marry one's first cousin, wanting to choose one's own husband, choosing a socially "inferior" or non-Muslim (or non-Sikh or non-Hindu) husband; or leaving an abusive husband. There were statistically significant regional differences for this motive. For example, in North America, 91 percent of victims were murdered for being "too Western" as compared to a smaller but still substantial number (71 percent) in Europe. In comparison, only 43 percent of victims were killed for this reason in the Muslim world.

Less than half (42 percent) of the victims worldwide were murdered for committing an alleged "sexual impropriety;" this refers to victims who had been raped, were allegedly having extra-marital affairs, or who were viewed as "promiscuous" (even where this might not refer to actual sexual promiscuity or even sexual activity). However, in the Muslim world, 57 percent of victims were murdered for this motive as compared to 29 percent in Europe and a small number (9 percent) in North America.

What the Age Differences Mean

This study documents that there are at least two different kinds of honor killings and/or two different victim populations: one made up of female children and young women whose average age is seventeen (Table 3), the other composed of women whose average age is thirty-six (Table 5). Both kinds of honor murders differ from Western domestic femicide.

In the non-immigrant West, serious domestic violence exists which includes incest, child abuse, marital rape, marital battering, marital stalking, and marital post-battering femicide. However, there is no cultural pattern of fathers specifically targeting or murdering their teenage or young adult daughters, nor do families of origin participate in planning, perpetrating, justifying, and valorizing such murders. Clearly, these characteristics define the classic honor killing of younger women and girls.

The honor murders of older women might seem to resemble Western-style domestic femicide. The victim is an older married woman, usually a mother, who is often killed by her husband but also by multiple perpetrators (30 percent of the time). Worldwide, almost half (44 percent) of those who kill older-age victims include members of either the victim's family of origin or members of her husband's family of origin. (See Table 5.) This is extremely rare in a Western domestic femicide; the husband who kills his wife in the West is rarely assisted by members of his family of origin or by his in-laws.

However, in the Muslim world, older-age honor killing victims are murdered by their own families of origin nearly two-thirds of the time. This suggests that the old-world custom has changed somewhat in Europe where the victim's family of origin participates in her murder almost one-third (31 percent) of the time. Thus far, in North America, no members of the family of origin have participated in the honor killing of an older-age victim. Whether North America will eventually come to resemble Europe or even the Muslim world remains to be seen, as this will be influenced by immigration demographics and by other factors. Finally, nearly half the older-age victims are subjected to a torturous death. However, the torture rate was at its highest (68 percent) in Europe for female victims of all ages. The torture rate was 35 percent and 51 percent in North America and in the Muslim world, respectively.

Worldwide, younger-age victims were killed by their families of origin 81 percent of the time. In North America, 94 percent were killed by their family of origin; this figure was 77 percent in Europe and 82 percent in the Muslim world. (See Table 3.) In North America, fathers had a hands-on role in 100 percent of the cases when the daughter was eighteen-years-old or younger (See Table 4). Worldwide, younger-age women and girls were tortured 53 percent of the time; however, in Europe, they were tortured between 72 and 83 percent of the time—significantly more than older-age women worldwide.

Western Responses to Honor Killing

Many Western feminists and advocates for victims of domestic violence have confused Western domestic violence or domestic femicide (the two are different) with the honor killing femicides of older-age victims. Representatives of Islamist pressure groups including the Council on American-Islamic Relations (CAIR) and the Canadian Islamic Congress, various academics (e.g., Ajay Nair, Tom Keil), activists (e.g., Rana Husseini), and religious leaders (e.g., Abdulhai Patel of the Canadian Council of Imams) have insisted that honor killings either do not exist or have nothing to do with Islam; that they are cultural, tribal, pre-Islamic customs, and that, in any event, domestic violence exists everywhere.[7] Feminists who work with the victims of domestic violence have

---

7 See, for example, *SoundVision.com*, Aug. 24, 2000; Musaji, "The Death of Aqsa Parvez Should Be an Interfaith Call to Action"; Elmasry, *Fox News.com,* Dec. 12, 2007;

seen so much violence against women that they are uncomfortable sin-gling out one group of perpetrators, especially an immigrant or Muslim group. However, as we have just seen, Western domestic femicide differs significantly from honor killing.[8]

Former National Organization for Women (NOW) president Kim Gandy compared the battered and beheaded Aasiya Hassan[9] to the bat-tered (but still living) pop star Rihanna and further questioned whether Hassan's murder was an honor killing:

> Is a Muslim man in Buffalo more likely to kill his wife than a Catholic man in Buffalo? A Jewish man in Buffalo? I don't know the answer to that, but I know that there is plenty of violence to go around—and that the long and sordid history of oppressing women in the name of religion surely includes Islam, but is not limited to Islam.[10]

At the time of the Hassan beheading, a coalition of domestic vi-olence workers sent an (unpublished) letter to the Erie County district attorney's office and to some media stating that this was not an hon-or killing, that honor killings had nothing to do with Islam, and that sensationalizing Muslim domestic violence was not only racist but also served to render invisible the much larger incidence of both domestic violence and domestic femicide. They have a point, but they also miss the point, namely, that apples are not oranges and that honor killings are not the same as Western domestic violence, including femicides.

One might argue that the stated murder motive of being "too West-ernized" may, in a sense, overlap substantively with the stated and un-stated motives involved in Western domestic femicide. In both instanc-es, the woman is expected to live with male violence and to remain silent about it. She is not supposed to leave—or to leave with the children or any other male "property." However, the need to keep a woman isolated, subordinate, fearful, and dependent through the use of violence does

Carroll, *FoxNews.com*, Oct. 14, 2008.

8 Chesler, "Are Honor Killings Simply Domestic Violence?" (Chapter 34); "A Civilized Dialogue about Islam and Honor Killing: When Feminist Heroes Disagree," *Chesler Chronicles*, Mar. 2, 2009; "Jordanian Journalist Rana Husseini on 'Murder in the Name of Honor: The True Story of One Woman's Heroic Fight Against an Unbelievable Crime,'" *Democracy Now*, Oct. 21, 2009.

9 *Fox News*, Feb. 16, 2009.

10 Kim Gandy, NOW president, "Below the Belt. No Woman, No Culture Immune to Violence against Women," Feb. 20, 2009.

not reflect a Western cultural or religious value; rather, it reflects the individual, psychological pathology of the Western batterer-murderer. On the other hand, an honor killing reflects the culture's values aimed at regulating female behavior—values that the family, including the victim's family, is expected to enforce and uphold.

Further, such cultural, ethnic, or tribal values are not often condemned by the major religious and political leaders in developing Muslim countries or in immigrant communities in the West. On the contrary, such communities maintain an enforced silence on all matters of religious, cultural, or communal "sensitivity." Today, such leaders (and their many followers) often tempt, shame, or force Muslim girls and women into wearing a variety of body coverings including the hijab (head covering), burqa, or chadari (full-body covering) as an expression of religiosity and cultural pride or as an expression of symbolic resistance to the non-Muslim West.[11] Muslim men are allowed to dress like Westerners, and no one challenges the ubiquitous use of Western technology, including airplanes, cell phones, the Internet, or satellite television as un-Islamic. But Muslim women are expected to bear the burden of upholding these ancient and allegedly religious customs of gender apartheid.

It is clear that Muslim girls and women are murdered for honor in both the West and the East when they refuse to wear the hijab or choose to wear it improperly. In addition, they are killed for behaving in Western or modern ways when they express a desire to attend college, have careers, live independent lives, have non-Muslim friends (including boyfriends with whom they may or may not be sexually involved), choose their own husbands, refuse to marry their first cousins, or want to leave an abusive husband. This "Westernization" trend also exists in Muslim countries but to a lesser extent. Allegations of unacceptable "Westernization" accounted for 44 percent of honor murders in the Muslim world as compared to 71 percent in Europe and 91 percent in North America.

Tempted by Western ideas, desiring to assimilate, and hoping to escape lives of subordination, those girls and women who exercise their option to be Western are killed—at early ages and in particularly gruesome ways. Frightening honor murders may constitute an object lesson to other Muslim girls and women about what may happen to them if they act on the temptation to do more than serve their fathers

---

11 *BBC News*, Oct. 5, 2006; Aisha Stacey, "Why Muslim Women Wear the Veil," *Islam-Religion.com*, Nov 15, 2009.

and brothers as domestic servants, marry their first cousin and breed as many children as possible. The honor murder of women already living in the West may also be intended as lessons for other female immigrants who are expected to lead subordinate and segregated lives amid the temptations and privileges of freedom. This is especially true in Europe where large Muslim ghettos have formed in the past few decades. It is particularly alarming to note that in Europe 96 percent of the honor killing perpetrators are Muslims.

The level of primal, sadistic, or barbaric savagery shown in honor killings towards a female family intimate more closely approximates some of the murders in the West perpetrated by serial killers against prostitutes or randomly selected women. It also suggests that gender separatism, the devaluation of girls and women, normalized child physical, psychological, and sexual abuse; arranged child marriages of both boys and girls; sexual repression; misogyny (sometimes inspired by misogynist interpretations of the Qur'an); and the demands made by an increase in the violent ideology of jihad all lead to murderous levels of aggression towards girls and women. One only has to kill a few girls and women to keep the others in line. Honor killings are, in a sense, a form of domestic terrorism, meant to ensure that Muslim women wear the Islamic veil, have Muslim babies, and mingle only with other Muslims.

Since Muslim immigration and, therefore, family networks are more restricted in North America than in Europe, honor-killing fathers may feel that the entire burden for upholding standards for female behavior falls heavily upon them and them alone. This may account for the fact that fathers are responsible 100 percent of the time for the honor murders of the youngest-age victims. In Europe and in the Muslim world, that burden may more easily be shared by sons and brothers, grandfathers, uncles, and male cousins.

What Must Be Done

How can this problem be addressed? Immigration, law enforcement, and religious authorities must all be included in education, prevention, and prosecution efforts in the matter of honor killings.

In addition, shelters for battered Muslim girls and women should be established and multilingual staff appropriately trained in the facts about honor killings. For example, young Muslim girls are frequently lured back home by their mothers. When a shelter resident receives such a phone call, the staff must immediately go on high alert. The equivalent of a federal witness protection program for the intended targets of honor killings should be created; England has already established such a program.[12] Extended safe surrogate family networks must be created to replace existing family networks; the intended victims themselves, with enormous assistance, may become each other's "sisters."

In addition, clear government warnings must be issued to Muslim, Sikh, and Hindu immigrants and citizens: Honor killings will be prosecuted in the West, and perpetrators, accomplices, and enablers will all be prosecuted. Participating families may also be publicly shamed. Criminals may (and should) be deported after they have served their sentences.

Western judicial systems and governments have recently begun to address this problem. In 2006, a Danish court convicted nine members of a clan for the honor murder of Ghazala Khan.[13] In 2009, a German court sentenced a father to life in prison for having ordered his son to murder his sister for the family honor while the 20-year-old son was sentenced to nine and a half years.[14] In another case, a British court, with the help of testimony from the victim's mother and fiancé, convicted a father of a 10-year-old honor murder after the crime was reclassified;[15] and, for the first time, the Canadian government informed new immigrants:

> Canada's openness and generosity do not extend to barbaric cultural practices that tolerate spousal abuse, "honour killings," female genital mutilation or other gender-based violence. Those guilty of these crimes are severely punished under Canada's criminal laws.[16]

Islamic gender apartheid is a human rights violation and cannot be justified in the name of cultural relativism, tolerance, anti-racism, diversity, or political correctness. As long as Islamist groups continue to deny, minimize, or obfuscate the problem, and government and police officials accept their inaccurate versions of reality, women will continue to be killed for honor in the West.

---

12 James Brandon and Salam Hafez, *Crimes of the Community: Honour-based Violence in the UK* (London: Centre for Social Cohesion, 2008), pp. 136-40.

13 *Brussels Journal*, July 2, 2006.

14 *Deutsche Welle* (Bonn), Dec. 29, 2009.

15 *The Guardian* (London), Dec. 17, 2009.

16 *The National Post* (Don Mills, Ont.), Nov. 12, 2009.

The battle for women's rights is central to the battle for Europe and for Western values. It is a necessary part of true democracy, along with freedom of religion, tolerance for homosexuals, and freedom of dissent. Here, then, is exactly where the greatest battle of the twenty-first century is joined.

Table One: Entire Population (N = 230)

Region	Worldwide	North America	Europe	Muslim World
Average Age	23	25	22	23
By Percentage				
Killed by Family of Origin[1,2]	66	49	66	72
Family Position[1]				
—Daughter/ Sister	53	50	49	56
—Wife/ Girlfriend	23	27	34	17
—Other[3]	24	33	27	27
Paternal Participation[4]	37	53	39	31
Multiple Perpetrators	42	42	45	41
Multiple Victims[1]	17	30	7	21
Tortured[1]	53	39	67	49
Motive[4]				
—"too Western"	58	91	71	43
—"sexual impropriety"	42	9	29	57

1 Significant according to a chi square test.
2 Family of origin includes fathers, mothers, brothers, grandfathers, uncles, and male cousins.
3 "Other" includes mothers, aunts, cousins, and no familial relation.
4 Significant according to a Pearson correlation test.

Table Two: Women Only, All Ages (N = 214)

Region	Worldwide	North America	Europe	Muslim World
Average Age	23	26	21	23
By Percentage				
Killed by Family of Origin[1,2]	69	52	66	75
Family Position[1]				
—Daughter/ Sister	56	52	53	58
—Wife/ Girlfriend	24	28	37	17
—Other[3]	20	20	10	25
Paternal Participation[4]	39	52	42	33
Multiple Perpetrators	18	30	7	21
Multiple Victims[1]	18	30	7	21
Tortured[1]	54	35	68	51
Motive[4]				
—"too Western"	58	89	73	44
—"sexual impropriety"	42	11	27	56

1 Significant according to a chi square test.
2 Family of origin includes fathers, mothers, brothers, grandfathers, uncles, and male cousins.
3 "Other" includes mothers, aunts, cousins, and no familial relation.
4 Significant according to a Pearson correlation test.

Table Three: Females 25 Years of Age and Younger (N = 129)

Region	Worldwide	North America	Europe	Muslim World
Average Age	17	18	18	17
By Percentage				
Killed by Family of Origin[1,2]	81	94	77	82
Family Position[1]				
—Daughter/ Sister	74	94	67	73
—Wife/ Girlfriend	14	0	20	14
—Other[3]	3	6	13	13
Paternal Participation[4]	54	88	54	46
Multiple Perpetrators	46	75	46	38
Multiple Victims[1]	17	30	8	20
Tortured[1]	53	25	72	47
Motive[4]				
—"too Western"	57	88	74	38
—"sexual impropriety"	43	12	26	62

1 Significant according to a chi square test.
2 Family of origin includes fathers, mothers, brothers, grandfathers, uncles, and male cousins.
3 "Other" includes mothers, aunts, cousins, and no familial relation.
4 Significant according to a Pearson correlation test.

Table Four: Females 18 Years of Age and Younger (N = 68)

Region	Worldwide	North America	Europe	Muslim World
Average Age	15	15	14	13
By Percentage				
Killed by Family of Origin[1,2]	89	90	86	90
Family Position[1]				
—Daughter/ Sister	82	100	78	79
—Wife/ Girlfriend	8	0	9	6
—Other[3]	10	0	9	15
Paternal Participation[4]	70	100	68	61
Multiple Perpetrators	39	80	32	32
Multiple Victims[1]	25	29	16	30
Tortured[1]	55	30	83	58
Motive[4]				
—"too Western"	55	80	67	41
—"sexual impropriety"	45	20	33	59

1 Significant according to a chi square test.
2 Family of origin includes fathers, mothers, brothers, grandfathers, uncles, and male cousins.
3 "Other" includes mothers, aunts, cousins, and no familial relation.
4 Significant according to a Pearson correlation test.

Table Five: Females 26 Years of Age and Older (N = 51)

Region	Worldwide	North America	Europe	Muslim World
Average Age	36	40	31	37
By Percentage				
Killed by Family of Origin[1,2]	44	0	31	65
Family Position[1]				
—Daughter/Sister	24	0	13	37
—Wife/Girlfriend	55	89	87	26
—Other[3]	21	11	0	37
Paternal Participation[4]	8	0	13	7
Multiple Perpetrators	30	11	43	30
Multiple Victims[1]	9	29	8	5
Tortured[1]	45	44	53	44
Motive[4]				
—"too Western"	56	88	69	38
—"sexual impropriety"	44	12	31	62

1 Significant according to a chi square test.
2 Family of origin includes fathers, mothers, brothers, grandfathers, uncles, and male cousins.
3 "Other" includes mothers, aunts, cousins, and no familial relation.
4 Significant according to a Pearson correlation test.

The author wishes to thank Jonathan Francis Carmona, a graduate student at Hunter College, CUNY, for the statistical tests for this study, and Prof. Howard Lune, director of the Graduate Social Research Program at Hunter College.

Middle East Quarterly
Spring 2010

- 53 -
Are Honor Killings Domestic Terrorism?

My second study about honor killings was posted this week at *Middle East Quarterly* (see Chapter 52). The second study is a groundbreaking examination of 230 victims on five continents.

So far, the study has been picked up widely on the web, and I've been interviewed in the *Hindustan Times* (!) and the *Edmonton Sun* about honor killings. I was just interviewed by the most excellent Lauren Green on Fox News on their *Strategy Room* program about "faith and terrorism." I was encouraged to position honor killings as a form of domestic, Islamist terrorism. In reality, the same radically Islamist mindset responsible for 9/11 or the Mumbai massacre tends to keep women in burqas, niquab, or hijab, segregated and subordinate. Such fundamentalists tend to follow radical Islamist mullahs who preach militant jihad and who do not preach against honor related violence, including honor killings.

Fox News had convened a panel to discuss the relationship between "faith and terrorism." We began by discussing the interview with Hussein Ibish, formerly the director of the American-Arab Anti-Discrimination Committee, now the executive director of the Foundation for Arab American Leadership. Ibish made a series of false claims, all of which sounded reasonable, "fair," and logical, and he did so in excellent American English. For example, he said that Muslims were persecuted by pagans when Mohammed was alive and that's why there are some Qur'anic verses that encourage or permit violence.

Poppycock!

Muslims under Mohammed were busy raping, pillaging, plundering, and enslaving the so-called pagans, trying to convert them; Mohammed and his soldiers genocidally slaughtered the Jewish tribes of Arabia. So what Ibish is really saying is that when Muslims cannot convert another faith group to Islam, Muslims feel "persecuted" and therefore resort to violence.

Nothing's changed.

But one more point: When Mohammed was in a weak position, he counseled "peace." When he was in a strong position, he counseled "no mercy, full jihad ahead."

I stressed that many terrorists, both home-grown and otherwise, are not motivated by poverty, unemployment, or lack of education. Remember that Bin Laden is a billionaire, the Christmas Day failed bomber Abdul Muttalab comes from a wealthy family, and Mohamed Atta was educated (as were Fort Hood Major Nidal Hasan and Times Square bomber Faisal Shahzad). Mental illness does not "cause" terrorism. The Saudi Wahhabi Salafist world-wide funding of mosques, madrassas, and Middle East Institutes does. Iranian funding of Hamas and Hezbollah funds and indoctrinates terrorism.

If a true and "peaceful" Islam—a pro-woman Islam—has been hijacked by maniacs, then true and peaceful Muslims must stand up to them. If one's interpretation of faith can encourage a man to drive a car bomb into Times Square, it can also give good people the faith and courage to stand up and fight the extremists in their midst.

Faith can empower people to combat radical evil in a way that nothing else can.

5/9/10

- 54 -
Stabs Wife 250 Times—Murderer's Identity Carefully Concealed

L ast week, Google directed me to a newspaper in Australia, where I read about a man who stabbed his wife 250 times, killing her. The report went on to allege that this killer also ate his wife's liver and lungs while their four year-old daughter watched. This fiend was sentenced to only 15 years to life. Although this man stabbed his wife 250 times, he hotly denies being a cannibal. That bad he's not. Even monstrous killers have pride.

What is wrong there Down Under, I wondered. And then—I read the most amazing bit of information. This heinous murder had not taken place in Australia but in my own backyard, in Queens, New York, three years ago, in 2007. And, while the crime and 2010 sentencing were viewed as newsworthy in Australia, the sentencing had not been covered in the (hardcopy) liberal New York mainstream media.

Who would commit such a savage murder? Was the murderer a domestic version of Jeffrey Dahmer who raped, murdered, then ate children and young men? But Dahmer and his ilk are not often married to women and do not have children. A serial killer might do this to a girl or woman whom he does not know, someone whom he believes is a prostitute. Again, these psychopaths do not prey upon their wives.

The murderer's name is Mohammed Solaiman; his victim's name was Shahida Sultanna. *The New York Post* and the *Daily News* covered the sentencing. *The New York Times* did not.

The Paper of Record did cover this murder, briefly, in 2007, when it happened—but in an article that also covered another Queens-based murder—as if to say that the borough of "Queens" was the true subject. Needless to say, no reporter dared note the murderer's ethnicity, culture, or religion. Journalists might not view this information as relevant, or they may already know that their editors will simply take it out as "racist" profiling.

In court, Solaiman's lawyer claimed that Solaiman, who was 49 years old at the time of the crime, was an "abused" husband whose 32-year-old wife had verbally and physically "abused" him for six years.

A number of Muslim wife-killers and daughter-killers do feel that they are the true victims, that they were only defending themselves after a female relative has "dishonored" them; these adult men felt "attacked," and were forced to "defend" themselves.

Ellen Sheeley, the author of a study on honor killings in Jordan, wrote that every single honor killing she'd investigated in Jordan was a torture-killing. She writes:

> Just in Jordan alone, each year about 20 of these crimes are reported in the English-language press. Anecdotally, I can't remember a single one that wasn't unspeakably torturous and violent for the victim. The predominant *modus operandi* is complete and utter overkill.

Pajamas Media
5/17/10

- 55 -

An Honor Killing By Proxy: Another Kind of Tragedy in Gujarat

At the end of last week, a British-Pakistani father, mother, and daughter were murdered in cold blood by their Pakistani relatives while the victims were praying in a cemetery at the end of a funeral. "Mohammad Yousaf, 51, his wife, Parviaz, 49, and their daughter, Tania, 23, from Nelson, in Lancashire, were killed in the eastern city of Gujarat when tensions over the breakdown of the marriage between their eldest son and their niece ended in tragedy."

This Gujarat is in Pakistan, not India; the Indian Gujarat was the tragic site of barbaric mass murders, most notably in 2002, when a Muslim mob stopped a train and burned 59 Hindus (mostly women, children, and seniors) alive. Retaliation was swift and ended with 790 Muslims and 254 Hindus dead.

This is the "peaceful" Gujarat.

The murder of the Yousaf family in a cemetery qualifies as an honor killing, but one of a slightly different sort. The families of origin did not kill their son or their daughter for getting divorced. The father, mother, and daughter who were killed were not the actual "guilty" parties. In a sense, this is an honor killing by proxy. The father and mother were guilty of permitting their son to divorce his first cousin; perhaps they had simply failed or were unable to stop their son from doing so. Their nephew was one of the four shooters. He avenged his sister's "shame" by shooting down the sister of the brother-cousin who had divorced the shooter's own sister. He was "saying" that his own sister was as good as dead, was now "damaged goods" and would never find another hus-

203

band. He was merely dispensing an "eye for an eye" form of justice.

From the shooter's (and his own family-of-origin's) point of view, traditional family order had been broken, Western mores had possibly destroyed it all. The Yousafs had lived in Lancashire for thirty years. Maybe they no longer believed in arranged, cousin marriage. Maybe they now believed in allowing their children to "choose" their life partners or to divorce them. Maybe this preference, or choice, was seen as interfering with future cousin marriages and with future family immigration plans.

According to a relative, the murdered daughter, Tania, was a married mother of two who worked at Pendle Borough Council. "She was a bundle of fun. Her friends are ringing up and everyone is hurting." A spokesman at the British High Commission in Islamabad said that the police were investigating the case.

Will this be treated as the murder of a British family in Pakistan? Will the British government pursue it—and if so, how? Will they extradite the killers to stand trial in England? Will Western governments start protecting its citizens from such tribal, cultural, and/or religious customs?

Britain already has the power to extradite British female citizens of Pakistani origin who have been kidnapped and held against their will if they can find them and if the kidnapped victim asks to be repatriated. Will Britain now go further? This case bears watching.

Pajamas Media
5/24/10

- 56 -
Why is the *Washington Post* Afraid to Use the Words "Muslim" and "Honor Killing" in the Same Article?

I n the last seven years, the print version of the *Washington Post* has covered honor killings sparingly, tangentially, briefly, and only in passing.

For example, in 2004, in a *Washington Post* article which argued that the United States should grant political asylum to women fleeing violence, the authors note that "Persecution is a high standard to reach, involving extreme and offensive conduct, such as honor killings, sexual slavery and rape." However, there is no discussion of what an honor killing is or who commits such murders. Two years later, in 2006, the *Post* ran a small item under "World in Brief" which reads as follows:

> A 14-year-old Pakistani girl died of an infected wound a month after being shot four times in an attempted 'honor killing' in Karachi, police said. Nur Jehan was shot in the stomach, leg, knee and arm and left for dead by her relatives, who accused her of having sex with a young man.

In the summer of 2007, the *Post* ran a three-paragraph piece about the high-profile honor murder of a young Iraqi Kurdish woman in England. Later that same year, in the fall, the Post ran a full-length AP story about how Kurds in Iraq are attempting to stop the practice of honor killing their daughters. The piece is based on the story of one unmarried woman who was refused an abortion by every doctor she consulted, tried to kill herself, then chose to keep her pregnancy a secret, moved to a hidden location—all to avoid being honor-murdered and to avoid "shaming" her family so that her unmarried sisters would still be able to find husbands.

Fair enough: This is journalism-on-the-ground, in Iraq, during a war, and the piece mainly focuses on one woman's plight; no serious analysis of the problem is offered. Still, one must ask: Why not refer back to the honor murder of an Iraqi Kurdish woman in the West, in England—a case covered in the newspaper's own pages? For a fact-driven piece, why is there absolutely no mention of the social class or religion correlated to these honor killings? Is that utterly irrelevant to understanding these tragic cases?

In late 2008, the *Post* did a story about an Indian couple who potentially face family violence for having married "out of caste," which defied the cultural values of their families. This couple, like other such couples, face being honor-murdered by their families. Here, the *Post* is not shy about telling us that these are Hindus and that to violate caste norms means risking being honor-murdered.

Just yesterday, May 25, the *Post* again did a full-length story about an Indian couple whose marriage was ruled "incestuous" (they were from the same clan); thus, the "groom was strangled and the bride forced to drink pesticide. Their bodies were dumped in a canal." Although the killers were tried and convicted, clan members have vowed to raise money to pay for an appeal. Here, we are told that both the couple and their murderers were Hindus.

Why does the *Washington Post* find it relevant, safe, politically correct, to say that "Hindus" commit honor murders but not relevant, not safe, not politically correct to say that "Muslims" do so as well? Indeed, it is quite clear that, while Hindus and Sikhs do commit honor murders, the majority of such murders seem to be Muslim-on-Muslim crimes—definitely in the West and probably worldwide.

The *Washington Post* apparently failed to cover thirty-seven honor killing victims who were murdered right here in the United States and Canada in the last twenty years. The one American-based honor killing that they did cover was filed by the Associated Press and concerned the honor murder of Noor Almaleki in Arizona. The story focused on the decision not to subject her murderer (who was also her father) to the death penalty. It was a brief story, and the author fails to mention that this, too, was a Muslim-on-Muslim crime. Both the 2007 AP story about honor killings among Iraqi Kurds, and the brief 2006 piece about the Pakistani honor killing, fail to mention that the murderers and the victims are all Muslims.

Another point: The latest article about a Hindu honor killing in far-off India was composed of 909 words. The single piece about the honor killing in Arizona was composed of a mere 113 words.

Once, the *Washington Post* prided itself as the crusaders who broke the story of Watergate and helped impeach a President. Given their current stand on honor killings and their failure to use the word "Muslim," I am reminded that glory fades so quickly.

Pajamas Media
5/26/10

- 57 -

"Soft" Censorship: Honor Killings That You Won't Read About

The mainstream media rarely covers them. More often, local media does, but even local media does so walking-on-egg-shells, careful to quote from at least one apologist and one know-nothing. Usually, the (hardcopy) mainstream media covers such events weeks later, only briefly, or as a way to "spin" possible prejudice against the perpetrators involved. Sometimes they are mentioned, but only in passing. Rarely do follow-ups appear. Usually, a wire service piece is used, and no original reporting is done. Sometimes, the newspaper's blog might refer to a piece which first appeared in another newspaper which, in turn, has mentioned the subject only in passing.

I am talking about how rarely the American mainstream media covers honor killings committed in North America.

For example, there was no mention of the 2006 honor murder of 20-year-old Canadian-Afghan Muslim, Khatera Sadiqi, and her fiancée, Feroz Mangal, by her brother, Habibullah, in the *New York Times, Washington Post, Los Angeles Times*, or in the *Wall Street Journal*.

True, this took place in Canada, not in the United States. That might explain it. Ah, no so fast.

One could only read about the very high profile 2008 Dallas-based honor killings of the two Egyptian-American Muslim Said sisters, Sarah and Amina, in a single paragraph of 60 words, which was buried in a piece of 911 words in the *New York Times*. There was nothing in the *Los Angeles Times* and nothing in the hardcopy version of the *Washington Post*, although some blogs appeared at their website which referred to another newspaper article which had mentioned these murders in passing.

Guess what? *The Wall Street Journal* was out to lunch on this one too.

To their credit, FOX News systematically reported on the Said sisters and also ran a documentary devoted to their case. And, of course, the blogosphere was lit up like Times Square about this case. Special kudos to *PajamasMedia, Frontpage, Newsrealblog, Islam in Europe, Europe News, Human Rights Service, War to Mobilize Democracy, Atlas Shrugs, JihadWatch,* and all the many other blogs that have been tracking honor killings worldwide.

Nevertheless, the father-murderer of these two young girls who were murdered for being "too western" remains safely at large, perhaps back home in Egypt raising another family or two.

The New York Times also failed to cover the 2008 honor killings of American-Pakistani Muslim Sandeela Kanwal in Atlanta, Georgia; and American-Ethiopian Muslim, Hawlett Mohammed, in Alexandria, Virginia—but they covered, at length, the 2008 murder of Hindu-American Monika Rani, who was burned alive in Oak Forest, Illinois, by her father because she married below her caste. This honor killing merited 470 words in the Gray Lady.

Likewise, the *Los Angeles Times* did not cover the Kanwal or Mohammed honor killings. The hardcopy *Washington Post* did not cover Kanwal but they did refer to the nearby Virginia-based Mohammed honor killing briefly.

In 2009, the gruesome beheading of Aasiya Z. Hassan was covered—but only five days later by the *New York Times*—and then mainly to explain that Islam had nothing to do with it and that anyone who believes to the contrary is misguided or prejudiced. The *LA Times* covered it a day later but only in passing in a "News in Brief" section. *The New York Times* also discussed this case at its blog but mainly in order to highlight the "soul searching" that this beheading had caused among Muslims of good will. The Paper of Record failed to discuss "Mo" Hassan's long and awful history as the savage batterer of three wives.

Aasiya Hassan merited a brief blurb in the *Los Angeles Times* and was merely noted in passing in a *Wall Street Journal* blog.

What is going on here?

Perhaps no op-ed writer has yet come forward who is able and willing to connect the dots? Not so, not true. For example, recently, I tried to interest the four major mainstream media outlets mentioned above in an op-ed piece about my own recent findings about how and why honor killings might be escalating in the West and how honor killings are not the same as Western domestic violence. All four mainstream media venues turned down my query—and separately, the query of a like-minded colleague.

Right now, there is "breaking news" about several honor killing cases in Canada which is, after all, our next door neighbor; so far, all is quiet on Canada's southern border.

Sunday morning, June 13, 2010, a Canadian-Afghan Muslim mother tried to kill her 19-year-old daughter in Montreal because she had stayed out too late Saturday night—but you probably haven't read about this in the *New York Times*, the *Washington Post*, the *Los Angeles Times*, or the *Wall Street Journal*. (Of course, Canadian papers are covering this).

On June 14, 2010, the Canadian-Pakistani Muslim father and brother who murdered 16-year-old Aqsa Parvez at the end of 2007 (for being "too Western"), finally pled guilty. You will not have read about this in mainstream American papers.

Why is such "soft" censorship important? Because law enforcement officials, public policy experts, professors, smaller newspapers, endangered victims, and both their helpers and advocates might have absolutely no idea that the problem is serious; their legislative or fundraising attempts will not be taken seriously and will be seen as raising "non-issues," or tilting at invisible windmills.

Our fear of criticizing murder because it has been committed by an immigrant of color who might be a Muslim (we do not want to be seen as "racist Islamophobes"), trumps our commitment to uphold the law for all who live here, even if they, too, are immigrants of color who also happen to be Muslims—and female.

Pajamas Media
6/16/10

- 58 -
Hindu Honor Killings in India

Honor killings occur quite rarely in the Indian diaspora in the West. Many Hindu human rights activists whom I queried hotly denied that Hindus ever commit honor/honour killings. One such gentleman insisted that "anyone who says Hindus do this is a Marxist or a Muslim troublemaker."

Nevertheless, according to the Indian media, at least ten separate cases of suspected honor killings took place—the bodies of 16 victims were discovered, or arrests were finally made—in June 2010 alone. More than one family member, often two to three relatives (a father, brother, uncle, grandmother, mother) or the village council (*khap panchayat*) were arrested as conspirators or murderers. Five male and female couples (ten victims) were killed while together; three killings were women-only; one killing was male-only.

The victims were mainly young and ranged in age from twelve to twenty four years old. The motives in all ten cases concerned the family's need to control marriage and reproduction. The idea of choosing one's own life partner was viewed as abhorrent, as something that only whores do.

However, in contrast to Muslim practices, these ten Hindu families found it unacceptable, a criminal act, to marry a cousin or someone from the same family or clan. In other words, while some of the honor killings were due to marrying someone from a different caste, even the right caste mate might not be acceptable if he lives in the same village or is too closely related to the bride.

These killings are shockingly savage. Young daughters are beaten, even hacked to death—or they are electrocuted.

In one June, 2010 killing, Pushpa, a 19-year-old Hindu Indian girl, was hacked to death by her brother while she slept because she had refused an arranged marriage and eloped with her lover. Her brother had managed to lure her back from hiding. The dead girl's mother told the police about the crime and asked them to arrest her son.

On June 13, 2010, 19-year-old Asha Saini and her 19-year-old boyfriend, Yogesh Kumar, were found dead in a house in Delhi, India. Police said that the two had been stabbed, gagged, and electrocuted. Police arrested the father, mother, aunt, nephew, and uncle of the girl for the crime. The family apparently objected to the relationship because the boyfriend was of a different caste. Indians were appalled and outraged that the honor killing took place not in a far-flung province but in their capital city.

If Hindus also commit honor killings, then it is not merely a Muslim phenomenon and may be understood as related to tribal customs. On the other hand, India was also semi-colonized by Islam and that battle continues. These recent Hindu honor killings all took place in the north of India, which is closer to Pakistan.

Why do Indians commit very few honor killings in the West? Why is this custom not "exported?" Are the kinds of Hindu Indians who immigrate to the West not like the Hindus who remain back home and who honor kill?

NewsRealBlog
6/29/10

- 59 -
Hindu Honor Killings Article Challenged by Hindu Human Rights Activists

E arlier today, I published a piece about Hindu honor killings. These murders were not "dowry burnings" which are usually committed by a mother-in-law and husband against a bride. In those cases, the motive is greed. The in-laws, usually the mother-in-law and the husband, want a new dowry. Hindu-on-Hindu honor killings are not committed by in-laws.

However, the Indian police, (unlike the Pakistani or Afghan police), made arrests. In one earlier instance, five members of a single family were sentenced to death; the leader of the village council who helped hatch the plot was sentenced to life in prison; and the driver of the car used in the crime received a seven year sentence. The Indian Home Minister P. Chidambaram is on record as saying: "The vilest crimes are committed in defending the honor of the family or women and we should hang our heads in shame when such incidents take place in the 21st century." Chidambaram also recommended some concrete actions to combat honor killings, including wider recruitment of women police officers.

Nevertheless, because I wrote about the phenomenon, I've already been criticized by some Hindu human rights activists. Here is part of one letter:

Is this Hindu honor killing or a social evil among Hindus? This we have to understand carefully. There is nothing Hindu about Hindus who do honor killings. (Hindus) worship woman as God and give (the) feminine the most highest altar, superior to man. Just Google for Kali (the representation of the universe in its material aspect standing on dead Shiva or the substratum to Universe), Durga (goddess of Energy/Shakthi), Saraswati (goddess of knowledge), Lakshmi (goddess of Wealth). As in any society, there are social evils, that develop among people living in certain regions who happen to belong to a certain religion. While this has to be condemned as crimes, it is very naive to compare this (to) Muslim honor killings whose scriptures sanction second class (or worse) citizenship to women, whose "prophet," who serves as an example to Muslims has married a 6 year old girl while he is 50 etc. There are crimes against women in the West too, but we do not associate it with Christianity.

I told him that nowhere in my piece do I mention "Hinduism" as a key factor or as a factor at all in these honor killings. If anything, I present these killings as a tribal custom—not as a religious one. And, I pointed out, the fact that goddesses are worshipped in Hinduism has not helped lower caste girls nor has it helped abolish the caste system. The rule of Goddesses has not even allowed certain Indian girls, both rich and poor, to choose their own husbands.

Another Hindu human rights activist believes that the sudden flurry of attention towards—and/or the actual honor killings of Hindus—is possibly being orchestrated by foreigners or Islamists to "make Hindus look bad."

My Hindu critic also strongly believes that these honor killings have been influenced by Muslim ways. (That may or may be true—but so what?) They also believe that Hinduism, the religion, in which the "female principle" is worshipped, can in no way have inspired such mistreatment of women.

Religion may not have the power to tame the savage misogynist beast; religion itself may be the source of much misogyny. These are the two prevailing and opposing views on the subject.

Pajamas Media
6/29/10

- 60 -
Potential Honor Killing Victim Wants Charges Dropped Against Brother, Father

Afshan Azad, "Harry Potter" Actress, Tries to Reverse Course. Afshan Azad, the lovely and graceful actress who appears in four of the Harry Potter movies, has, in real life, been threatened with death and allegedly attacked by her father and brother. Her sin? She is a British Muslim of Bangladeshi origin who stands accused of dating a Hindu man. Yes, this alone is a capital crime in Islam.

The actress, whose father and brother threatened to kill her and who "badly bruised" her over her relationship with a Hindu man, has been begging the court to release her brother and father who have now been jailed for five weeks. According to the *Daily Mail*:

> The actress has tried on three occasions to retract her statement and has pleaded with the Crown Prosecution Service not to proceed with the matter…This is a desperately sad situation. She never wanted her father or brother locked up.

Afshan does not refer to her own forced flight and five week "confinement" in London hiding with friends. Her brother, Ashraf, takes absolutely no responsibility for what he did and in fact blames unnamed others for the consequences of his own actions and those of his father Abdul. Ashraf has been quoted as follows:

> We are going to get trouble from the community now. It is bad news for our safety, her safety. My younger brother is

going to get harassed at college. All our family is going to be harassed by the community because of this. Her career could be ruined. When she goes to a premiere or something, they are going to ask her about this not about the film.

I can only imagine the pressure that Afshan's mother Nelofar and her other brothers and extended family members have been exerting on poor Afshan. Just as incest victims—not their attackers—are blamed and ostracized; just as battered women who finally get orders of protection, or even kill in self-defense, are blamed and ostracized; just imagine the pressures being brought to bear on Afshan.

I would strongly advise Afshan not to go home—ever again. Here's what I wrote, in part, at *National Review's The Corner*:

While the British police are exceptionally sensitive to this problem and have helped potential honor-killing victims, the problem is vast and growing. Afshan Azad now needs to be in hiding and protected, on a permanent basis, from her own family. Perhaps she and her actor friends could lead a campaign against honor killings. I would be honored to join them.

Afshan: You are playing the part of Padma, a powerful witch, in the next Harry Potter movie. How would Padma handle this situation? Channel her strength. Defend yourself, protect yourself. As to your longing to be loved by and reunited with your family—perhaps you must give it up, tragic and unjust as that might seem. Even if you give up your Hindu boyfriend, it is too late. You have already shamed your family publicly. Their honor will require nothing less than your death.

Why not contact the women in Britain who are campaigning against honor killing? They will support you. Why not contact Diana Nammi, the co-founder of the London-based International Campaign Against Honour Killings?

Pajamas Media
7/5/10

- 61 -
Afshan Azad Retracts Nothing

Potential honor killing victim, Harry Potter actress, Afshan Azad, may not have been the one who asked that charges against her father and brother be dropped. One of my wonderful readers, a legal secretary, read the British media more carefully than I did and pointed out that Afshan herself is simply not on record as saying that she wanted the charges dropped or that she wanted to retract anything. While she may have said this, we have absolutely no record of her having done so. I did not note that this quote about dropping the charges was attributed to the lawyer, John Wolfson, who is representing the jailed father and brother.

On both July 3 and again on July 4 the lawyer, John Wolfson, said that Afshan had asked that charges be dropped. I was wrong to attribute Wolfson's words to the victim. In an exchange with the sharp-eyed legal secretary, she told me:

> I have not been in contact with Ms. Azad. (If I were, I would give her the exact same warning you're giving her). I simply smelled a rat yesterday when I read the report that she'd tried "three times" to retract her statement. My first reaction was exactly like yours—I believed it and I was horrified. But when I scrolled down the body of the text, I discovered that wasn't Ms. Azad who'd said it—it was instead the attorney for her father and brother—Mr. John Wolfson. The lawyer for the potential honor murderers is quoted as saying:

> "But lawyer John Wolfson, who is defending the father and son, insists the actress is already regretting her statement,

and has tried to retract it through the Crown Prosecution Service three times."

He tells the Daily Express, "This is a desperately sad situation and she has never wanted her father and brother to be locked up. She has tried on three occasions to retract her statement and has pleaded with the Crown Prosecution Service not to proceed.

"I sincerely hope for the family's sake that this can be quickly and happily resolved. My client and his father have already denied the charges and will maintain that plea."

According to my reader:

This is the oldest (and dirtiest) trick in the legal world–a lawyer trying to save his client by destroying the veracity of the accuser. The lawyer for the father and brother is desperate; his clients are facing huge jail sentences for attempted murder. The lawyer's only hope is to make the accuser retract her statement–"oops! It was all a misunderstanding." Please don't feel bad that you've been duped. I would have had the exact same reaction as you—had it not been for the fact that I've been a legal secretary for decades.

Sadly, Ms. Chesler, you ARE accurate in pointing out that victims of abuse often plead for mercy for their abusers. You are also sadly accurate in revealing that those abusers inevitably reward their victim's mercy with murder. Last but not least, you are sadly accurate in saying that Ms. Azad can never go home. So long as her family clings to the "religion of peace," they will do their best to kill her—and they will do so with no remorse or shame.

Ms. Chesler, your advice to Ms. Azad is spot on. Bless you for that. She should contact Diana Nammi for help. You are also sadly, totally accurate in telling Ms. Azad that she can never go home again.

Pajamas Media
7/6/10

- 62 -
Muslim Honor Killing Elephants in the Room at the *New York Times*

Yesterday I posted a piece at FOX about the mainstream media's extensive coverage of honor killings—but only if they are committed by Hindus and in faraway India.

Today, three days after their weekend front page story about a Hindu honor killing, the Gray Lady again devotes five paragraphs of an editorial about the same Hindu honor killing in India. Lest we forget, the editors repeat the fact that the Indian case involved "Brahmin Hindus" whose "caste" consciousness is part of the "Hindu religion." However, true to form, they do not mention the religion of any other "honor" or "horror" killers in the places they list such as the Middle East, Italy, Sweden, Brazil, and Britain.

Amazingly, they do not even list honor killings in the United States, which are increasingly known to law enforcement. But "Brazil?" Surely, they jest. Seventy-four percent (74%) of Brazilians are Catholics; 15% are Protestants; 7.4% are listed as having "no religion"; 2.2 % are Mormons, Jehovah's Witnesses, or Spiritists; .05 % are Jews; .02% are Muslims and .002% are Hindus.

Is the *New York Times* actually confusing a "passion" or "machismo" killing (by an adult man who targets an adult woman) with a family-of-origin "honor" femicide which primarily targets young girls? I have had this very argument with a feminist who is brilliant in her understanding of Western-style domestic violence. Still, she believes that the Brazilian doctrine of "machismo," in which a man kills his girlfriend or wife in a fit of jealous passion because she is sleeping with another man—is the same as an "honor" femicide.

Here are the names of five known honor killing victims in North America. Four of the five are young girls killed by their father and/or father and brother. Only one is an adult woman who was killed by her husband: Sarah and Amina Said; Noor Almaleki; Aasiya Hassan; Feroz Mangal and Khatera Sadiqi; Aqsa Parvez.

All are Muslims, none are Hindus.

Pajamas Media
7/13/10

- 63 -
Muslim Women Are on Fire

I n Afghanistan, the women are setting themselves on fire, choosing an awful, fiery death rather than one more awful beating at the hands of a husband and a mother-in-law. Amazingly, when the mainstream media has finally written about this tragedy in Afghanistan, it still carefully manages not to use the words "Muslim" or "Islam." For example, see *Time* magazine's recent coverage of this very subject. And, see my previous pieces on what such "soft censorship" is really about when the American mainstream media consistently fails to describe a Muslim-on-Muslim honor killing in the West as such.

In Kabul, when battered women run away, their own families refuse to take them back and the government puts them in jail and treats them as criminals. In a rather moving documentary, *Daughters of Afghanistan*, Sally Armstrong shows us what happened to one young Afghan woman who refused to take the beatings anymore and upon a lawyer's advice dared return to her family of origin. Her own father clapped her up into solitary, perhaps for the rest of her life, to live in a cold, dark room with one bricked-up window.

This happened in 2002, after the Taliban fell.

But the Taliban mentality in Afghanistan long predated the Taliban phenomenon. In 1961, I remember meeting a rather genial relative who had come down from the Khyber Pass region to meet me, his first American woman. Apparently, he, too, was a merciful fellow who had married his brother's widow—but then shut her up in solitary. I was told that he fed and clothed her and that this alone saved her from a far more dismal fate. I did not understand then—or now—why this poor widow-wife could not have shared the family tasks and remained among the living. Entombed, buried alive—like Verdi's great operatic heroine, Aida. Without a name, without even a number, the fate of this unknown prisoner haunts me still.

These tragedies are no longer confined to Third World countries.

Given massive Muslim immigration to the West, we have massive Muslim female resistance to being subordinated and buried alive under burqas—resistance which is punished by Muslim-on-Muslim honor killings in the West.

Families of origin carefully plan these murders. Mothers often play a key role in luring their daughters back home, in strangling or stabbing them, and in helping their murderers escape. If you want to understand how mothers can actually mistreat, persecute, and collaborate in the murders of their daughters, please read my book *Woman's Inhumanity to Woman*.

Just yesterday, Aset Magomadova, a Calgary-based mother who strangled her 14-year-old daughter, Aminat, with a headscarf in 2007, finally received a "suspended sentence" and three years probation. The mother is a Muslim refugee and widow from Chechnya; her other child, a teenage son, is suffering from muscular dystrophy, and she herself was wounded in the war—her foot was partly blown off. The girl was allegedly on drugs and suffered from serious behavior problems. Victim advocates are outraged at so light a sentence. The judge did not believe that Magomadova actually meant to kill her rebellious daughter. The judge sentenced the murderer to "counseling for grief, depression, and anger management."

The question remains: Was everything possible done for a troubled teenage Muslim girl who was "acting out?" If not, why not? But, for whom is "everything done?" If anyone in an official position understood that a Muslim girl is at special risk, especially if she is "wild;" if the media used the word "Muslim" where appropriate—perhaps services tailored to Muslim immigrants from war-torn regions might now exist.

This past week, the Canadian "federal government affirmed its zero-tolerance stance against "honour killing," declaring such "barbaric cultural practices" as "heinous abuses" that "have no place in Canadian society." They are considering adding "honour killing" as a separate charge to the Criminal Code. Honor killings are referred to as "culturally driven" violence against girls and women.

Expect such tragic "culturally driven," "South Asian immigrant" and "Muslim" problems to proliferate in the West. The questions: Are we equipped to handle such problems? Are we morally bound to do so?

How expensive will our intrinsic altruism and outreach to the "wretch-ed of the earth" actually be?

NewsRealBlog
7/17/10

- 64 -

Leave Us and We'll Kill You:
Islam and Apostates in America

M any battered women stay with their batterers because they have been warned that if they ever leave, turn to the police, or "tell" anyone what is really going on, their batterer will then kill them.

Cult members are routinely warned that if they break free and "tell" anyone about abusive cult practices, not only will they be shunned, stalked, and punished, but their relatives, including children, who are still prisoners of the cult, or true believers, will be punished too.

By now, many Westerners may believe this is true about batterers and about cults—but they will not believe that it is also true about fundamentalist Islam. Trained in favor of religious tolerance, concerned that if one religion is restricted that all religions might be; genuinely uninformed about non-western religions such as Islam, Hinduism, Buddhism, Taoism, Shintoism, etc., they assume that all religions are alike in terms of their virtues and that sinners of every religious persuasion exist despite—not because of—their religion.

When it comes to Islam such views may be wrong.

Many Muslims are not religious. Many Muslims who are religious are not fanatic fundamentalists or radicals and tend to lead (or would like to lead) quiet, peaceful lives. But an increasing number of Muslim religious and political leaders are quite hostile to human rights and freedom of religion as universal values. These leaders point to passages in the Qur'an or Hadith that justify cross-amputation, stoning, child marriage, polygamy, and wife-beating as religious rights. They believe that infidels should either convert, be killed, or are to be held hostage—im-

225

poverished, jailed, murdered, or exiled.

Fundamentalist/political/radical Muslims are clear that any Muslim who criticizes or exposes any gross violation of human rights committed by Muslims or by Muslim political or religious leaders, must be defamed and silenced—and that any Muslim who actually converts to another religion must be killed, on sight, by any Muslim, or preferably by a member of their own family, who is expected to cleanse their shame and restore their honor and the honor of Islam by murdering this apostate.

In 2001, "Sabatina James," (a pseudonym), fled from Austria to Germany and went into hiding to escape being honor-murdered by her family after she converted from Islam to Christianity. Her family had immigrated from Pakistan. "Sabatina's" troubles began when she was 15 years old because she dared to wear lipstick and blue jeans. She was mercilessly beaten for these crimes. When she rejected marriage to a cousin, "Sabatina" was sent to a Qur'anic school in Lahore, where she was repeatedly flogged. She finally agreed to the marriage—but only in order to be able to return to Austria. Then, when she was 19 years old, she fled.

In 2002, Marlyn Hassan, who was eight months pregnant with twins, was stabbed to death in New Jersey by her husband for refusing to convert from Hinduism to Islam. Her husband also killed his mother-in-law and sister-in-law who were present at the time.

In 2009, Iraqi-born Vian Bakir Fatah was stabbed to death by her Iraqi ex-husband in Norway. Her "crime"? She had converted to Christianity and had a new boyfriend. Her ex-husband murdered her in the presence of their four children.

We certainly know that Christians have been—and are still—savagely persecuted in Muslim lands. I and many others have written about this often. Authors Nonie Darwish and Ibn Warraq have both spoken out about this issue. Darwish, a Muslim convert to Christianity, has challenged the major Muslim American organizations to denounce the Islamic belief in death-for-apostates. Thus far, no organization has done so.

While about 50,000 Christians convert to Islam in America each and every year, we know very little about the estimated 20,000 American Muslims who turn to Christianity each year. In 2002 (a lifetime ago), Julia Duin wrote an informative article on this subject. She interviewed Muslim apostates and the pastors who converted them to Christianity and described the punishments to which they were all routinely subjected. At best, families disown them, they lose custody of their children, they must use pseudonyms, disappear, live in hiding, and can never safely see their relatives again.

Muslims who convert to Christianity in America do so secretly and usually talk to reporters using pseudonyms. Those who raise questions about Islam online report being hacked, sent viruses and death threats. Pastors who convert Muslims to Christianity report being "watched" by many mosques. Muslim converts in America who wear crosses are sometimes recognized on the street or at work by Muslims from their former circles who then verbally and physically attack them; they are also threatened with death.

According to several sorces, a Saudi princess who converted to Christianity in America was whisked away by limousine and never seen here again. An Iranian male convert to Christianity applied for political asylum "because he knows he can't return to Iran and be safe…(but) his family in America and Iran are in danger from family members who will shun them and deprive them of any inheritance."

According to Mina Nevisa, an Iranian Muslim convert to Christianity, who wrote a book about her experiences, both she and her female cousin were attending an underground church in Teheran. Nevis fled Iran together with her husband. Her cousin was not so lucky. "She was arrested on charges of apostasy and taken to Evin prison, where she was raped, tortured, and then killed by firing squad. The pastor was also killed."

I hope that American judges, lawyers, mental health professionals, and immigration officials will educate themselves about this. Why? Because without doubt, they will soon be handling the cases for police protection, witness protection program status, and political asylum which Muslim converts to Christianity (apostates) are bound to bring in America.

Pajamas Media
8/2/10

- 65 -

Is Wanting to Marry the One You Love a Crime?

The *New York Times* finally got it right and put the news on their front page. The Afghan Taliban is back in business, and they just ordered two hundred men to stone two human beings to death for the crime of loving each other and wanting to marry. The all-male mob happily obliged them; it included the couple's closest relatives and neighbors.

Amazingly, the Newspaper of Record does not use the word "Muslim." They refer to "religious authorities," "a religious court," and to "religious scholars," but they name no religion. Is it Buddhism, perhaps, which once flourished widely in Afghanistan? Or, is the unnamed religion paganism, perchance? Alexander the Great was a proud pagan, and he cut through Afghanistan on his way to India, leaving pagan practices, blonde hair, and green eyes in his wake. The Sassanids, who once also ruled in Afghanistan, were Zoroastrians.

Afghanistan, once the crossroads of the world, was not a Muslim country until Arab Muslims colonized the entire Middle East and Central Asia by the sword from the seventh century on; this bloody, proselytizing task was completed by the tenth century. Islam is now the religion which rules Afghanistan, the very religion which the *New York Times* will not name.

This omission is ridiculous since everyone knows that the Taliban are Muslims and indeed, like most Muslim-majority countries, are increasingly engaged in stoning, beheading, amputations, floggings, acid attacks, and nose and ear cutting against any co-religionist, male or female, who dares to defy any and every tribal norm. In their view, Muslim "honor" demands such punishments.

Why not turn to the real moderate Muslims who are anti-Islamicists and allow them to "speak for" the Muslim Street? This is what the contributors to Zeyno Baran's excellent collection, *The Other Muslims: Moderate and Secular*, implore. This is precisely why you should read Zuhdi Jasser's piece on the Cordoba Mosque at Ground Zero.

Some say that we cannot eliminate the concept of honor but that we must, instead, replace one concept of honor with another. Kwame Anthony Appiah suggests this in his new book, *The Honor Code: How Moral Revolutions Happen*. He believes that the practices of dueling, the Atlantic slave trade, and Chinese foot-binding changed when people's attitudes towards them changed. "Honor must be turned against honor killing." Thus, people—outsiders and dissidents—must educate people about the dishonorable nature of honor killings.

I am not sure how to do this or how long such an educational program might take--or cost.

One suggestion: It is not enough to sentence entire families or clans for having collaborated in an honor killing. Certain European countries are already doing that, and they are deporting the criminals after their sentences have been served. We may have to go further. If Appiah is right, then potential honor killing families must know that their entire extended family, including those relatives who have played absolutely no role in the murder, will also be deported.

As much as I shrink from collective punishment, (it defies the best Western legal thinking about individual rights and responsibilities), only something this spartan might, potentially work. Imagine being responsible for the deportation of 30-100 relatives, only 20 of whom actually collaborated in the honor killing of a girl. Imagine the shame and dishonor that would accrue to the family responsible for such a massive deportation.

Think about it.

Pajamas Media
8/17/10

- 66 -

John Esposito, Saudi Arabia's Man-On-Campus, Opposes Honor Killings When Hindus Commit Them

I t was only a matter of time before someone would try to make some political hay out of the curious obsession that the mainstream media has with honor killings when they are committed by Hindus.

The *Huffington Post* has given none other than John Esposito the bully pulpit on this one. Professor Esposito teaches Islamic Studies at Georgetown, where he is also the founder and director of the Prince Alwaleed bin Talal Center for Muslim-Christian Understanding. ("Hath not a Jew eyes?" Why are Jews not included in this project of understanding?)

From 1988-1992, Esposito served as the President of The Middle East Studies Association of North America (MESA). This association is a radically left, pro-Palestinian, anti-Zionist, and anti-Semitic group. It is certainly not a feminist group. Martin Kramer's excellent book, *Ivory Towers on Sand*, examines MESA's activities and point of view.

Who else, who better, to speak for women, who can better express a feminist point of view? And on an American left-liberal website? This is the high ground that Esposito seeks to claim. He is now concerned with "violence against women." He writes:

> Gender equity and violence against women are two issues rightfully attracting more attention in the main-

stream press, but in the court of public opinion, Islam is seen as an instigator of women's oppression. Studies show that gender equity is cited as a reason for the public's mistrust of Islam...such violence refers to crimes committed against females and cuts across numerous faiths, cultures and societies.

Therefore, to redeem the honor of Islam and earn his Saudi money, Esposito describes an honor killing, assuming that most readers will assume that it has been committed by Muslims. But, he explains, this tragedy has been perpetrated by Hindus!

Women are murdered in so-called honor killings every day. On Saturday, the first-ever Indian Peoples' Tribunal on so-called "Honour Killings" gathered prominent lawyers and activists from major Indian non-government organizations, including the Human Right Law Network, the Women's Legal Forum and the Women's Christian Association of India, to raise awareness for these crimes. The event followed an incident earlier this summer when two young people from different backgrounds pledged to marry one another but were killed by their loved ones. Family members perpetrated the so-called honor killing to restore their communal standing. Some praised the murderers as heroes, and authorities treated the crime with impunity.

Were the victims Muslim?

No. That's the point.

Shamelessly, Esposito actually holds the Indian government's rapid and high profile response to honor killings against it to make his point that Hindus, as well as Muslims, actually commit honor killings.

Esposito is right when he says that "violence against women cuts across numerous faiths, cultures, and societies." The work of Second and Third Wave feminism has proven that to be so. However, Christians, Jews, Buddhists, Bahai, Zoroastrians, Shinto, etc. do not commit honor murders. Hindus, but only in India, do so; it is mainly Muslims, both in the West and in Muslim-majority countries, who engage in this foul practice. I challenge John Esposito to deny this. I challenge him to show me what steps the Saudi, Libyan, Sudanese, Somali, Iraqi, Pakistani, Afghan, and Iranian governments have taken to put an end to this abomination. I challenge John Esposito to find me 100 imams and 100 mullahs who would be willing to issue a *fatwa* against all those who conspire in or perpetrate the torture and murder of their family's own women.

Pajamas Media
9/6/10

- 67 -

Taming the Wild East: Arab Honor Killings in Israel

Israel has a relatively good record in terms of helping potential honor killing victims escape and survive and in arresting and prosecuting honor killers.

For example, in 2007, Hamda Abu-Ghanem, 18, was shot to death in Ramle, Israel by her brother because some men in her town had referred to her as a prostitute. She was the eighth woman to have been murdered in her extended family in seven years, and the family's women finally went public. In a plea bargain, an Israeli court sentenced the brother to sixteen years in prison.

In 2007, 21-year-old Nadia Abu Amar of Jerusalem was murdered by her three brothers and her uncle because she refused to marry the man she was engaged to and because she got her father arrested and convicted for assault. One of the brothers received a sentence of 27 years in prison, one received a 12 year sentence; the other two perpetrators received six-year sentences.

In 2008, a court in Nazareth, Israel, sentenced Khaled Muslemi to 14 years in prison for attempting to murder his sister in an honor killing because he had heard rumors that she had been behaving promiscuously. The Israeli court stated:

> The despicable, repetitive phenomenon of murder...of innocent women under the pretence of "honor killings" must be condemned in the harshest manner possible...Acts such as the defendant's bear no honor. They bear only shame and

233

disgrace. The court is disgusted by the defendant's decision to be his sister's executioner.

Such sentences are not often handed down in Mecca, Islamabad, Kandahar—or in Amman, or under Palestinian Authority (PA) control on the West Bank or under Hamas in Gaza.

In 1997, in a small village in Jordan, 21-year-old Rania Arafat was honor-murdered by her younger brother, who was chosen precisely because minors receive a reduced sentence. Her aunts ordered her murder because she refused an arranged marriage and then dared to elope with an Iraqi man of her own choosing. Rania's killer probably did not spend more than a few months in jail.

In 2003, Rofayda Qaoud of Abu Qash in the PA areas was murdered by her mother Amira Qaoud, who put a plastic bag over her head and sliced her wrists with a razor. Her crime? Rofayda had been raped by her two brothers and impregnated. Her mother-killer, Amira, was expected to receive at most three to five years in prison. It is not clear if she did so.

In 2005, a group of Hamas gunmen shot 20-year-old Yusra al-Azzam to death after they found her picnicking on the beach with a man. The man, it turned out, was her fiancé. Hamas disavowed the killings but released the killers because they were related to a powerful Gaza clan. The Mufti of Gaza later ordered that 25,000 Jordanian dinars ($35,000) of "blood money" be paid to the al-Azzam family.

The Israeli police report that 11 of the recent murders, (three in the last month alone), which took place in Lod were honor murders; they have arrested two professional killers who were hired by families to "cleanse their shame." Both cases involved women engaging in unacceptable relationships with men.

The Arabs in Lod claim that the "violence" is due to a lack of social services. In Arabic, the media only refers to "violence," not to "honor killings." Ari Cadri, the attorney for the suspects, is threatening to sue the media for claiming that the "the two suspects were hit men or operating a business for honor killings."

Here's the background.

Eighty percent of the Lod population is Jewish. Twenty percent is Arab. In the 1960s, a large number of Bedouin began moving to Lod looking for grass for their sheep. At first they settled in tents. Later they built wooden huts, then sheet-metal houses, then regular concrete houses, and finally villas. According to a source who must remain anonymous, "All that time, the state did nothing to move them back to the Negev. Nobody knows why, maybe because the local authorities did not complain since they employed some of these Bedouin for very low salaries."

In the last decade, through the media and education, and by dint of living with a more modern Jewish population, these Bedouin were exposed to modernity. Their daughters started dressing in modern ways, started adopting a modern lifestyle, and started to go to high schools and universities. According to my source: "The men could not stand this and started to kill them for bringing shame on the family by dressing in modern style, by going to school or by refusing to marry their cousins."

In addition, the Bedouin traditionally tend to resort to violence whenever a dispute erupts due to the realities of living in a harsh and unforgiving desert. They do not expect the police, social workers, or a central government to solve their conflicts or to enforce their customs. According to my source, "Even a generation after leaving the desert they still retain a Bedouin mindset, which is well expressed by the Bedouin proverb: 'You can take the Bedouin out of the desert, but you can't take the desert out of the Bedouin.'"

In a sense, what is happening in Lod is a miniature version of the problem that Europe now faces with a non-integrated Muslim population. Illiterate, unskilled immigrants from rural areas of Turkey, Morocco, Algeria, Pakistan, Bangladesh, Afghanistan etc. have flooded Europe. They watch Jihadic programs via satellite television, and attend fiery reactionary sermons. Many, not all, have little desire to become modern or western; they view doing so as an act of shameful surrender. Many, not all, are now also theologically and politically radicalized. They are also honor murdering their women and attacking the police, both verbally and physically, accusing their adopted countries of "racism" and "discrimination," and demanding a place for their customs: Sharia law, face-veiled women, gender-segregated public facilities, halal food, etc.

Lod=the Parisian banlieus; Lod=the refugee camps in Germany; Lod=the Arab-only neighborhoods in Rotherham and Bradford.

NewsRealBlog
10/29/10

- 68 -

Romeo and Juliet in Muslim Iraq

Romeo and Juliet are alive and well in Dokan, Iraq—well, not exactly. Romeo (Aram Jamal Rasool) was murdered in an honor killing. Juliet (Sirwa Hama Amin) gave birth to her legal husband Romeo's son, but was also permanently shunned by her own family—the very family who killed her beloved Romeo. Juliet now lives in a house filled with weapons and is escorted by armed guards provided by Romeo's family when she leaves the house.

This Juliet can never marry again. She is a dishonored woman. She can never see her relatives again—except perhaps for a moment, when they murder her; perhaps not even then, for her family may send a paid assassin to cleanse its shame.

The honor murder of a man, not a woman has, seemingly, catapulted the case into the American media. Finally, at long last, even the *New York Times* has written about an honor killing committed in a Muslim country: Iraqi Kurdistan. In the past, the same American mainstream media refused to write about honor killings committed in the United States—but mainly about honor killings perpetrated by Hindus in India.

However, once again, in this latest article the word "Muslim" or "Islam" is never used. This article, written by John Leland and Namo Abdulla, goes further than this mere omission. It's clear political objective appears in the title and subtitle: "A Killing Set Honor Above Love: A Stern Tribal Code Grips Iraqi Kurdistan."

Just in case you fail to understand their point, in the fourth paragraph, the journalists quote Qadir Abdul-Rahman, one of Juliet's uncles as saying, "The girl and boy should be killed. It's about honor. Honor is more important for us than religion."

236

And there you have it. "Muslims" do not commit honor killings—and when they do, it has nothing to do with Islam. The murderers are not described as Muslims. They are identified as tribal elders. When such unidentified people commit honor killings the murders are due to a "deep seated tribal honor code."

Perhaps this is true. If so, then why not drop "Hindu" and "Sikh" from the articles about Hindu and Sikh honor killings?

This is part of a pattern. Recently, in Sweden, the media did not note the religion or ethnicity of the man who physically attacked a male physician who was examining his wife who had just given birth. The woman was bleeding to death and the unnamed and poorly described assailant remained unknown.

How many ethnic Swedes would attack a doctor because he is a man trying to save a woman's life? I offered to write an op-ed piece about honor killings for the *New York Times*, a venue in which I had frequently appeared in the past. The editors turned the idea down cold, as did the *Washington Post*.

NewsRealBlog
11/22/10

- 69 -
Will Honor Killing Threats Keep Harry Potter Actress in Permanent Hiding?

Afshan Azad, 22, the high-profile Harry Potter actress, remains in hiding after refusing to appear in a London court. As I've noted previously, Ms. Azad had been dating a Hindu man. Her father, Abul Azad, 53, and her brother Ashraf, 28, called her a "prostitute" and tried to force her into an arranged marriage with a Muslim man. In May of 2010, her brother also beat her and her father threatened to kill her. She escaped her family home and has been in hiding ever since. According to the Telegraph, she refused to testify against her family, saying that doing so would endanger her further. Apparently, the British police tried but failed to persuade Ms. Azad to testify.

Ms. Azad's refusal to appear makes sense. She is already in great danger for having associated with a non-Muslim man. Add to that the public and shameful exposure of her family in this matter. Having her male relatives jailed would mean a torturous death sentence for her.

My previous studies have shown that immigrants to the West, including and especially immigrants from South Asia, (Ms. Azad is of Bangladeshi descent), continue to perpetrate gruesome honor killings in the West.

The level of violence towards girls and women in South Asia can be barbarous and quite unbelievable.In 1998, Zahida Perveen's husband, in a fit of rage, bound her hand and foot and then, using a razor and a knife, proceeded to cut out her eyes and slice off her ears and nose. Zahida's crime? Her husband suspected that she was having an affair with a brother-in-law. At the time, Zahida was three months pregnant.

In 2004, a tribal council in Pakistan in the Punjab ordered that a young girl be publicly gang-raped then paraded naked through her village—a punishment for an alleged crime committed by her brother. This case became known worldwide when the girl did not kill herself but instead pressed charges.

Girls in South Asia and of South Asian descent living elsewhere are routinely killed for far less than choosing their own husbands. She may be a young, modern, and popular actress who lives in the West and who plays the part of a young and charming witch, but all of Harry Potter's magic cannot protect her from the normalized violence towards women both in Pakistan and among South Asian immigrants in the West.

The British police have acted properly. The law stood ready to condemn this threatened honor killing, this specific form of family-style femicide. However, how can Afshan remain "underground" and still ply her trade as an actress?

South Asian immigrant honor killings are not confined to illiterate, uneducated, and impoverished families. On the contrary. Some powerful, well-educated, and wealthy families punish their well educated daughters honor murdering them. (Samria Imran Sarwar's family was both wealthy and educated.) The fact that Afshin Azad was "allowed" to work as an actress does not mean that she was allowed to socialize with a non-Muslim or to marry a non-Muslim man of her own choosing.

NewsRealBlog
12/21/10

- 70 -
Al Qaeda Female Suicide Killer?

According to the Arabic media, in the course of questioning a suspected male Al Qaeda terrorist, the Iraqi police in Diyala were given the name of an Iraqi woman, Shahlaa Al-Anbaky, as someone who would soon be perpetrating a suicide bombing. The police immediately went to look for her in Mandali, a town sixty miles northeast of Baghdad. On Christmas Eve, 2010, when they could not find her, they pulled her father, Mohammed Najm al-Anbaky, a small-time trader of chickens and sheep, in for questioning.

According to the English language press, once in police custody, Mohammed admitted that he had killed his daughter as a matter of "honor" because she was presumed to have a "boyfriend" in Al Qaeda. This Mohammed was also reported to have killed one of his sisters in 1984 as a matter of "honor." Mohammed admitted that he had strangled Shahlaa and then, for good measure, had slit her throat. Finally, he had buried her in his own backyard—not in a good Muslim cemetery—just as if his daughter was one of his chickens or sheep.

In this case, English-language readers only learn that the "honor" killing of a woman has taken place in the Arab Middle East. Arabic-language readers learn that the police were not investigating an honor killing at all but were, rather, looking into a possible terrorist attack by an Al Qaeda operative.

Indeed, earlier this year, the so-called "First Lady of Al Qaeda" (Haila Al-Qusayyer) was arrested in Saudi Arabia presumably for recruiting girls and women to become human bombs. In addition, in December, 2009, the wife of Al-Qaeda's second-in-command, Ayman Al-Zawahiri, issued a call for Muslim women to support violent jihad:

Jihad is [incumbent] on every Muslim man and woman…
and [we women] should keep ourselves in the service of the
Mujahideen, and we should fulfill whatever they ask of us,
may it be through monetary aid to them or any service or information or suggestion or participation in fighting or even
through a martyrdom operation. How many sisters have
performed martyrdom operations in Palestine and Iraq and
Chechnya, and vexed the enemy, and caused them a great
defeat!!

Meanwhile, back in Baghdad and Baquba, Iraq, we learn that Mohammed Najm Al-Anbaky is the kind of father and brother who is not
ashamed to have murdered his female relatives for "honor" and that in
neither instance was he arrested for such cold-blooded murders.

Would this kind of man view a woman's membership in Al Qaeda
as "dishonorable" or is his belief that his daughter may have had a "boyfriend" the prime motive for murder?

Female human bombs, like their male counterparts, may be brutally brainwashed or threatened with blackmail by wealthy, educated,
serial killers by proxy. The recruits may be clinically depressed, or frustrated by lives in which they have known little tenderness, no love, and
absolutely no hope of change.

As noted before, Wafa Idris, the first Palestinian Arab human
bomb, was probably in a clinical depression. Her first and only child
had been a stillborn and, as a result, she was now sterile. Her husband,
who was also her first cousin, had divorced her over this and had already
taken a second wife. She was mocked by family and friends and she understood that she had no future in Palestinian society. As a divorced and
infertile woman, she was doubly "tainted." Her bleak prospects—due to
Islamic and Palestinian misogyny and not to the Israeli-Palestinian conflict—were used to trap her into redeeming her dishonor by becoming
a murdering martyr.

In 2002, Idris blew herself up in the middle of Jerusalem, injur-
ing one hundred people and murdering an eighty-one year old man.
The fact that she was a trained paramedic in no way gave her pause (or
anything to live for). The Saudi Ambassador to London wrote a poem
glorifying her deed as exceptionally praiseworthy. However, I doubt that
she was a Western-style political revolutionary. Idris grew up in a tribal,
Islamic society in which women are expected to sacrifice themselves in
terrible and medieval ways.

The case of Reem al-Riyashi suggests a similar and horrifying scenario. Several Israeli sources have discovered that this young mother of two very young children "was forced to carry out the suicide attack as punishment for cheating on her husband." Allegedly, al-Riyashi's husband was a Hamas activist and her lover was a Hamas operative who had carried out the love affair for the express purpose of recruiting her. According to the British *Sunday Times*, al-Riyashi's husband himself drove her to the border crossing. Neither her husband nor her so-called lover valued her as anything other than a weapon that belonged to them.

In 2004, pretending to be crippled, al-Riyashi killed herself and four Israelis at the Erez crossing. Her "choice" was either to be honor murdered for having had an affair—or to go out in a repentant blaze of glory.

Such jihadic terrorism is a death force battling life and the life instinct. Female human bombs have recently (in 2010) blown themselves up in Baghdad in women-only areas, especially where women are on religious pilgrimages and have small children with them. At such a moment in history, the Muslim jihadists are showing us that one may be raised as a (presumably) peaceful woman; one can even become a biological mother; or be trained as a paramedic—and none of this will matter. Hate and death will triumph over normal, rational decency, and against all positive human instinct.

I was recently told about a ranking Hamas official whose son had been treated for cancer by Jewish doctors in an Israeli hospital. They saved the boy's life. He was asked whether this had in any way changed his political and religious views about Israel and Jews. "Absolutely not," said the ungrateful, possibly unnatural father.

We deny this at our peril.

FrontPage Magazine
12/28/10

Reality Banished, Propaganda Enshrined

I f you have lived among tribal Muslims, (and I have), you will understand that western concepts of objective truth do not exactly exist. But, for that matter, if you have lived long enough among western multi-cultural relativists (and I have, I have), you will come to a similar conclusion. Hence, consider the following.

A military friend tells me that "When you're taking flak you know you're over your target."

From that point of view, I am certainly over my target. The systematic "disappearance" of truth-telling when it comes to Islam may have led to an upcoming international conference at Australian National University in Australia: "Honour Killing across Culture and Time."

> Honour-motivated violence is a trans-historical and cross-cultural phenomenon, yet it has recently become a metonym for Islamic and anti-modern cultures.

Yes—it is a trans-historical and cross-cultural phenomenon, but that is because Islam has colonized every continent and, unlike Christianity and Judaism, has failed to abolish this form of misogynist barbarism.

The conference description is couched in postmodern language which asks: "How is honour embodied and performed in ways that lead to gendered violence?" "How do status anxieties and social asymmetries contribute to honour killing?" "How do anti-violence strategies negotiate competing claims of human rights and cultural relativism?" "How are personal and familial honour-related killings distinguished from collective public and state violence?"

And there you have it.

"Social asymmetries," (no doubt caused by western imperialism, colonialism, white racism, and capitalism), are probably responsible for "honour killing;" and the American wars of aggression in Iraq and Afghanistan are far more violent than individual, domestic "honour killings."

Clearly, this conference wants to defend Islam from being seen as the only group which is violent towards women. Such a perception is deemed to be "racist" and "Islamophobic."

A scholar and a writer usually has no way of knowing whether her work saves real lives. For some time now, I've been privileged to have been asked to testify, via affidavit, in a number of averted honor killing cases. All but one of these cases are still underway. Earlier this week, I received very good news which I would like to share.

It concerns the African woman who refused to become an elderly Muslim man's sixth wife; who had secretly converted to Christianity; and married another African Christian man and fled to the United States on a forged passport. My affidavit has, apparently, thus far, kept this poor soul in our blessed country. Her advocate told me that she has just heard from the prisoner's husband.

> He told me that it was your affidavit and my letter that has kept X in the US thus far. There were 42 other refugee claimants in the prison with her—but she was given a special paper that none of the others received. It was information about remaining in the US. Most of the others have now been deported, but X remains in prison. The lawyer says she has a very good case for going to the half way house in Y—set up for people such as X. Hers is a convoluted case to say the least…but her husband sends his gratitude to you for getting involved and endorsing what we know to be true for women in (this African country)."

This is all I have to say to the conveners of the conference in Australia and to those who criticize my work on honor killing. Why not save some lives, then get back to me with your politically correct theories?

NewsRealBlog
1/28/11

- 72 -
Testifying for the Victims in Flight from Honor Killing

She is marked for certain death.

Her final hearing takes place on Friday, January 14, 2011. If American Immigration decides to deport her back to her Muslim family in Africa, she will, without doubt, first be genitally mutilated and then honor murdered for insisting on remaining a Christian, for having fled an arranged Muslim marriage—and for having secretly married a Christian man.

I doubt she will be able to take her case to the United Nations. After all, that august body has condemned free speech/truth speech as hate speech, especially where Islam is concerned. Incredibly, presumably "progressive" European countries have increasingly launched criminal investigations against their own politicians, human rights activists, and academics for daring to tell the truth about Islamic gender and religious apartheid if that truth shows Islam in a negative light.

On January 24, 2011, the distinguished Lars Hedegaard, the President of the Danish Free Press Society and the International Free Press Society, will stand trial for telling the truth about Islamic gender apartheid. According to Ahmed Mohamud, the Vice President of The Danish Free Press Society, and Katrine Winkel Holm, Chief Editor of *Sappho*, the Society's magazine, both Lars Hedegaard and Jesper Langballe, a member of the Danish Parliament, are accused of committing "hate speech." Langballe exposed honor killings among Muslims; and, on December 3, 2010, he was convicted for doing so.

I have been called upon to testify in court cases for potential Muslim honor killing victims who are seeking asylum in America. Will I, too, someday be tried as a "racist"? Will such asylum seekers themselves be one day tried as "Islamophobic" criminals for exposing the horrendous violence they have escaped in the hope that the West will be a sanctuary for them? What will happen to them and to their advocates if telling the truth about Islam becomes a punishable offense in America?

To date, the highest profile apostate and potential honor killing case concerns the teenager Rifqa Bary. I was privileged to work with her lawyers both in Florida and Ohio. Bary's lawyers managed to keep her out of her family's clutches and obtained for her a "fast track" to a green card and to citizenship.

Within a fourteen month period, I was approached by three sets of lawyers and by one advocate.

I submitted an affidavit for a second asylum-seeker whose case may be unique. She fled a Western European country because she feared that her father and other male relatives would murder her for having secretly converted from Islam to Christianity. I urged the judge in her case to understand that just because a woman has fled from a European democracy does not mean that she has necessarily fled from a Western environment. Her immigrant family inhabits a bubble in which wife-battering is routine, living on welfare is seen as more dignified than taking a menial job, and spying on one's daughter to be sure that she never talks to men or has any non-Muslim friends is not considered invasive but one's duty.

This young woman told me that her father flew into instant rages over the smallest things; he once hit her mother when she brought him food not to his liking. He threw a table at his daughter because she was too quiet. He would then threaten her with a knife and say, "I'm not afraid of the police because I can kill myself too." If mere silence could set off this level of violence, one can only imagine how he might respond if he discovered that she had converted to Christianity.

I also submitted an affidavit on behalf of a third woman who is desperately trying to stay in the United States. She cannot risk returning to her South Asian country. Her crime? She dared to marry a man whom she loved but who belonged to a different sect of Islam; she did so against her parents' wishes. Her family is an elite and prominent family which would risk a loss of reputation if they did not punish such a defiant daughter.

Last week, a Canadian advocate and a professor of anthropology contacted me on behalf of a fourth woman. She is a convert to Christianity who was born and raised in the killing fields of Congo. Her father worked hard to end the dictatorial Mobutu regime and was therefore murdered by Mobutu's death squads. Her mother fled to a neighboring African country, where she married a Muslim man who insisted on marrying his new stepdaughter off to an elderly Muslim man; in turn, her chosen husband insisted that she first be genitally mutilated. This woman had already learned about the horror of genital mutilation firsthand when a friend of hers died from an infection after the "procedure" was inflicted upon her.

To understand what she is running away from, here is an account of one genital mutilation that recently took place in Cairo, Egypt:

> Our ears were assaulted by maniacal screams coming from one of the open shops that lined the alley…We looked in the direction from which came those screams to see a middle-aged woman seated in a barber chair, a child on her lap, and a man on his knees in front of the child. I assume the little girl was the daughter of the woman in the barber chair, who was restraining the girl and spreading the child's legs open, while the man on his knees was the barber who owned that barber shop. He leaned forward, concentrating on the space between the girl's legs, where he was working with a straight razor. The barber proceeded with businesslike indifference to the little girl's shrieks, as did the people in the street, who went about as if carving off a clitoris were something they saw every day, and as if the horrendous suffering the child expressed so loudly were a normal refrain in the raucous symphony that is Cairo. I stood motionless, transfixed by the crime I was watching, cursing myself for not charging into that barbershop, grabbing the little girl, and running away as fast as I could. A few moments later, the barber tossed a small red mass of bloody flesh into the gutter, a human clitoris for chickens to eat…

In flight from such barbarism, this poor soul fled Africa and arrived in the U.S. about six months ago with a falsified passport and a falsified visa which indicated that she was a single woman. According to her anthropologist-advocate, she had no choice—she could not tell anyone that she had secretly married another African Christian who now lived in Canada because she would not have been allowed to leave her African country as a married woman without permission from her Muslim father or husband. She could not risk asking her mother for such a letter; that would involve the mother in what would be seen as a conspiracy against her new Muslim family.

She was caught in a Catch-22 trap.

Thus, when this valiant soul tried to cross the border into Canada, she was closely questioned. However, she was both afraid to lie and afraid to tell the truth. Instead, she simply wept. Once the Canadian authorities understood that she had a husband in Canada and that her passport listed her as single, they turned her away. Ayaan Hirsi Ali herself chose--or was forced to lie to Dutch authorities when she first arrived there; despite her having risen to become a member of Parliament, this lie ultimately led to a serious attempt to deport her.

Back to our unnamed hero. Shortly after being barred from entering Canada, and for unknown reasons, American immigration authorities arrested her and have been keeping her in detention for the last month.

Her anthropologist-advocate attended her initial hearing and tried to visit her in detention. She told me: "The security was unbelievable, and all deadly serious. Even I was intimidated. I can only imagine how she, a tiny woman, must feel--handcuffed for the duration. We could not even visit with her. Just a quick 60 seconds to hug her before the hearing, then about 30 seconds while waiting for the elevator before she was taken back to jail."

If only the perpetrators of Islamic gender apartheid—and not their victims—faced this kind of treatment. But they do not.

She is now facing deportation. Her final hearing will take place this Friday. Her Canadian advocate believes that Canada would probably accept her but it will still take some time to convince the government to readmit her since she has already been turned back at the border. Her lawyer has advised her advocate, her husband, and his family not to show up for the final hearing—advice which troubles me because it is important for the judge to see that she has supporters who find her story credible and who are ready to take responsibility for her.

One must also ask: Should the West, including the United States and Canada be taking in so many persecuted victims from other countries? That's certainly what America is about—but can we afford to subsidize this rescue work? Can we afford not to?

Update: Alas, on the day before the Immigration Judge would have been legally forced to release her to her waiting husband (also a Christian African), he called some authority in Congo who, in an apparently drunken moment, assured the Judge that the Congo would take her with or without proper paperwork. She was on a plane back to a never-ending war, to be lost forever to her loving husband and her Canadian advocates.

How could this have happened? Poor lawyering, no money, an terrified inability to deal with the Canadian Immigration authorities about certain understandable inconsistencies in her story.

Clara, for that is her name, did not know how to explain that her passport did not and could state that she was married because her mother had wanted her daughter to undergo FGM and to become the fourth wife of some grandfather. But, Clara was already secretly married and had converted to Christianity. Had she said so, it would have endangered her mother's life. Thus, miraculously, with the help of a Christian underground, she obtained a Congolese passport as a single, Muslim woman.

At the border, Clara's main Canadian advocate said that she only wept when she was questioned and could not speak.

I think of Clara from time to time; I am haunted by her terrible fate. If you know anything about the Congo you'll understand.

FrontPage Magazine
1/13/11

- 73 -
Inside the Mind of an Islamist

1. *When Is The Aggressor Not The Aggressor? When He Has Been Forced to Defend His Lost Honor*

On February 12, 2009, immediately after stabbing his unarmed wife 40 times with two large hunting knives and then brutally beheading her, he became calm, relieved. For the first time in years, he felt "peaceful." Only then did he feel "safe from the Evil Dragon Terrorist" which is how he referred to Aasiya Zubair Hassan, the wife he had viciously battered for seven years.

Muzzammil Syed Hassan insists that he, not she, was the "abused" and long-suffering spouse.

How is this possible? How can a man with a long and terrible history of physically and psychologically battering three wives and physically and psychologically abusing his children as well—he once punched his 13-year-old son in the nose—say this and believe it with his whole heart? In pre-trial interviews, Hassan described having suffered immense psychological abuse and humiliation. He said:

> "All abuse happens behind closed doors, thus NO witnesses," Hassan stated in his most recent letter. "All abuse is psychological, emotional wounds are not visible, thus NO evidence. . . . What a perfect crime! Only the poorly trained abusers use physical violence and get caught, for physical abuse leaves behind evidence."

Like other batterers, Hassan is not merely saying that Aasiya "provoked" him to kill her but that she had been torturing him for seven years: cleverly leaving no marks. Finally, afraid of being exposed—either as a batterer or, in his eyes, as a battered spouse, both humiliating possibilities for a leader of the Muslim-American community—Muzzammil said that he "snapped." He had to kill her to restore his peace of mind.

And so, he took control.

2. *Where Else Have We Heard Such Reasoning?*

An Al-Qaeda, Hamas, or Muslim Brotherhood leader will insist that his campaigns of murder and propaganda are really campaigns of "self defense" against the Zionist, infidel, Nazi, Apartheid Enemy. Since their holy Muslim lands, which they define as part of their honor and often as encompassing the entire world—psychologically, their missing phantom limb—have been taken and occupied by infidels, they must send human homicide bombs so that what belongs to them is returned, so that they are made whole and no longer humiliated in history.

Thus, Islamist acts of beheading (journalist Daniel Pearl, would-be businessman Nicholas Berg, civil engineer Kenneth Bigley, contractor Eugene Armstrong, engineer Jack Hensley, engineer Paul Marshall Johnson, Jr., etc.), and blowing up innocent civilians on aircraft, at cafés, on the streets, at work in the World Trade Center, are not "aggressive" acts, but are, rather, "defensive" acts, desperate attempts to ensure that the impure infidels will flee, so that their Muslim property, purity, and honor can be restored.

Blowing up Israeli civilians is even more an act of "self-defense," since, as they see it, there are no innocent Israelis, all are complicit in the allegedly "genocidal crimes" against the Palestinian and Arab people. Blowing up other Muslim civilians, using children as soldiers—well, some Muslims are not "true" Muslims, some Muslims are working with the enemy infidel, some Muslims are whores—and they all deserve to be killed anyway.

Before we get into Muzzammil's personal history, we need to understand something about the country he comes from: Pakistan.

3. *Where Could Muzzammil Syed Hassan Have Learned That Extreme Violence Towards Women Is Normal?*

For the first seventeen years of his life Hassan grew up in Pakistan, where the level of violence towards girls and women was and still is

251

rather unbelievable.

In 2009, I received an extraordinary report which documented honor killings in Pakistan. My Pakistani informant, of the SW Community Development Department, in Sind, Pakistan, sent me an unpublished paper in which he describes and explains a murderous Pakistani culture very carefully. He writes:

> Women in Pakistan live in fear. They face death by shooting, burning or killing with axes if they are deemed to have brought shame on the family. They are killed for supposed "illicit" relationships, for marrying men of their choice, for divorcing abusive husbands. They are even murdered by their kin if they are raped. The truth of the suspicion does not matter—merely the allegation is enough to bring dishonor on the family and therefore justifies the slaying. The lives of millions of women in Pakistan are circumscribed by traditions which enforce extreme seclusion and submission to men. Male relatives virtually own them and punish disobedience with violence.

According to my informant, most honor killings in Pakistan are unreported and go unpunished.

> The isolation and fear of women living under such threats are compounded by state indifference to and complicity in women's oppression. Police almost invariably take the man's side in honor killings or domestic murders, and rarely prosecute the killers. Even when the men are convicted, the judiciary ensures that they usually receive a light sentence, reinforcing the view that men can kill their female relatives with virtual impunity. There are few women's shelters, and any woman attempting to travel on her own is a target for abuse by police, strangers or male relatives hunting for her. For some women suicide appears the only means of escape.

> In [Pakistani] communities an 'honor killing' is considered a just punishment, not a crime.

> Male control does not only extend to a woman's body and her sexual behavior but all of her behavior, including her move-

ments, her language and her actions. In any of these areas, defiance by women translates into undermining male honor and ultimately family and community honor. Severe punishments are reported for bringing food late, for talking back or for undertaking forbidden trips, etc. A man's honor defiled by a woman's alleged or real sexual misdemeanor or other defiance is only partly restored by killing her. He also has to kill the man allegedly involved. Since [the woman] is murdered first, the [man] often hears about it and flees, aided by the fact that unlike the woman, he is both familiar with the world outside the house and can move freely in it. But [men] who escape will not be able to return to normal life. Nobody will give such a man shelter; he remains on the run until he and his family are ready to negotiate with the victim, the man whose honour the [man] defiled. The balance is restored by negotiating compensation for damages.

Moreover, there are few safe places for a woman to escape to. Seeking help outside the family is fraught with danger for a woman. Not only does society blame a woman for being targeted for murder—the popular perception being that she must somehow deserve it—but by seeking outside help she risks being sent back to her husband or father in whose custody she is perceived to belong. Most important by seeking help outside, she adds shame to her husband and his family by making the issue public. No Kari ["black" woman marked for honor-killing] who escapes is ever forgiven, even if her innocence is recognized; some men are known to have traveled hundreds of miles to find and kill Karis, even years after the alleged misdeed. The sheer scale of the phenomenon in Pakistan makes it a case apart.

In this informant's view, although such crimes of honor are a pre-Islamic practice, the increase in religious fundamentalism has led to an increase in honor killings. Honor killing victims "remain dishonored even after death. Their dead bodies are thrown in rivers or buried in special hidden Kari graveyards. Nobody mourns for them or honors their memory by performing the relevant rights."

This is the culture that nurtured Muzzammil Hassan, the culture that also nurtured his wife Aasiya—which explains why, after she obtained an order of protection and had Muzzammil ejected from their home (his home, his land, his property), she still did his laundry and indeed, was bringing him clean clothing at his office at Bridges TV, where he lay in wait for her with his two pitiless hunting knives.

4. *Can Living in America Erase the Pakistani Within?*

In America, he liked to be called "Mo" and "Steve." The Big Guy weighed nearly 300 pounds, or twice his wife's weight—and he just wanted to fit in, be a regular American. He came here when he was 17 and excelled. In 1996, he received an MBA from the Business School at the University of Rochester; he then became a banker in Buffalo, New York. Big "Mo" was ambitious. He wanted to present Muslims in a positive light. In 2004, together with his wife Aasiya, he founded Bridges TV, an English-language Islamic network to combat alleged anti-Muslim bias in the American media. He found several million dollars in backing.

But Hassan could not stop being a Pakistani Muslim man. He still felt entitled to control, monitor, harass, and physically batter his third wife. When he physically punished her, he viewed this as "correcting" her mistakes. When she went to the hospital and filed a police report—she had black eyes, bruises, cuts—he viewed her exposing him as "humiliating attacks," indeed, as "terrorist attacks." When she said that she was going to file for divorce, he viewed that as "killing him;" in addition, he began to fear that these police and hospital reports plus a divorce with such facts out in the open might jeopardize his dream of a pro-Muslim television network. Her attempts to defend herself from his physical violence, e.g. sitting on her, trying to run her car off the road, beating her so viciously that his son from a previous marriage who lived with them had to use a whole roll of toilet paper to stanch the flow of blood, dragging her across their driveway, blackening her eyes, breaking windows, etc., were experienced *by him* as "abusive."

In my studies published at *Middle East Quarterly*, I found that one feature of an honor killing, as perpetrated in the West, is sometimes "overkill." The victims are tortuously murdered, burned, raped, mutilated, stoned, even beheaded, as was the case with Aasiya. At trial (which is still ongoing) it became clear that Muzzammil attacked his unarmed wife with two hunting knives and stabbed her at least 40 times before he beheaded her—a signature Islamist-era gesture.

Clearly, female-initiated divorce is not acceptable, neither in Pakistan (where women are killed for far less than demanding a divorce) nor in America. Muzzammil Hassan was a three-time loser in terms of marriage with his reputation and credibility on the line. If it emerged that he beat his wife, badly, and constantly subjected her to psychological torture, he feared he would lose his backers and their image of him as a good man.

5. *Is Muzzammil Hassan "Crazy" in Western Terms?*

Muzzammil is a male batterer who is also Pakistani and Muslim. He has been brought up to believe that he is entitled to whatever he needs, thinks he needs, or wants. Anyone who deprives him of what he needs or wants, is a dangerous "terrorist" enemy, especially if she is a woman.

According to Muzzammil, he and Aasiya made a "contract" which included certain terms, i.e. that she never turn to the police, never threaten divorce, never report him to Child Protective Services. Each time she does so, he is being "killed;" his world is "collapsing;" his pride is wounded; his failure to control his wife is becoming known. He in no way can acknowledge the harm he has done to her and their children.

Prosecutor Colleen Curtin Gable forces him to admit that he was "not in any danger" when he attacked an unarmed woman. And she forces him to admit that he had "killed" his wife. Acidly, and precisely, she notes that "In three-and-a-half days of testimony," Hassan spent about "two seconds on the actual murder."

That is because he wanted the judge and jury to hear "his side," "the whole truth." Thus, he spent all his time trying to arouse pity, sympathy, and understanding for how he had suffered, not how his wife and children may have suffered. He is the only one who matters.

Muzzammil takes no responsibility for his actions or how they affect others. He referred to the murder as "things happened." As to the 40 stab wounds which preceded his beheading of her, he responds, dully, disassociated, "If the wounds are there, then I did it, ma'am." But he has "no recollection of specific things happening." All he knows is that when it was all over, "defending himself," he felt no "remorse," but only "relief that he managed to escape a (diseased) terrorist." He says: "I was face to face with evil."

Muzzammil Syed Hassan is unapologetic, brash, brazen, belligerent, and incredibly aggressive. Acting as his own lawyer, he wanted to personally question the judge, the prosecutors, and his own children on the stand. (He did cross-examine his daughter Sonia, who looked down and at the jury the entire time.) Muzzammil admitted that he called the district attorney "dumbo," his wife "Darth Vader," a "monster," and an "evil dragon." He also called the court "voodoo justice" and a "kangaroo court."

Muzzammil has the mind, heart, and soul of both an overly pampered baby and a domestic terrorist. But his lack of remorse, concern only for his own image, his willingness to do anything, including murder, to punish those who have tarnished his image teaches us all something about the mind of an Islamist jihadist.

NewsRealBlog
2/6/11

- 74 -
Jury Finds Honor Killer Muzzammil Hassan Guilty—Mainstream Media Sends No Reporters

The verdict is in. The jury found Muzzammil Hassan guilty of second-degree murder. Sentencing will take place on March 9th; the minimum sentence for second-degree murder in New York State is 15 years and the maximum is 25 years to life. The District Attorney has said that he will push for the maximum sentence.

This man has now orphaned two children, those whom he fathered with Aasiya, and traumatized the two children whose mother was one of Muzzammil's previous victims.

This is a victory for the American jury system, which in this case valued the life of a woman more than she would have been valued in her native Pakistan.

I congratulate the jury on its just and swift (50 minutes) decision. And I congratulate the prosecution on a job well done. But, in my opinion, Aasiya Zubair Hassan's killer should have been charged with first-degree murder. New York State has abolished capital punishment and reserves first-degree murder charges for murders involving special circumstances, such as torture, multiple murders, or the killing of a police officer. In my opinion, 40 stab wounds and a beheading deserves to be considered torture. But whatever the charge would have been, it could not bring back this much-sinned against woman.

The New York Times, the *Washington Post*, the *Wall Street Journal*, and the *Los Angeles Times* all failed to send a reporter to cover this trial.

The Wall Street Journal carried an 879-word Associated Press story on its website, while the *New York Times* ran 269 words from the same story in its hardcopy version in a 2 x 7 inch spot at the bottom of page A24 of the New York section.

The AP reporter herself does not refer to this as an honor killing, leaving it up to one of her interviewees, a lecturer at the University of Buffalo, to make the case that the murder was "a mix of domestic violence and honor killing." In her past reporting on this case, she only went so far as to write that the murder "gave rise to speculation" that it was an honor killing.

The conservative media has been covering honor killings in America; the left-liberal mainstream media has been reluctant to do so. But millimeter by millimeter, inch by inch, the mainstream media is slouching toward acknowledging that honor killings committed by Muslims do exist and are taking place in North America.

NewsRealBlog
2/7/11

- 75 -
Justice Served in an American-Islamic Honor Killing

Arizona Judge Roland Steinle has just sentenced Faleh Almaleki to 34½ years in prison. According to live reporting from the courtroom, the judge noted that Almaleki showed no remorse after the murder, he did not forgive his daughter, he did what suited his own purpose. The judge also said this was the hardest case he had to face in his six years on the bench. He found no mitigating factors and sentenced Almaleki to 34 and 1/2 years: 15 years for the aggravated assault of Khalaf, 3 and 1/2 years for leaving the scene of an accident, and 16 years for the second-degree murder of his daughter. He was facing a maximum total of 46 years.

As we may recall, Faleh made his escape with the help of his wife, Seham, Noor's mother, and their son, Ali. Seham made sure Faleh had his diabetes medicine with him; perhaps she packed a little bag for him too. Seham was no kinder to Noor than her father was. Seham cursed Noor on a regular basis and made life at home so impossible that Noor left. She moved in with the sympathetic Amal, whose son, Marwan, Noor may have begun to date. Seham soon cursed the woman who dared give Noor shelter.

Noor's crime was that she had refused to remain in an arranged marriage in Iraq, (where her father had sent her), wanted to live in America, insisted on dressing like a modern, American girl. In her family's eyes, she was a "whore," a "disobedient" daughter who deserved to die. Their honor depended on her death.

I cannot imagine what it might be like growing up in a family and

259

in a culture where you know, in advance, that your own parents, brothers, sisters, first cousins, and uncles might be the ones who might one day kill you. I would think that "trust" and "intimacy" would be difficult and that reality-based paranoia would prevail. The laws in America allow for conspirators to also be tried. Thus far, that has not happened here. Neither Tissy Said nor Seham Almaleki, (both the mothers of honor killed daughters), have been tried as collaborators in their daughters' murders. This has happened in Europe.

As we have seen, in 2004, Great Britain also began re-classifying old murders. In 2006, in London, Banaz Mahmod was raped and strangled to death by two of her cousins and a hired gun at the order of her father and uncle. Her "crime" was that she had left an arranged marriage. The two cousins fled to Iraq after the murder; they were the first suspects ever to be extradited from Iraq to Britain. All five men involved were sentenced to life in prison; the men will be eligible for parole after 17-23 years.

The kinds of Muslims (or Sikhs and Hindus) who commit honor murders on our soil are importing barbarism and criminal misogyny. The remedies will be costly and take a great deal of time and will include a combination of careful screening procedures, combined with citizenship, police, judicial, social work education—and the enforcement of Western laws.

FrontPage Magazine
4/15/11

76

Honor Killings, Jew-Hatred & UN Think

H ina Jilani is a Pakistani women's rights activist, an advocate of the Supreme Court of Pakistan, a former U.N. Special Representative of the Secretary-General on Human Rights Defenders, and a co-author of the infamous and famously retracted Goldstone Report.

Dear Hina Jilani:

Greetings! I am familiar with and an admirer of your work as a Pakistani feminist and human rights lawyer, one who has gone on record opposing both honor killing and rape and the inadequate legislation against such crimes in Pakistan.

In 1999, you handled a high profile honor killing case, that of a Pakistani woman, Samia Imran (aka Samia Sarwar), whose physician mother and politically powerful father arranged that she be shot to death in your office because she dared to seek a divorce from a dangerously violent Pakistani husband. I wrote about this case in 2004-2005 and have written about it again any number of times since then.

I have tried to imagine what you and your staff have felt. I am friendly with a Turkish-German lawyer whose battered 15-year-old client was shot to death in her office in Berlin; the lawyer herself was shot and left for dead as well. Clearly, the lawyer lived. But we did talk about the effect this murder has had on her forever after.

Perhaps you are familiar with my work in general and in the area of honor killings; perhaps not. I have published fifteen books, including the landmark *Women and Madness* and *Woman's Inhumanity to Woman*. I have published two studies, written hundreds of articles, delivered speeches, given interviews, and written affidavits for girls and women who are now seeking asylum in the United States because they are at risk of being honor murdered in Southeast Asia, Africa, and Europe. Once, long ago, I lived in Kabul, Afghanistan and moved in Muslim circles.

Under other circumstances, we might have met, worked together, perhaps even befriended each other.

Sadly, that is now not the case.

Yesterday, the Pakistani Supreme Court upheld the acquittal of five of the six men who were convicted in the 2002 tribal-council ordered gang-rape of Mukhtar Mai, perhaps the bravest woman in Pakistan, perhaps the bravest woman in the world. Instead of killing herself or turning bandit as did the notorious Phoolan Devi after a similar gang-rape in India, she instead pressed charges and opened a school and a shelter for other similarly battered and raped Pakistani women.

We both know that Mukhtar Mai is supremely endangered by the release of these higher-caste rapists, as are all the women of Pakistan.

In February of 1983, you and your sister Asma spent 20 days in prison for demonstrating on behalf of a young blind girl named Safia Bibi. She—the rape victim—had been jailed in Pakistan for adultery.

Thus, I was shocked—enormously saddened—when I realized that, as a long-time UN employee/professional you are also one of four people on the United Nations Fact Finding Mission on the Gaza Conflict which produced the Goldstone Report and which is now insisting that it be implemented, Goldstone's recantation be damned. (I assume that you've read the many powerful and credible critiques of this Report.)

Here is why I am writing.

You know that false but lethal slander leads to the honor murder of girls and women in Pakistan, in the Islamic world, and among Muslim immigrants to the West. Yes, Hindus and Sikhs do commit honor murders in India, but rarely in the West, and their motives seem to be different. Allegations of "sexual impropriety," true or false, vague or specific, are behind so many honor murders of Muslim girls and women in Pakistan and in other Muslim-majority countries.

Hina, please understand: The lies and slander that have been generated against Israel are every bit as false and unjust as the lies told to justify the honor killing of girls and women.

I once worked at the United Nations. In my opinion, it is completely ineffective save in two areas:

It has legalized Jew-hatred with a vengeance and it has provided a High Life for many Third World/developing world professionals who wish to be well paid to live in the West and yet also wish to retain or achieve reputations as champions of justice. Therefore, I understand the price you would have to pay if you broke with UN-Think or with Third World Think which is so intensely anti-American, anti-Western, and anti-Israel—the convenient scapegoats for all the crimes and ills of the Arab and Muslim world.

Nevertheless, please think about the implications of my analogy.

Like an honor killing victim, Israel is being slandered so that the terrorist violence against it will be seen as justified and legitimate. When Israel exposes the Big Lies or tries to defend its civilian citizens against such pitiless violence, like the raped girls and women in Pakistan and other Muslim-majority countries, Israel is blamed. She provoked it. She knew the rules. She knew she was meant to die if she stepped out of line by a millimeter; surely she knew that being born female was a capital crime, a death sentence.

Israel dares to live—and on sovereign Jewish land. It exists surrounded by Arab and Muslim countries that believe she has no right to exist and who have sworn to kill her.

Unlike Pakistan, or other Muslim countries, Israel actually prosecutes rapists. This includes the former president of the country, Moshe Katsav, who, on December 30, 2010, was convicted by a Tel Aviv court and sentenced to seven years in jail, beginning on May 7, 2011.

More important: Israel has given shelter to girls and women in flight from being honor murdered in Gaza and the West Bank, where honor murders are endemic and soaring due to Islamism, not to Israeli policies of self-defense.

Most recently, in March of 2011, Hamas beat, tortured, and arrested eight women journalists in Gaza, including Asma Al-Ghul, a prominent advocate against honor killings. She had been arrested before for appearing on the beach, dressed in Western clothing, with male colleagues and friends; she had actually dared to laugh and to swim in her clothing. She asked me to edit and publish her work on honor killings and I did so.

As a feminist and human rights activist, I assume you are aware of the extent to which honor killings are committed among Israeli Muslim Arabs ("Palestinian" citizens of Israel) and the extent to which Israel prosecutes such crimes. For example, seventeen years ago, Nadil Abu Hadir, an Israeli Muslim Arab citizen who lived in Jerusalem, honor killed his sister; he stabbed her to death in broad daylight in the central bus station and in full view of her three children. He then fled to Bethlehem, where the Palestinian Authority sheltered him for seventeen years. Only recently was he tried and convicted by an Israeli court for this crime and sentenced to life in prison. He was also ordered to pay each of his sister's children 100,000 shekels.

According to the Palestinian Center for Human Rights, there were nine honor killings committed in Gaza in the first seven months of 2009. That is, nine known honor killings. As you know, most honor killings remain unknown. In Gaza, the most an honor killer can receive is three years; they are often sentenced to far less.

Here is what I'm asking. Why are you prosecuting Israel so vigorously? Why are you not using your power at the United Nations to prosecute Pakistan for its abominable record in terms of human rights and women's rights? Will prosecuting only Israel help Muhktar Mai or the world's women in some way that I cannot fathom?

Hina: I am not sure you will read this letter, but if you do, please contact me. We share many interests, even passions, but we most definitely part company on the relationship of the United Nations to the sovereign state of Israel and about what really happened in Gaza. I would like to talk this through with you if you are open to such a dialogue.

All best,
Phyllis Chesler

NewsRealBlog
4/22/11

77

Jessica Mokdad, 20, Killed by her Stepfather

B in Laden may be dead but, as many have noted, his ideology is still very much alive. Indeed, it landed on our shores long ago. It is most definitely here now.

Women in burqas and in severe hijab are increasingly commonplace on our city streets as are other more barbaric gender apartheid practices. This includes heartless honor killings—femicides.

Over this past weekend, there was a new honor killing in America. To their credit, the Associated Press (AP) did a short online story which was picked up by CBS and by local Minnesota and Michigan newspapers.

Otherwise—silence.

The victim's name was Jessica Mokdad. She was 20 years old. Her killer was her stepfather, Rahim A. Alfetlawi, 45 years old. According to the assistant principal, Jessica was a "standout student" at Coon Rapids High School in Minnesota. "She was a quiet student who was very confident in who she was and proud of being a Muslim."

Why was she killed? Because, according to the police, her stepfather believed she was "not adhering to Muslim customs." And, because her biological father was "letting her be a little more Americanized than what [the defendant] wanted."

What's different about this case is that Jessica fled to the safety of her biological father's home in Grand Blanc, Michigan. Thus, her own father was supporting her, as was her paternal grandmother, in whose home she was when Alfetlawi found her and shot her with a 9mm handgun.

Like Muzzammil "Mo" Hassan in Buffalo, (who beheaded his

wife), Atfetlawi calmly went to the police and admitted killing his step-daughter. Like Faleh Almaleki in Arizona (who ran his daughter down with a two ton jeep), Alfetlawi also hedged his bets and claimed that the gun went off "accidentally."

Mokdad was planning to attend college.

Why is the mainstream media silent about this outrage? Why are Muslim-American organizations silent?

Why are Muslim women's organizations also silent? Please speak out. Why is her mother, Wendy, silent? Was she complicit in this decision as were the mothers of the Said sisters in Dallas and Noor Almaleki in Arizona?

NewsRealBlog
5/4/11

- 78 -
Muslim Mothers Who "Honor Kill" Their Daughters

Two Muslim mothers, both widows, both living in Uttar Pradesh in India, helped each other murder their grown daughters, Zahida, 19, and Husna, 26, for having committed the crime of marrying Hindu men.

They held their daughters down and slowly strangled them to death. The poor dead darlings actually believed they were entitled to marry non-Muslim men for "love," and that ultimately, their mothers and Muslim community would accept them back. This is typical of many honor killing victims. While these two young women knew enough to contact the police for help—and the police actually got their mothers to sign an agreement that they would not "harm" their children—it was only a piece of paper. The daughters' longing for reconciliation and naïve hopefulness was their undoing. Their mothers agreed not to hurt them and sweet-talked them into returning, but once the girls were home, they became prey for the kill.

But life without a family network is unthinkable for someone whose identity is not individual, but rather, is located in collective. Progress and "modernity" may be coming to India, but slowly.

Neither mother, Khatun or Subrato, has expressed the slightest remorse. Both feel justified because their daughters brought shame to their families. According to the police, Khatun said: "We killed them because they brought shame to our community. How could they elope with Hindus? They deserved to die. We have no remorse."

This is cold-hearted, but such tribal woman-on-woman crimes are typical in many parts of the world.

Clearly, this is an extreme case of woman's inhumanity to woman. We expect women, mothers especially, to be able to defy social custom for the sake of saving their children. The reality is just the opposite. The slightest transgression, especially by women, will upset huge networks and topple all social stability. No one will marry someone from a "shamed" family; that family will be forever ostracized, impoverished, and may also die out genetically. Mothers, fathers, and relatives are loyal to their tribal social customs rather than to any one individual, even if that individual is their own child. The sacrifice of the individual in service to the greater tribal and ethnic-religious social structure is what tribal civilization is about.

Woman's inhumanity to woman is also a common phenomenon in India where mothers-in-law routinely assist their sons in burning their daughters-in-law to death. As I've noted previously, this is known as a "dowry killing," which is perpetrated so that another new bride can bring another dowry into the impoverished and/or greedy family. There is a special wing in a prison in New Delhi for such mothers-in-law. In addition, female infanticide was a long-time practice in both India and China. Both women and men steal children in India and sell them to be adopted abroad or, more frequently, to be groomed into sexual slavery either at home or abroad.

Surveys have shown us that women in India believe that women deserve to be beaten. Perhaps women simply expect this to happen. Many Hindu and Muslim mothers refuse to accept severely battered child-daughter brides back into their home. In Afghanistan, such little brides sometimes kill themselves.

To its credit, the Indian Supreme Court has recently declared that "It is time to stamp out these barbaric, feudal practices which are a slur on our nation."

FrontPage Magazine
5/18/11

Abbas' Fake Honor Killing Outrage

L ast month, Palestinian President, Mahmoud Abbas, "scrapped the laws" which guaranteed "leniency" for honor killers. Family honor will no longer be a mitigating factor in such cases. On the West Bank and in Gaza, family murders of Muslim girls and women routinely draw sentences of six months or less.

Abbas was apparently driven to this unusual act by public outrage about an alleged honor killing which took place near Hebron on the West Bank.

Over a year ago, on April 20, 2010, 20-year-old Aya Baradiya disappeared. Her paternal uncle, 37-year-old Iqab Baradiya, and two accomplices had kidnapped her, bound her hand and foot, and threw her down a well, leaving her to die a slow and painful death. Her remains were not found for more than a year.

Aya was a religious woman who wore a hijab. Her university classmates described her as "chaste and noble-minded."

What crime did she commit? Aya wanted to marry a man. Her suitor went through the traditional channels. Her parents approved of the match but wanted her to wait until she graduated. Her uncle, 17 years older than she was, strongly disapproved of the engagement. And so he killed her.

Although the media are now reporting her murder as an honor killing, it is not a classic honor killing.

For example, her uncle did not immediately confess. Although some honor killings are disguised as "suicides" or accidents and never made public, in general, those that do come to light often involve proud confessions. Honor killers confess as a way of publicizing that they have "cleansed their shame."

In Aya's case, there was no "shame" that had to be cleansed.

In addition, Aya's parents and siblings did not collaborate in the decision to murder their daughter, knew nothing about it, were haunted by her disappearance, and played absolutely no role in her murder. In fact, when Aya did not return home from university, her parents immediately reported her missing.

One suspects that her uncle may have had a highly inappropriate interest in his niece. His behavior suggests that he had an unnatural proprietary interest in her sexual and reproductive future and acted as if his niece was more like his daughter over whom he had the power of life and death.

How ironic that President Abbas, who has thus far been unmoved by the epidemic of honor killings among Arabs on the West Bank, in Gaza, and in Israel proper, (where Israeli police make arrests), has now ostensibly decided to do the right thing vis-à-vis honor killings—when no honor killing has occurred. But is he really doing the right thing?

Aya's murdering uncle has demonstrated the cruelty of Arab men towards Arab women; this includes the innocent women in their own immediate and extended families as well as women in general. Aya Baradiya was murdered—but it was not an honor murder. Please read my studies on honor killings in order to understand what one actually is. The following are some examples of genuine honor murders among Arabs on the West Bank, in Gaza, and in Israel, which apparently left President Abbas unmoved. I have written about some of these femicides earlier.

In 2003, Rofayda Qaoud of Abu Qash in the West Bank was murdered by her mother Amira Qaoud, who put a plastic bag over her head and sliced her wrists with a razor. Her crime? Rofayda had been raped by her two brothers and impregnated. According to her mother, the family's honor demanded that she sacrifice her daughter for the violent crimes of her criminally psychopathic sons.

In 2007, Hamda Abu-Ghanem, 18, was shot to death in Ramle, Israel, by her brother and her cousin because some men in her town had referred to her as a "prostitute." She was the eighth woman to have been murdered in her extended family in seven years and, in an unprecedented move, the family's women finally went public.

In 2007, 21-year-old Nadia Abu Amar of Jerusalem was murdered by her three brothers and her uncle because she refused to marry the man she was engaged to and because she got her father arrested and convicted for assault.

In 2009, Fadia Najjar of Gaza City, a divorced mother of five, was bludgeoned to death by her father because she owned a cell phone. He suspected that she was using it to call a man outside of the family. The day after the murder, he turned himself into police.

According to Asma Al-Ghul, an Arab feminist who has focused on Arab honor killings, Najla' A., 24, a divorced woman living in Rafah in Gaza, was strangled by her extremist brother while sleeping because she used to be away from home for long hours, which ignited rumors about her behavior. After the police discovered what had happened, her family bribed the police and they let the brother go. (Al-Ghul does not date this case.)

In typical Arab style, President Abbas has said he has done something but he has really done nothing. He has not yet signed his vow into law or published it. Abbas has used the unexpected outcry against the (non-honor) murder of a young woman who is being called a "martyr," and whose reputation was above reproach, to stage a symbolic but actually toothless response to the very real epidemic of honor killings among ("Palestinian") Arabs. According to experts, judges do not rely upon the "mitigating factor" provision when they hand down lenient sentences for honor murderers. According to *Haaretz*, a newspaper with which I generally do not agree, here are the facts about what Abbas did (and didn't) do:

> [A] review of the draft of the presidential decree indicates that judges in Palestinian courts, who showed leniency toward murderers—handing down sentences ranging from six months to three or four years in prison in such cases—did not necessarily rely on the two problematic clauses mentioned above, but rather, on other articles not even mentioned in the presidential decree.

In addition, there is this: Aya is being presented as a "chaste" and "noble" girl who did nothing wrong according to Arab standards. What about those Arab girls and women who refuse to veil or to accept arranged marriages? Or who are seen as too "Western?" Do Abbas and Arab society still believe that such women deserve to be honor murdered? In what way are their civil and personal rights protected under the rule of the Palestinian Authority or under Hamas's rule in Gaza?

In this instance, the Associated Press reporters have further misled the public by failing to understand that Aya Baradiya's murder, however heinous, was not an honor killing—at least not in the classical sense. They present the facts but fail to analyze them properly.

Furthermore, why did the AP reporters chose to quote Suha Arafat and Hanan Ashrawi, two prominent Arab Palestinian women who masquerade as feminist activists but who have done nothing to combat or expose honor killings in Palestinian society? Suha claims that she tried to persuade her late husband, Yasser Arafat, the terrorist leader, to do something about the problem, but there is no record of this. As for Ashrawi, I searched far and wide for anything that she might have said or done about honor killings before AP quoted her, but there appears to be nothing. Her 1995 memoir, *This Side of Peace: A Personal Account*, doesn't contain a single reference to honor killings.

Both claim to have secretly aided Muslim would-be honor killing victims. Again, the only networks I know about are Israeli Jewish feminist networks and Christian feminist networks. Like Edward Said, Ashrawi is a Christian, and yet somehow I doubt she would have jeopardized her only-woman status on the Executive Committee of the PLO to help the most vulnerable of her gender in distress. Finally, the only "safe" place an Arab girl or woman can be easily spirited away to is… Israel.

Suha Arafat and Ashrawi are propagandists, ideologues, uber-nationalists, who have justified terrorism and demonized Israel. This is their strong suit. They are not feminist activists. Next time, AP should interview Asma Al-Ghul, who was among the eight female journalists who were arrested, beaten, and tortured by Hamas this past March in Gaza.

FrontPage Magazine
6/22/11

- 80 -
Guilty: Afghan Muslim Family in Canada Convicted in Honor Killings

On Sunday, January 29, 2012, two years and seven months after the bodies of four Canadian women all from the same family were found murdered, after a ten week trial, and after fifteen hours of deliberations, a seven-woman, five-man jury voted "guilty" to first degree murder for three members of the Shafia family.

Although I myself initially hailed this as a possible turning point in Canada (in terms of the nation's failed multicultural policy), I now wonder why the life sentence, which in Canada means 25 years without parole, was not 25 years without parole for each life coldly snuffed out.

The three Shafias: Mohammed Shafia, 58, Tooba Yahya, 42, and Hamid Shafia, their son, were tried under Canadian law for premeditated murder and for conspiracy to commit murder; no special "honor killing" related law was needed. This is as it should be and yet, if such a special law did exist, there might have been an "enhanced penalty" which might have maximized the sentences. However, Canadian law in general is lenient. They have no death penalty and there has been no capital punishment in Canada since 1962.

Still, true justice should have resulted in a 25 year sentence for each murder: one for Geeti, 13, one for Sahar, 17, one for Zainab, 19, and one for Rona Amir Mohammed, 52, instead of what amounts to about a minimum of 6½ years for each life taken.

Nevertheless, the case was vigorously pursued by the Canadian authorities on behalf of justice for four freedom-loving Muslim girls and women.

The Shafias are a prosperous family of polygamous Afghan immigrants who fled Afghanistan in 1992, took up residence in various Arab states and in South Africa, and then came to Canada in 2007.

Clearly, this was an honor killing and one that a biological mother, biological father, and biological older brother perpetrated.

On June 30, 2009, when the bodies of the dead girls and woman were discovered in the family's Nissan in the Rideau Canal, the accused wept uncontrollably and went through an exaggerated public display of mourning.

However, privately, post-massacre, the police recovered wiretaps of Mohammed Shafia saying that his daughters had "hurt [him]..and betrayed...and violated us immensely. God curse their generation, they were filthy and rotten children. To hell with them and their boyfriends… May the devil shit on their graves."

On wiretap, Mohammed said that if he had it to do over again he would. His self-pity, self-righteousness, and cruelty are typical of the kinds of men who commit such murders.

The atmosphere in her household was filled with terrible and unceasing tensions: paternal demands that his daughters behave as if they were still living in Afghanistan (or in the Muslim Middle East), and not in Canada; daily physical, psychological, and verbal battering; the second wife's continuous cruelty towards the first wife; a brother whose job it was to stalk and monitor his sisters' behaviors.

The first wife, Rona Amir's crime, in addition to her infertility, was that she supported Tooba Yahya's three daughters in their desire to assimilate and westernize.

Like Palestina Isa, Geeti, the youngest, had told her teachers that she wanted to be placed in foster care.

Clearly, the system failed these at-risk teenagers.

According to Dr. Salim Mansur, a Muslim Canadian professor and author, Canada's multi-culturalism policy is ultimately "racist." It keeps immigrants confined to their "group" and does not encourage members to become "individuals" and "citizens" of a modern liberal democracy.

Although some have called for a special "honor killing" law, it is important to note that the Shafias were tried and convicted under existing Canadian law. They were not tried for committing a culturally approved "honor killing," but for having conspired to commit a cold-blooded and pre-planned murder on Canadian soil.

It is important to note that for the first time the *New York Times*, the *Washington Post*, and the *Wall Street Journal* covered an honor killing case which involved Muslim perpetrators in North America. However, the *Wall Street Journal,* the *New York Times, CNN, BBC*, and the *Washington Post* all shied away from using the term "Muslim," but indicated that the perpetrators of these honor killings were "Afghans" and "immigrants;" they sometimes utilized the term honor killing but usually either in quotes or preceded by the phrase "so-called."

The *Huffington Post* has published more than twenty articles in the last 24 hours on this trial. A quick review suggests that very few articles use the word "Muslim." Some of the journalists include Supriya Dwivedi, Danielle Crittenden, Stephanie Levitz, and Ayaan Hirsi Ali.

There has been something of a silence, at least so far, on the part of the various North American Muslim associations.

However, CAIR's Canadian chapter did a television interview about the Shafia case in 2011 in which its very severely hijabbed representative, Maryam Dadabhoy, argued against the use of the term "honor killing." She compared it to "domestic violence" and pointed out that far more incidents of domestic violence are occurring in Canada and elsewhere than are "racialized" honor killings.

Interestingly, *Al Jazeera* in English released few statements about the trial, but in its live coverage of the verdict, the reporter used the term "Muslim" and seemed supportive of the ruling.

Why do I obsess about the use of the word "Muslim"? I do so because too many Westerners are confusing this simple descriptor with an insult; too many Westerners have been intimidated by false concepts of politically correct, anti-racism into never describing a Muslim as anything other than a victim. Well, there actually are four Muslim victims in the Shafia case and they are all female. In order to honor that truth and hopefully to prevent further such honor killings, we must speak accurately.

Not all Muslims honor kill their daughters. But those who do are rarely punished in Muslim-majority countries. It is important that moderate and modern-oriented mullahs and imams call for the abolition of women's subordination in mosque sermons. In 2011, the Canadian chapter of CAIR announced that Canadian Muslim leaders should issue a call against domestic violence. In my opinion, this should include an end to the normalized battering of daughters and wives, an end to the overly strict supervision of female behavior, and an end to forced marriage.

I am not that optimistic. Canadian CAIR has finally issued a statement on the Shafia decision in which, as usual, they mainly point out

that "everyone," "all religions" suffer equally from such "domestic violence" tragedies, etc. Thus, they take no responsibility for the ways in
which Muslims and Muslim immigrants exert a very specific kind of
control over women and ultimately kill them when and if their women
disobey their Old World tribal, ethnic, and religious customs.

Since the verdict has been announced, the lawyer for Hamid Shafia
is appealing his guilty verdict on the ground of "media bias and hearsay
evidence." The lawyers for Hamid's parents have also vowed to appeal.

Pajamas Media
2/2/12

- 81 -
The Honor Killing That Never Happened

Like many others who were carefully selected, I, too, recently received a very shocking email from one Arsalan Akhtar (arsalan.akhtar21@gmail.com). He accused a rather distinguished Pakistani public figure of having honor killed his daughter. The email also claimed that the Pakistani media had covered this killing up at the request of very high government officials. I immediately tried to contact Arsalan Akhtar, but to no avail.

Many bloggers (who shall remain nameless) reproduced this email without confirming whether it was true or not.

Given what we know about Pakistan the entire episode seems entirely possible. Pakistan is a very dangerous place for women. Acid is thrown right into the faces of young girls and wives who are seen as even slightly "disobedient." Recently, an exceptionally beautiful Pakistani wife who had suffered this awful fate finally killed herself. She had endured over three dozen plastic surgeries on her face in Italy. Her suffering was simply too great. The fiend who did this to her was her husband and because he comes from a rich and powerful family, he has never been charged. Pakistan is a place where anything terrible can—and probably has—happened.

It is difficult to accurately estimate the number of honor killings that take place in Pakistan as the vast majority are believed to go unreported. In 2010, according to the Human Rights Commission of Pakistan, 800 women were killed for honor in Pakistan. This figure likely represents only the tip of the iceberg.

According to the Aurat Foundation, a Pakistani human rights organization: "At least 675 Pakistani women and girls were murdered during the first nine months of the calendar year 2011 for allegedly defaming their family's honor." Almost 77 percent of such honor cases ended in acquittals.

A similar study, published in 2011 by the Research and Development for Human Resources Women Rights Cell, found that 605 women and 115 men in Sindh, Pakistan were honor murdered or murdered in domestic disputes that same year.

Pakistan is also the capital of what may be called the "honor killing industry." Female relatives are killed for money. A father may kill a daughter, claim it as an honor killing, then try to extort blood money from the man who has allegedly dishonored the victim. The scenarios can grow very complicated. According to Muhammad Haroon Bahlkani, an officer in the Community Development Department in Sindh, a "man can murder another man for unrelated reasons, kill one of his own female relatives, and then credibly blame his first victim for dishonoring the second. Or he can simply kill one of his female relatives, accuse someone rich of involvement with her, and extract financial compensation in exchange for forgoing vengeance."

But would a Pakistani public figure engage in such filthy and dishonorable behavior? The answer is yes.

For example, as I've previously noted, in 1999, a very powerful Pakistani family had their daughter, Samia Imran, contract murdered in her feminist divorce lawyer's office. Samia's crime? She dared to seek a divorce from her violent husband who was also her cousin. Her father, Ghulam Sarwar, the President of the Peshawar Chamber of Commerce, and her mother, Sultana Sarwar, a gynecologist, were never even charged. Violent demonstrations broke out against her *lawyers*, whom the police refused to protect.

In addition, the lawyers were condemned to death by the usual religious fanatics; the Chamber of Commerce supported the murder. Members of Pakistan's upper parliamentary house demanded that the two women lawyers be punished. To this day, Samia's parents remain shamefully free.

However, in addition to never hearing back from Arsalan.Akhtar, something about his accusations didn't feel right. The accusations were too perfect, too big, too astonishing. Therefore, I asked Benjamin Ismail, the Director of the Asia Desk (which includes central Asia) of Reporters Without Borders, to ask one of his journalists to look into the matter. He did.

The email was fraudulent, a hoax, a case of political malice. The reporter spoke to the allegedly murdered daughter. She is outraged. I am not naming her or her father here because I do not want to taint their reputations any further.

What is the lesson to be learned?

The internet tempts us to simply "play telephone" with information. In addition to making things up, both well-meaning and self-aggrandizing bloggers also reproduce whatever crosses their screen. Investigative journalism is a thing of the past. Research is also passé.

This is an era of in which amateurs with poor impulse control twitter the day away. Big Liars, both anti-jihadist bloggers and crafty jihadists, rule the roost. They are tremendously aided by technology. Their word goes viral, global, in an instant.

Consider this a cautionary tale.

Pajamas Media
4/13/12

- 82 -
Hindu vs. Muslim Honor Killings

A lthough the overwhelming majority of honor killings world-wide occur within Muslim communities,[1] one would not know this by reading the mainstream media. Fearful of being labeled "Islamophobic," the American press has given only glancing attention to the widespread, honor-related ritual murder of Muslim women in the Middle East and South Asia while treating periodic honor killings among Muslim immigrants in the West as ordinary domestic abuse cases.

Over the last few years, however, the media has published a flurry of articles about Hindu honor killings in India, the only non-Muslim-majority country where these murders are still rampant.[2] Apologists for Muslim culture and civilization rushed to herald the upsurge in reported Hindu (and Sikh) honor killings as evidence that the practice is "a universal problem, not an Islamic issue."[3]

While India is a striking exception to Islam's near monopoly on contemporary honor killings, the following preliminary survey shows Hindu honor killings in India to be different in terms of motive and in what defines a violation of honor from those of Muslims in neighboring Pakistan. Though no less gruesome, the Hindu honor killings seem largely confined to the north of India and are perpetuated by sociocul-

---

1 Phyllis Chesler, "Worldwide Trends in Honor Killings," *Middle East Quarterly*, Spring 2010, pp. 3-11.

2 For example, see *The New York Times*, July 9, 2010, June 4, 2011; *The Washington Post*, Nov. 22, 2008.

3 John L. Esposito, "Honor Killing: Is Violence against Women a Universal Problem, Not an Islamic Issue?" *The Huffington Post*, Sept. 4, 2010.

tural factors largely specific to India. The millions of Indian Hindus who have immigrated to the West do not bring the practice along with them.

The recent spike of honor killings in India is likely the product of a clash between traditional and modern values, intensified by high economic growth and increasing social mobility. The spike may also reflect growing media coverage of this crime. The democratically elected government of India has taken important, if long overdue, steps to combat the practice of honor killing, and some progress has been made.

Not so in Pakistan where officials at all levels of government are either unable or unwilling to cope with honor killings. For Pakistan and many other Muslim countries, which have yet to experience the social stresses of rapid modernization or build the kind of political institutions that can eradicate a practice so deeply rooted in traditional beliefs—especially as Islamists now dominate—the worst may be yet to come.

The Social Milieu

Honor killing is the premeditated murder of a relative (usually a young woman) who has allegedly impugned the honor of her family. It tends to predominate in societies where individual rights are circumscribed by communal solidarities, patriarchal authority structures, and intolerant religious and tribal beliefs. Under such conditions, control over marriage and reproduction is critical to the socioeconomic status of kinship groups and the regulation of female behavior is integral to perceptions of honor, known as *maryada* in many Indian languages and as *ghairat* in Urdu and Pashto.

In such an environment, a woman who refuses to enter into an arranged marriage, seeks a divorce, or fails to avoid suspicion of immoral behavior will be viewed by her family as having dishonored them so grievously that her male relatives will be ostracized and her siblings will have trouble finding suitable spouses. Killing her is the only way the family can restore its honor, regardless of whether she actually is or can be proven guilty of the alleged offense. In sharp contrast to other forms of domestic violence, honor killings are frequently performed out in the open, and the perpetrators rarely act alone. Unni Wikan, a social anthropologist and professor at the University of Oslo, observed that an honor killer typically commits the murder "as a commission from the extended family."[4] The lead author of this article documented this in

4 Unni Wikan, "The Honor Culture," Karl-Olov Arnstberg and Phil Holmes, trans., originally published as *En Fraga Om Hedre*, Cajsa Mitchell, trans. (Stockholm: Ord-

2009[5] and 2010[6] for honor killings both in the West and in Muslim-majority countries.

Though neither Islam nor Hinduism directly sanctions honor killing, both play a role in legitimizing the practice in South Asia—if for no other reason than that such societies have not prosecuted this crime, have issued light sentences, or have failed to use their religious authority to punish and abolish it. Hindu society is divided into religiously mandated castes, membership in which is hereditary and effectively permanent. At the lowest rung of the ladder are roughly 150 million Indians who are called Dalits (the oppressed), commonly known in the West as "untouchables." Although many Dalits have reached high political office, notably former president K. R. Narayanan,[7] they are still held in low regard by many other Indians.[8]

According to Hindu religious law and tradition, marrying or having sexual relations with a member of a different caste is strictly forbidden. So, too, is romantic involvement with someone from the same sub-caste (*gotra*),[9] a proscription that contrasts notably with Muslim cultures where first cousin marriage is widely preferred. The vast majority of Hindu honor killings target young Indians suspected of violating one of these two commandments. In northern India, the murders are often explicitly sanctioned or even mandated by caste-based councils known as *khap panchayats*.[10] Although the Hindu Marriage Act of 1955 made inter-caste and intra-*gotra* marriages legal, both remain unacceptable to the large majority of Indian Hindus. According to a 2006 survey, 76 percent of the Indian public oppose inter-caste marriage.[11] In some areas of the country, any marriage not arranged by the family is widely regarded as taboo. "Love marriages are dirty ... only whores can choose their partners," one council leader told an Indian reporter.[12]

---

front Forlag AB, 2005).

5 Phyllis Chesler, "Are Honor Killings Simply Domestic Violence?" *Middle East Quarterly*, Spring 2009, pp. 61-9.

6 Chesler, "Worldwide Trends in Honor Killings," pp. 3-11.

7 *The New York Times*, July 26, 1997.

8 "Caste-based Discrimination in South Asia," European Commission (Brussels) and the International Dalit Solidarity Network, June 2009; "Broken People: Caste Violence against India's 'Untouchables,'" Human Rights Watch, Washington, D.C., Apr. 1, 1999.

9 *The Australian* (Sydney), Apr. 3, 2010.

10 *Times of India* (Mumbai), Mar. 30, 2010.

11 *The New York Times*, July 9, 2010.

12 *Times of India*, Sept. 8, 2009.

Although Islam does not specifically endorse killing female family members, some honor killings involve allegations of adultery or apostasy, which are punishable by death under Sharia (Islamic law). Thus, the belief that women who stray from the path can be rightly murdered is consistent with such Islamic teachings. The refusal of most Islamic authorities to unambiguously denounce the practice (as opposed to merely denying that Islam sanctions it) may encourage would-be honor killers.

While the Qur'an preaches the equality of all Muslims (or at least all Muslim males), and Islamic leaders frequently bemoan the evils of India's caste system, vestiges of caste identification are evident among some Pakistani Muslims, who are descended from Hindus who were forcibly converted to Islam in the Middle Ages and were part of India before 1947.[13]

Empirical Trends

It is difficult to accurately estimate the number of honor killings that take place in Pakistan and India as the vast majority are believed to go unreported. In 2010, there were roughly 900 reported honor killings in the northern Indian states of Haryana, Punjab, and Uttar Pradesh alone while 100-300 additional honor killings took place in the rest of the country.[14] Also in 2010, according to the Human Rights Commission of Pakistan, 800 women were killed for honor in Pakistan.[15] Both figures likely represent only the tip of the iceberg. According to the Aurat Foundation, a Pakistani human rights organization: "At least 675 Pakistani women and girls were murdered during the first nine months of the calendar year 2011 for allegedly defaming their family's honor." Almost 77 percent of such honor cases ended in acquittals.[16] A similar study, published in 2011 by the Research and Development for Human Resources Women Rights Cell, found that 605 women and 115 men in Sindh were honor murdered or murdered in domestic disputes that same year.[17]

In order to compare and contrast honor killings in India and Paki-

---

13 See Yoginder Sikand, "Islam and Caste Inequality among Indian Muslims," *Asianists' Asia*, first published in *Qalandar* (Paris), T. Wignesan, ed., Mar. 2004; Anatol Lieven, *Pakistan. A Hard Country* (New York: Public Affairs, 2011), pp. 101-2.

14 *The Hindu* (Chennai, Madras), July 11, 2010.

15 *Dawn* (Karachi), Aug. 9, 2011.

16 *Business Reporter* (Karachi), Jan. 5, 2012.

17 Ibid., Jan. 9, 2012.

stan, a sample was taken of 75 Hindu honor killings in India, including 50 cases that were specifically caste-based and 25 where the motive was not clearly specific to caste. The Indian cases were compared to 50 Muslim honor killings in Pakistan and 39 Pakistani Muslim honor killings in the West. Hindu honor killings in the West have been too rare to allow for valid statistical comparisons.[18] The researchers relied on English language media reports for data,[19] selecting the first cases that met the criteria of being a Hindu or Muslim honor killing and about which most of the following seven variables were known: location/religion; gender of victim; motive; the presence or absence of torture; age; number of victims per incident; and whether it was the woman's or the man's family who committed the killing.

The average age of all of the victims in this study, both male and female, was 22, with no statistically significant differences among the groups. Overwhelmingly, it was the women's families that committed the honor killings even in cases in which there were male victims. In India, 94 percent of the killings were carried out by the woman's family of origin. Four percent were killed jointly by both the man's and the woman's families of origin; in one case it was the allegedly shamed husband of a woman who did the killing; in no cases was it just the man's family of origin. In Pakistan, the woman's family of origin was responsible for 78 percent of the killings while husbands of "adulterous" wives accounted for another 16 percent. In 3 cases (6 percent) it was the man's family of origin that committed the murder. The number of husbands who were killers was highest in Pakistan because a large percentage of the Pakistani victims (30 percent) had been accused of adultery. Among Pakistani Muslims in the West, 97 percent of the killings were by the woman's family. This is to be expected, as it is women who are considered the keepers of male and family honor and the responsibility for enforcing society's honor code falls on the women's families.

---

18 Chesler, "Worldwide Trends in Honor Killings," pp. 3-11.

19 For Indian Hindu cases: *The Times of India, The Hindustan Times* (New Delhi), Press Trust of India News Service (Delhi), *The Independent* (London), *The Washington Post*, Reuters, *The Hindu, Indian Express* (Chennai, Madras), *Outlook India* (New Delhi), *Thaindian News* (Bangkok), Indo-Asian News Service (New Delhi), and the BBC. For Pakistani cases: Associated Press, *The Pakistan Daily Times* (Lahore), stophonourkillings.com, *The Daily Telegraph* (London), *The News International* (Karachi, Lahore and Rawalpindi/Islamabad), *The Regional Times of Sindh* (Hyderabad and Karachi), *Dawn*, and *Pakistan Today* (Lahore). The Indian honor killings took place between 2001 and 2011; those in Pakistan between 1999 and 2011. The Pakistani honor killings in the West took place between 1998 and 2009.

A number of statistically significant differences are notable.

Gender of Victims. In 40 percent of the cases, Indian Hindus murdered men while Pakistani Muslims murdered men only 14 percent of the time in Pakistan and 15 percent of the time in the West. The higher percentage of male victims in India underscores the fact that Hindu honor killings are more often about caste purity than female-specific sexual purity. While sexual purity is traditionally a female responsibility, the religious mandate to maintain strict boundaries between castes is an obligation for all Hindus, both male and female.

Motivation. The reported motivations underlying the killings varied significantly across the three groups. The researchers identified four major motives among Indian Hindus: caste-specific motives, "immoral character," "contamination by association," and non-caste-specific illicit relationships, which included interfaith relationships, adultery, pregnancy out of wedlock, and illicit relationships that were considered shameful for unspecified reasons. "Contamination by association" victims were killed not because they had done anything wrong but because of their association with the guilty party (mostly children of mothers who had been accused of violating sexual norms).

"Immoral character" victims were considered rebellious or licentious but were not suspected of being romantically involved with a specific individual. For example, Pakistani-Canadian Aqsa Parvez was murdered by her father and brother because she did not wear a hijab (head covering).[20] A 14-year-old Indian girl, S. Rajinilatha, was murdered by her father not because she was involved with any particular man but merely because she wrote love poetry.[21] Meena, an 18-year-old Hindu girl, was shot to death because she left her village for three days, and her family was not satisfied with her explanation of where she had been.[22]

In the case of Pakistani Muslims, the researchers identified three motives: illicit relationships, "contamination by association," and "immoral character." Only 4 percent of Muslim victims in Pakistan were killed because they were romantically involved with someone from a different caste, and caste was never a motive among Pakistani Muslims in the West. Consequently, the motive in this small number of cases was

---

20 *The National Post* (Toronto), Dec. 12, 2007.

21 "'Honour' Killings on the Rise in Tamil Nadu," Stop Honour Killings, London, Sept. 16, 2010.

22 *Times of India*, Feb. 16, 2011; *Mid-Day* (Mumbai and Delhi), Feb. 15, 2011.

classified simply as "illicit relationship."[23]

The reported motivations of Muslim honor killers in Pakistan differed from those of Pakistani Muslims in the West. In Pakistan, 12 percent of the victims were "immoral character" victims. In the West, 65 percent of the victims were "immoral character" victims. This may be because there are so many more opportunities for "immoral" assimilation/independence in the West, and young Pakistani women living there may be pushing boundaries more forcefully.

There were also significantly more "contamination by association" victims among Pakistani Muslims, both in Pakistan and in the West, than among the Hindus in India. For example, one Pakistani Muslim case in the West involved the murder of an adult sister-in-law, her young child, and a father-in-law who happened to be in the battered wife's new home at the time. Only 4 percent of the Indian Hindus killed were "contamination by association" victims (n=3), compared to 22 percent of the Pakistani Muslim victims in Pakistan (n=11) and 19 percent of Pakistani Muslim victims in the West (n=7). The overwhelming majority of Hindu killings are caste-related, generally targeting young men and women shortly after they eloped and before they could have children. Pakistani Muslim honor killings are more often about obedience in general, especially sexual purity, and a woman's sexual and moral purity can be challenged for as long as she lives.

Torture. Some victims were killed in a manner clearly intended to maximize pain. For example, 17-year-old Anup Kumar of Haryana was electrocuted in 2011 for being in a relationship with a girl from the same sub-caste.[24] In Islamabad, 40-year-old Elahi Husain's brothers tied her to a tree and stoned her to death in 2007 for being in a relationship of which they disapproved.[25]

The torture rate for Hindus in India (39 percent) was significantly higher than for Muslims in Pakistan (12 percent). Many of the Indian Hindu victims in this study were burned alive, electrocuted, or hacked to death. Even in cases where there was no torture, the bodies of the victims were often desecrated,[26] grimly displaying the family's determination to restore its honor at all costs. It is possible that the torture rate in Pakistan is comparable to that in India and that Pakistani police and media are more circumspect in revealing gruesome details.

23 See Sikand, "Islam and Caste Inequality among Indian Muslims."

24 *Times of India*, Jan. 28, 2011.

25 *The Daily Telegraph*, Jan. 31, 2007.

26 Reuters, May 16, 2008; *The Economist*, Apr. 15, 2010.

Among Pakistani Muslim victims in the West, however, a stagger-ing 59 percent were tortured. Perhaps this is because the perpetrators feel so besieged and humiliated by the surrounding culture that they must take more extreme measures to reclaim their honor and because so many Pakistani girls and women are tempted to assimilate.

Pakistan's Actions on Honor Killings

In Pakistan, the fusion of Islamic beliefs, a patriarchal social order, and tribal segmentation have effectively reduced women to the status of chattel. Pakistan was ranked 133 out of 135 countries in the World Eco-nomic Forum's 2011 Global Gender Gap report.[27] A 2011 survey by the Thomson Reuters Foundation ranked Pakistan as the third most dan-gerous country in the world for women (India was fourth).[28]

According to Homa Arjomand, the Canadian lawyer who led the successful fight against the imposition of Sharia law in Ontario, the lives of most girls and women in Pakistan are routinely terrible. They can ex-pect that their husbands will rape and beat them savagely, often breaking their bones and knocking out their teeth; they may face extreme sadism during pregnancy as well as unhygienic and dangerous confinement as a permanent way of life; their families will not help them.[29]

The summary execution of female relatives for a wide range of sus-pected moral infractions is considered justifiable by many Pakistanis.[30] Tribal councils often sanction the practice[31] while local police turn a blind eye. Because of this impunity, honor killing is sometimes used as a pretext for other crimes. For example, according to Muhammad Haroon Bahlkani, an officer in the Community Development Department in Sindh, Pakistan, a "man can murder another man for unrelated reasons, kill one of his own female relatives, and then credibly blame his first victim for dishonoring the second. Or he can simply kill one of his fe-male relatives, accuse someone rich of involvement with her, and extract

---

27 *The Global Gender Gap Report 2011*, The World Economic Forum, Geneva, Nov. 2011.

28 "The World's Most Dangerous Countries for Women," Thomson Reuters Founda-tion, New York, June 15, 2011.

29 Homa Arjomand, "Effect of globalization of political Islam on women," www.nosha-ria.com, accessed Mar. 28, 2012.

30 See, for example, Asian Human Rights Commission, Hong Kong, May 12, 2011; *The China Post* (Taipei), Mar. 10, 2012; BBC Urdu, Aug. 29, 2008.

31 Lieven, *Pakistan*, pp. 101-2.

financial compensation in exchange for forgoing vengeance." Bahlkani has a name for this: the "Honor Killing Industry."[32]

In Pakistan, many honor killings are known as *karo-kari* killings, which literally means "black male" and "black female" in Urdu and refers to cases in which adulterers are killed together. However, according to Bahlkani, there is an escape clause, but only for the men who can run away, hide, or pay restitution. Women are confined to the home, and few people will shelter a female runaway.

Although senior Pakistani officials have frequently denounced the practice of honor killing, little of substance has been achieved in combating it. While the penal code was stiffened in 2005 to impose a 10-year minimum sentence for honor killing,[33] legislative initiatives to protect women from domestic violence have been repeatedly watered down or abandoned in the face of Islamist opposition. In 2009, Pakistan's National Assembly passed the Domestic Violence (Prevention and Protection) Bill, which strengthened legal protections against domestic violence for women and children. However, the Council of Islamic Ideology, a constitutional body charged with assessing whether laws are consistent with Islamic injunctions, issued a statement saying the bill "would fan unending family feuds and push up divorce rates." After this, the bill was held up in the Pakistani senate and allowed to lapse. According to Special Public Prosecutor Nghat Dad, "The government's attitude towards pushing for the cause has been hopeless ever since the Council of Islamic Ideology's opposition."[34]

Under Sharia-based provisions of Pakistan's judicial system, murderers can buy a pardon by paying blood money (*dyad*) to the victim's family. Since the family of honor killing victims are nearly always sympathetic to the honor killer as well as complicit to some degree, obtaining a pardon is usually just a formality.[35] Women's rights organizations in Pakistan have pressed parliament to disallow the practice of blood money in honor killing cases, but conservative Islamist groups have blocked the needed legislation.

Even when such arrangements do not take place, honor killers are rarely prosecuted for lack of cooperative witness testimony. For those few who happen to be convicted, a light prison sentence is far preferable

---

32 Correspondence with Muhammad Haroon Bahlkani, 2010, 2011.

33 *USA Today*, Dec. 28, 2005.

34 Iffat Gill, "Can legal reforms protect women in Pakistan?" *Worldpulse.com*, Portland, Ore., Mar. 29, 2011.

35 BBC, Mar. 2, 2005.

to dishonor. According to the Human Rights Commission of Pakistan in a recent report: "The legal, preventative, and protective measures needed to provide effective protection to women against violence perpetrated in the name of honor remained absent."[36]

India's Actions on Honor Killings

Indian society at large is no less misogynistic than that of Pakistan. Since boys are preferred and girls are seen as a burden, an estimated four to twelve million selective abortions of girls have occurred in India in the past three decades.[37] The 2011 Indian census found 914 girls for every 1,000 boys among children six or younger.[38] Dowry burnings, the practice of a man and his mother dousing his wife with cooking oil and burning her alive so that a new bride and dowry can be obtained, are as big a problem as honor killings in India.[39]

As the Indian media have fastidiously documented,[40] there has been a marked increase in the number of reported honor killings in recent years. In 2010, a government-funded study on the prevalence of honor crimes in India found that they are most common in regions dominated by *khap panchayats* and increasingly involve inter-caste, rather than intra-sub-caste marriages.[41] In these regions, local politicians turn a blind eye to the murders and resist efforts by the central government and parliament to deal with the problem while local police collude in honor killings[42] or help cover them up, often mischaracterizing the murders as suicides.[43] In 2011, theaters in Haryana refused to screen an Indian film on honor killings because of threats by *khap panchayats*.[44]

According to Prem Chowdhry of the Delhi School of Economics, honor killings were less frequent in the past "because elopements didn't

36 "State of Human Rights in 2010," Human Rights Commission of Pakistan, Lahore, Apr. 2011, p. 206.

37 Prabhat Jha, et al., "Trends in selective abortions of girls in India: analysis of nationally representative birth histories from 1990 to 2005 and census data from 1991 to 2011," *The Lancet*, May 24, 2011, pp. 1921-8.

38 *The New York Times*, May 24, 2011.

39 BBC, July 16, 2003.

40 *The New York Times*, July 9, 2010.

41 *The Tribune* (Chandigarh, India), May 14, 2011.

42 "India: Prosecute Rampant 'Honor' Killings: Amend and Enforce Laws to End Barbaric Practice," Human Rights Watch, New York, July 18, 2010.

43 See, for example, *Times of India*, Mar. 15, 2011.

44 *Indian Express*, July 30, 2011.

happen ... livelihood was so clearly tied to the land, and the land was so clearly enmeshed in these relationships."[45] Greater socioeconomic mobility has weakened these bonds. As *khap panchayats* struggle against modernization, preserving their traditional power means retaining control over reproduction, and they have resorted to violence to achieve this.

In sharp contrast to their Pakistani counterparts, Indian government officials have vigorously condemned honor killings in their country.[46] So, too, have liberal Indian media outlets,[47] some of which have done aggressive investigative reporting on the issue. In 2010, an undercover reporter working for the Indian television channel Headlines Today found two policemen from the northern state of Haryana who boasted about their willingness to hand over a young woman to be honor murdered. "Cut her into pieces and then throw her in some river," one said.[48] A number of Indian nongovernmental organizations are working to defend women from honor killings. The Love Commandos, with 2,000 volunteers and a 24-hour national hotline, are devoted to protecting newlyweds who defy their families.[49]

In 2010, Prime Minister Manmohan Singh ordered a cabinet-level commission to draft national legislation designed to eradicate honor killing.[50] The proposals included an amendment to the penal code allowing *khap panchayats* leaders to be prosecuted for sanctioning murders as well as the revocation of the 30-day notice period required by the Special Marriage Act, which has enabled families to track down and preemptively kill the couples.[51] In 2011, the Law Commission of India, under the Ministry of Law and Justice, drafted a new bill—The Endangerment of Life and Liberty (Protection, Prosecution and Other Measures) Act—designed to prevent *khap panchayats* from denouncing couples who violate caste restrictions. According to the bill,

> It shall be unlawful for any group of persons to gather, assemble or congregate with the ... intention to deliberate, declare on, or condemn any marriage or relationship such as

---

45 *The Australian*, Apr. 23, 2010.

46 See, for example, *Times of India*, Aug. 1, 2010.

47 "Barbarian Face," ibid., July 4, 2007.

48 *India Today* (New Delhi), Sept. 17, 2010.

49 *The Guardian* (London), Oct. 10, 2010.

50 *Times of India*, July 9, 2010.

51 "India: Prosecute Rampant 'Honor' Killings," July 18, 2010.

marriage between two persons of majority age in the locality concerned on the basis that such conduct or relationship has dishonored the caste or community or religion of all or some of the persons forming part of the assembly or the family or the people of the locality concerned."[52]

The fate of this legislation is uncertain, however, as the *khap panchayats'* control over local voting blocs has enabled them to blunt legislative reforms in the past. The government has made more progress on the judicial front. In 2010, India's Supreme Court instructed the governments in Haryana and six other states to take steps to protect potential honor killing victims.[53] In 2011, it decried honor killing as a "barbaric and shameful" practice that must be "ruthlessly stamped out."[54] The court also declared honor killings ordered by *khap panchayats* to be illegal and warned that government officials who fail to act against honor crime offenders will be prosecuted.[55]

Although fear of caste ostracism makes it difficult to find cooperative witnesses, Indian courts have begun aggressively prosecuting honor killers and their accomplices. In 2010, a Haryana court sentenced five men to death for the honor murder of a young couple who had married despite being members of the same sub-caste while giving a life sentence to the head of the *khap panchayat* that ordered their deaths.[56] In November 2011, an Indian court sentenced eight men to death and twenty others to life imprisonment for involvement in three honor killings.[57] Increasingly, local police officials have been suspended and even arrested for collusion in honor killings.[58]

India still has a long way to go. While the Indian government continues to face resistance and evasion of responsibility on the part of local officials, it has not encountered the same kind of virulent, often violent, opposition to women's rights typical of Pakistani Islamists. There is little doubt that the Indian government is determined to win what promises to be a long battle against honor killing. The Western media's interest in Hindu honor killings developed only after Indians themselves began

52 *The Hindu*, June 8, 2011.
53 *Times of India*, June 21, 2010.
54 BBC, Apr. 20, 2011.
55 "Crime and Punishment," *Times of India*, Apr. 27, 2011.
56 *The Australian*, Apr. 3, 2010.
57 *International Business Times* (New York), Nov. 16, 2011.
58 *The Australian*, Apr. 3, 2010.

exposing the practice and pressing for change.

Conclusion

Although Hindu honor killing is a gruesome and sordid affair, it differs in many important respects from honor killing in neighboring Pakistan, other Muslim countries, and Muslim communities in the West. Indian Hindus murder men for honor more often than do Pakistani Muslims, and they murder for reasons mainly related to concerns about caste purity.

Perhaps the most striking characteristic of Hindu honor killings is the fact that Indians abandon the horrific practice when they migrate to the West whereas many Pakistani Muslims carry it with them. The research for this is not entirely clear. Perhaps a different kind of Hindu immigrates to the West—one more educated and already pro-Western. Young Hindus in the West are no less prone to violating traditional social codes than are young Muslims, and their parents may be no less furious when they do, but Hindu families in the West do not feel the same degree of public humiliation and shame as they might experience back in India. Perhaps they are eager to preserve their cultural identity but not at the expense of alienating their adoptive communities. The absence of dreaded *khap panchayats* may mitigate the consequences of dishonor.

Due in part to the spread of radical Islamist ideology, Muslim immigrants in the West are either radicalized or socialize predominantly within similarly traditional or radicalized Muslim-only communities, and their conception of honor reflects this. Even affluent young women of Pakistani descent in the West can face the credible threat of death or severe bodily harm. Actress Afshan Azad, who played Padma Patil in the *Harry Potter* film series, was beaten and threatened with death in 2010 by her Pakistani father and brother for dating a non-Muslim.[59] If she can be victimized, anyone can.

While it is alarming that there are so many honor killings in India and Pakistan, there may yet be cause for hope. Every honor killing begins with a rebellion against tribalism and patriarchy—and with the fear that tribal and patriarchal values are under attack. Many of the victims in our study were people who believed that they could push traditional boundaries, that they could get away with asserting their rights. They were wrong, and they paid the ultimate price for that mistake, but the

---

59 *The Telegraph*, Dec. 20, 2010.

crucial factor is that they tried. More rebels will follow.

Phyllis Chesler is emerita professor of psychology and women's studies at the Richmond College of the City University of New York, author of fourteen books, and co-founder of the Association for Women in Psychology and the National Women's Health Network. Nathan Bloom, a recent graduate of the University of Chicago, is a former assistant to Phyllis Chesler. The authors thank Tchia and Avraham Snapiri of IDEA-Management and Economic Consulting Ltd., for performing the statistical tests for this study, and Petra Bailey for help in gathering the data.

Middle East Quarterly
Spring 2012

- 83 -

Honor Killings in the West and the God of Poetic Justice

On December 18th, the FBI offered a new reward of twenty thousand dollars for information leading to the capture of alleged honor/horror killing Egyptian-born father, Yasser Said. Two filmmakers, Xoel Pamus and Nenna Nejad, who are working on a documentary about the 2008 honor killing of Sarah and Amina Said in a suburb of Dallas, Texas, uncovered compelling evidence which they turned over to the authorities.

The United States has been forced to take honor killings seriously.

Earlier this month, the seventh honor killer involved in British-Kurdish Banaz Mahmud's 2006 honor femicide was finally caught and jailed in Great Britain. Also in December, Sarbit Kaur Athwal, who testified against her British-Sikh honor killing family, won a prize for her bravery—"The Ultimate Woman Warrior award."

This month was also a milestone of sorts for me in this same area.

One does not often get to learn how one's work has been used in the world as I just have, but this December, that is precisely what happened.

I have recently published three studies about honor killings. Based on my research, I have submitted courtroom affidavits for those in flight from being honor killed. My affidavits have often turned the tide—or so the lawyers tell me.

Here is how my work helped make a difference in a very high profile court case in Canada.

As I've written before:

On June 30, 2009, Mohammad and Tooba Shafia, a wealthy Afghan-Canadian immigrant couple, honor killed three of their biological daughters: Geeti, Sahar, and Zainab, as well as Mohammed's first wife, Rona, who lived with them. Hamed, the eldest son, participated in this carefully planned but ultimately bungled case of intimate human sacrifice.

On December 4th, Canadian Assistant Crown Prosecutor, Gerard Laarhuis, spoke about this high-profile case at Ayaan Hirsi Ali's Conference on Honor Violence in New York City. He confirmed that the Shafia daughters, who ranged in age from thirteen to nineteen, were viewed as "whores" by their parents and brother.

The girls believed they were living in Canada. Zainab did not want to marry her first cousin but someone of her own choosing. Their parents and brother believed that Afghans must behave as if they are still living in Afghanistan no matter where they are, geographically. The teenagers wanted to leave home. They bitterly resented parental punishment and brotherly stalking. They had boyfriends. The older teenage girls took photos of themselves wearing skimpy, sexy clothing—together with boyfriends.

According to Crown Prosecutor, Gerard Larhuuis, who successfully prosecuted this case: "In this family the concept of dying and death was with them all the time…these children knew they could die. The victim's crime? They wanted to be free." The women were spied on and tightly controlled. Rona, the first wife, was miserable and wanted to leave. Tooba, the second wife, hated her, and held her passport, but would not allow her to leave.

Rona is Mohammad's property. She is his to do with as he likes. No Afghan wife is allowed to divorce her husband, divorce is perceived as a great "dishonor." (Only husbands, not wives can initiate a divorce.)

The Shafia daughters violated another major taboo: They told other people—infidel outsiders and other family members—about what was happening to them. Prosecutor Laarhuis noted that the children and Rona had cried out for help many times (to teachers, relatives, children's services) but neither Canadian authorities or sympathetic family members interfered with what was going on.

The Canadian Prosecution and detectives did painstaking and brilliant work. Laarhuis believes (but cannot prove) that Tooba, their mother, sat with her daughters and co-wife in a car, and "kept everyone calm," as each girl, one by one, was taken out and drowned by her father and brother nearby, in a shallow body of water. Then, all four corpses were placed in a car and pushed into the Rideaux Canal; however, the car did not properly sink.

The jury unanimously found all three Shafias guilty. They were each sentenced to life in prison with no possibility of parole for 25 years. All three have appealed their sentences.

I was also at the Ayaan Hirsi Ali conference to deliver a lecture of my own. When I identified myself and asked Prosecutor Laarhuis a question he stopped, beamed with delight, and publicly stated—and then repeated in an email exchange with me several days later—that the Prosecution had relied heavily on my research in this area.

I am grateful to those who have supported and published my honor killing research, especially the Middle East Forum and *Middle East Quarterly* and to the God of poetic justice, that I, who was once held captive in Kabul and who nearly died there, have lived to do this work which helped prosecute the Afghan honor/horror killers of four Afghan women.

Jerusalem Post
12/24/13

- 84 -
Letter to the Editor – Honor Killings in the West

To the Editor:

"Two Star-Crossed Afghans Cling to Love, Even at Risk of Death" (front page, March 10) is a poignant story of just one Romeo and Juliet couple.

Afghanistan, Pakistan, India, the Arab world and the Muslim diaspora in the West have thousands of such cases, both known and unknown. Educated and wealthy families are as likely to engage in this crime as are poor or illiterate farmers.

Wealthy Afghan immigrants to North America have perpetrated honor killings, like the Shafia case in Canada, in which a wealthy biological father and mother and their biological son killed three biological daughters and a first wife because they were becoming too "Westernized."

While we may not be able to help the women in Afghanistan, we are honor-bound to do so in the West.

PHYLLIS CHESLER
New York

New York Times
3/16/14

- 85 -
Honor Killing in the *New York Times*— Silence on "Honor Killings"

To the Editor:

According to "In Spite of the Law, Afghan 'Honor Killings' of Women Continue" (news article, May 4), neither Sharia law nor Western law has any power over tribal law, which drives the honor killing of women. This is partly true since tribal law also drives religion-based and caste-related honor killings of women—and men—in India.

But tribal tradition is also viewed as "religious" by both Muslims and Hindus, and while the Indian government has condemned and passed increasingly strong legislation against honor killings, the same cannot be said of the Afghan government.

No Afghan mullahs cry out against this practice of human sacrifice. Such indigenous practices were not caused by the West or by foreign invasions. One wonders what it will take to end these murderous, misogynist customs.

PHYLLIS CHESLER
New York

New York Times
5/7/14

- 86 -
A Real War on Women

I just appeared for an hour on the BBC on the *World Have Your Say* program to talk about three separate cases in the news: the Pakistani woman who was just stoned to death for daring to marry the man she loved; the massacre in Isla Vista, California, fueled by a violently misogynistic manifesto; and the German tabloid exposure of Kate Middleton's bottom.

I appeared with some very wonderful speakers in Pakistan, the United States, and the UK on these issues.

As to the first story: Early today, a 25-year-old woman was stoned to death by twelve—yes, twelve—male relatives, beginning with her father and including her brothers and possibly cousins. They did so right outside the High Court in Lahore. This is a brazen statement about refusing to abide by any secular Pakistani law.

This victim's blessed name was Farzana Iqbal and bravely, tragically, she refused to marry her cousin and instead married the man she loved. One of the Pakistani women on the BBC program pointed out that none of the many bystanders rescued her or stopped these men from killing her.

A crowd gathered. No one dared intervene. The bystander phenomenon coupled with cultural approval for this act of barbarism, coupled with some vicarious enjoyment involved in seeing an "uppity" woman punished, coupled with the fear that if one intervened they, too, would be stoned, stayed the hand of one and all.

According to one news account, Farzana's husband claimed that her family had wanted money from him and, failing to get it, they killed her. This suggests that the family may have been poor. However, wealthy families in Pakistan also commit brazen honor killings. We have seen this in the 1999 case of Samia Imran/Samia Sarwar.

Samia's parents were wealthy. Her father, Ghulam Sarwar Khan Mohammed, was one of the most successful businessmen in the North West Frontier and the president of the Peshawar Chamber of Commerce; her mother, Sultana, was a gynecologist. They prided themselves on being modern and liberal.

Thus, they told Samia that she could leave her husband and return to school; they even had a hand in banning her husband from the home. Samia's parents were adamant: Whatever she did, she could never, ever get divorced. This meant that, at twenty-eight, Samia would have to had to resign herself to a life without intimate companionship. An affair would be out of the question. Samia told others that she feared her parents "would kill her" if she disobeyed them.

Bravely, but in retrospect, tragically, Samia decided to initiate divorce proceedings. She made an appointment with two leading feminist lawyers, Hina Jilani and Asma Jahangir. Within five minutes of Samia's entering their offices, her mother came in, accompanied by a hired hit man who shot Samia to death. Unbelievably, Samia's paternal uncle was there, too. The hit man proceeded to kidnap at gunpoint a woman, Shahtaj Qizalbash, who worked in the law office building.

Many Pakistanis were not angry that the Sarwars had murdered their own daughter. On the contrary, violent demonstrations broke out against her feminist lawyers—whom the police and the courts refused to protect. The two lawyers received death threats from religious extremists. Imran's family organized a meeting of the Peshawar Chamber of Commerce which supported the murder and issued fatwas demanding the lawyers be punished. Samia's father considers himself a "liberal." He is also a realist. He is not in a position "to change society. Everyone must have honor."

Please note: Absolutely no one has been prosecuted for this heinous crime.

I stayed on the BBC to discuss the mass femicide/homicide in Isla Vista, California, and the extraordinary internet outpouring from women about their own experiences of sexist verbal abuse, sexual harassment, rape, near-rape, domestic violence, etc. The murderer's manifesto was as hateful towards women as Hitler's *Mein Kampf* was hateful towards Jews. It is too chilling to read in full.

Some American feminist voices on the BBC program spoke about feeling relief that so many other women were responding to the hashtag

#yesallwomen; they also felt anxious and fearful about so much misogyny. Often, when one tweets something, that is the end of it. No legislation gets crafted and passed. One merely expresses oneself and feels stronger that one is not alone. I hope that the coming generation of feminists, both men and women, do more than that. I am counting on them to do so.

Our last topic was the German newspaper's publishing Kate Middleton's exposed bottom when the wind blew her dress up. Poor taste, beneath contempt said I—but proof, yet again, that no woman, however royal, is really spared this culture of public shaming. All women are equal in terms of eroticized body parts when it comes to providing fodder for tabloid rags.

Breitbart
5/27/14

A New Kind of American Tragedy

An American tragedy is taking place in a Brooklyn Federal Courthouse.

Both the defendant, standing trial for conspiracy to commit murder abroad in Pakistan, and the main witness against him, his daughter Amina, wept when they first saw each other. Amina's extended family stared at her with hostility. As she testified, Amina paused, hesitated, and sobbed. She and her father had been very close until he decided that she had become too "Americanized."

This Pakistani-American father of five, a widower, worked seven days a week driving a cab in order to support his children; this included sending his daughter, Amina, to Brooklyn College.

This is a successful American immigrant story—and yet, it is also one in which Western law has prevailed over murderously misogynistic tribal honor codes.

Mohammad Ajmal Choudry sent Amina to Pakistan so that she might re-connect with her "roots"—but he had her held hostage there for three years. During that time, Amina, an American citizen, was forced into an arranged marriage, ostensibly to her first cousin, who probably expected this marriage to lead to his American citizenship. Such arranged marriages, and arranged specifically for this purpose, are routine.

Amina, who grew up in New York from the time she was nine years old, did not want to be held hostage to this marriage. Indeed, Amina had found a man whom she loved and wished to marry. Plucky, American-ized Amina fled the arranged marriage within a month. With the help of a relative, the U.S. State Department, and ultimately, the Department of Homeland Security, Amina left Pakistan and went into hiding in the United States.

She had to. Her father had threatened to kill her if she did not return to her husband, give up her boyfriend, or return to her father. Mohammad may have pledged Amina's hand without her knowledge, long, long ago.

From Mohammad's point of view, his beloved daughter had betrayed and dishonored him. She had "un-manned" him before his family.

What did Mohammad Choudry then do? According to the Indictment filed in United States District Court/the Eastern District of New York on September 20, 2013, Choudry knowingly and intentionally conspired to commit one or more murders. He contacted and wired money to at least four conspirators in Pakistan, including some relatives. Since Amina would not come out of hiding, their job was to murder the father and sister of Amina's boyfriend. And they did just that. An eyewitness "observed Choudry's brother standing over the victims, holding a gun and desecrating the bodies."

The murders were committed in Pakistan "between January 2013 and February 2013." Mohammad Ajmal Choudry was arrested in New York on February 25, 2013. The trial began last week, in June, 2014. Amina testified that her father had vowed to kill her and every member of her partner's family if she did not do the right thing.

The price of love or of freedom for Amina—and for other women in her position—is very high. She will have no family of origin. If she ever weakens and tries to seek them out, she risks being killed by one of her siblings, uncles, or cousins. After all, Amina entrapped her father on the phone by allowing him to death threaten her and others—and by testifying against him.

Like female genital mutilation, honor murder is so entrenched a custom that, in addition to prevention and prosecution (at least in the West), what may be required is this: People may need to be taught courage, the art of resisting tribal barbarism. Families may have to be taught to go against tradition; withstand ostracism and mockery; endure being cut off by their families—for the sake of their daughters.

One fear that a "dishonored" family has is that they will not be able to marry off their other daughters or sons. Perhaps educating a pool of potential marriage mates into understanding that murder is not "honorable;" that daughters' lives are valuable, that such horror murders are not religiously sanctioned (if indeed, that is the case), and that enacting tribal honor codes are high crimes in the West.

This is how Molly Melching found grooms for some non-genitally multilated girls in Senegal, in Africa. It is certainly worth trying.

Breitbart
6/30/14

- 88 -

Family "Honor Kills" Indian Newlyweds for Marrying Without Parental Consent

A young Hindu couple in the Punjab dared to marry for love—but without permission from the bride's family.

Sandeep Rani and his wife, Khushboo, knew enough to flee their homes and to seek a court order of protection, which the Punjab and Haryana High Court granted them.

They did not know enough to go into permanent hiding or to move far, far away. Instead, they returned to their home village of Mugowal and showed their court order to the local police in Hoshiarpur. Apparently, the police chose not to protect them. However, the police claim that either the couple did not "accept protection" or did not advise the police as to their exact whereabouts. An investigation is underway.

On the night of January 3rd, the couple were killed by five masked men. They were horribly stabbed and hacked to death with knives and swords. This killing was up-close, ugly, and very personal.

One must ask why. According to our 2012 study in *Middle East Quarterly* ("Hindu vs. Muslim Honor Killings"), the main reason that Hindus perpetrate honor killings (and only in India, not in the West) is related to caste violations. Hindus are not supposed to marry out of their caste. However, this tragic couple belonged to the same caste—they were Dalits (formerly and shamefully known as the "untouchables" or as "the oppressed").

However, they apparently grew up in the same village. Perhaps they were members of the same sub-caste. Among Muslims, first cousin marriage is preferred. Hindus are not supposed to marry anyone from the same sub-caste (*gotra*). One wonders whether this was the killing offense. In addition, Hindus are not supposed to marry without parental or, really, paternal permission. They are not supposed to choose their own spouses. According to a Hindu Religious Council Leader, "Love marriages are dirty… only whores can choose their partners." Sandeep Rani's mother, Udham Kaur, has identified Khushboo's father, Sodhi Ram, as one of the killers. (She claims that his mask slipped.) Also, Sandeep Rani's father, Parkash, was stabbed when he tried to protect his son.

This suggests that the couple believed they had the support of Sandeep's parents and may explain why they returned. Impoverished Dalits cannot survive without extended family networks.

Thus, Hindu views about the importance of arranged marriage, the Hindu definitions of honor where marriage is concerned, the nature of poverty, the understandable attachment to and dependence on one's family and native village, coupled with police inaction, all led to this latest honor killing tragedy in India.

In contrast to their Pakistani counterparts, Indian government officials have vigorously condemned honor killings. In 2010, a Haryana Court sentenced five men to death for the honor murder of a young couple who had married despite being members of the same sub-caste, while also giving life sentences to the head of the *khap panchayat* (religious council) that ordered their deaths.

Let us also consider that while religious and tribal traditions remain barbaric, the secular democratic Indian government is at war against these customs, and that young lovers are also daring to push the traditional boundaries.

Breitbart
1/6/15

- 89 -
Model Awareness: *Cosmo UK's* Bold
Anti-Honor Killing Cover

The cover is shocking, gruesome, and bold. It features the face of a woman encased in plastic, being smothered to death. A video shows the plastic wrapping being ripped open, "signifying the release of women from violence."

Cosmopolitan magazine in the UK has released a mock-up cover of their February issue, designed by Leo Burnett Chase, as part of a campaign to raise awareness about honor killings. The cover is that of a 17-year-old British-Pakistani girl, Shafilea Ahmed, who was suffocated to death by her parents in 2003 for the crime of refusing an arranged marriage.

Cosmo has joined Karma Nirvana and the Henry Jackson Society in organizing an "inaugural Day of Memory for Britain's Lost Women, which will take place July 14—the day of Shafilea Ahmed's birthday."

Will mainstreaming a critique of honor killing reach those most likely to perpetrate so dishonorable a crime? Are the cover and planned campaign proof that some Europeans are ready to relinquish the failed doctrine of multi-cultural relativism, appeasement, and the "soft" double standard of racism? Is the British legal system finally ready to do whatever it takes to abolish this barbaric cultural practice?

Shafilea Ahmed was a young British-Pakistani girl whose only crime was that of becoming too "Western." Her parents allegedly sedated her without her knowledge and packed her off to Pakistan to meet her much older cousin to whom she had been promised in marriage. Shafilea responded by drinking bleach in a failed suicide attempt. She refused the marriage. Her mother, Farzana, was furious that she had "made a scene."

From her parents' point of view, Shafilea's body, virginity, and fertility were resources that belonged to her family, not to Shafilea herself. Shafilea had shamed the family. Her younger siblings would not be able to find spouses.

Shafilea endured years of being beaten and threatened, sometimes almost daily; she was often isolated and starved. Shafilea tried to get help. In her own words, found in an application for housing help, she wrote: "Regular incidents... One parent would hold me while the other hit me."

At the time, in multi-culturally correct Britain, there was no "help" for her. According to an editorial in the *Guardian*, "Her school, the police, and the social services in Warrington were all aware that there were difficulties in the family. She was 11 when she ran away for the first time."

When the beatings and abuse failed, Shafilea's family felt that they had to kill her because, clearly, they could not control her. Thus, her father, Iftikhar, a 42-year-old a taxi-driver, and her mother, Farzana, a 40-year-old housewife, murdered her in cold blood by smothering her in plastic. They forced all their children to witness the murder—and threatened to kill them if they ever told anyone.

The police found Shafilea's body in the River Kent, in Cumbria, but they had no witnesses. According to the *Telegraph*:

> For nine years Shafilea Ahmed's parents thought their surviving children were so terrified of them that they would never break ranks...To ensure there were no lapses, they were given a detailed "script" of what they should and should not say to friends, teachers and the police...about [their] sister's disappearance.

Such family silence is Mafia-like and usually unbreakable.

According to the *Daily Mail*, authorities knew that there was a suitcase packed in the Ahmed hallway which contained "gold bars and the children's passports... just in case [they] had to leave the country at the drop of a hat."

According to the *Guardian*:

> Intermittent attempts were made to offer (Shafilea) support, but they were repeatedly compromised by basic mistakes.

Her friends and tutors knew of her father's violent temper yet interviews were conducted while he remained in the same room. To avoid answering difficult questions the Ahmed parents claimed they were victims of racism.

The break came when Shafilea's sister, Alesha, came forward and when Chief Crown Prosecutor Nazir Afzal (CPP) took matters into his capable hands.

Farzana was an active perpetrator both in the murder and in the disposal of her daughter's body. Alesha told the *Daily Mail* that "their mother began the attack with the words 'Just finish it here,' before her father stuffed a plastic bag in Shafilea's mouth, holding it there until she stopped breathing."

According to Afzal, "Alesha arranged to have her own home burgled to get back at mom and dad. We arrested her. Once in police custody, she said that the reason she did this is because '[her] mom and dad killed [her] older sister in front of me. [Her] mum said '[She will] be next.'"

When I asked CCP Afzal what Farzana was like, he said this: "She was extremely strong, very charismatic, an established community leader, with a manipulative personality. As an uneducated woman in an arranged marriage, Farzana probably viewed her lifestyle as the only possible option for her daughters." This was true for millennia in Pakistan and is still true today in non-assimilated Muslim enclaves in the West.

According to the *Telegraph*, Alesha's testimony "threw the killers' carefully-constructed defence into disarray." In 2012, Farzana and Iftikhar were both convicted and jailed for life.

This is a tragic story about a girl who was betrayed by her family and cultural customs, who tried to save her own life, but was betrayed again by a British system that did not help her to do so.

However, Alesha became a hero when she decided to save her own life and bravely spoke out. CCP Afzal made sure this case was properly handled. Afzal has handled a number of honor killing prosecutions. Please note that both heroes are also Muslims.

Breitbart
1/20/15

- 90 -
Turkey Calls for Campaign Against 'Violence Against Women' While Honor Killings Remain Rampant

Turkish Prime Minister Ahmet Davutoğlu has announced an "extensive campaign against violence against women across the country, in the aftermath of the brutal murder of a university student in an attempted rape on a public minibus."

Three men, now in custody, have been accused of stabbing twenty-year-old Ozgecan Aslan to death, cutting off her hands while she was still alive (to make sure there was no DNA evidence on her fingernails—suggesting she fought back). Then, for good measure, they burned her body. Women are wearing black to mourn her murder. There are discussions underway about the death penalty for woman-murder.

However, violence against women in Turkey is not confined to stranger rape, stranger harassment, or stranger murder. On the contrary, intimate partner and family violence in terms of honor killings are rampant. In 2009, when Turkey was attempting to join the European Union (EU), Turkish girls were forced to commit suicide rather than have their deaths appear as honor killing statistics. At that time, under Turkish law, honor killers "could get a reduced sentence claiming provocation." Changing this law to ostensibly comply with European standards merely led to the forced suicide option and to a "spike" in honor killings, not only in rural Turkey, but also in Istanbul.

In 2011, government figures suggested that recorded honor killings increased "14-fold in seven years, hitting nearly 1,000 in the first seven months of 2009." Turkish women's rights activists insist that the "laws are not applied," that the "police are unwilling or unable to help vulnerable women," and that there "are not enough safe houses for women." Some experts suggest that a too-rapid modernization coupled with rural immigration to modern cities account for the spike in Turkish honor killings.

Turkish Muslims in Europe have perpetrated a series of high-profile honor killings.

For example, Turkish-Kurd Fadime Sahindal chose a Swedish way of life. She wanted a "higher education" and chose a white Swedish boyfriend. Her parents considered her "a whore," her brothers endlessly harassed her in public. Fadime took them to court, but was eventually forced to live in hiding. In 2002, her father finally found and shot Fadime to death. The Kurdish community in Sweden did not condemn him. "If a girl goes out with a boy without being married then she's a whore," said Kamaran Shwan, chairman of the Kurdish Association in Malmo.

In 1996, Hatin Surucu, a fifteen-year-old Turkish German citizen, was forcibly married to her cousin in Turkey. In 1999, she returned to Berlin, where she had been born, together with her son. Hatin broke with her family, refused to wear the Muslim head scarf, and lived with her child in a hostel. She became an electrical engineer. She said she "simply wanted to live her life." Hatin lodged frequent complaints with the Berlin police about her brothers' threats to kill her.

In 2005, Hatin was shot and died choking on her own blood. A bus driver discovered the body and called the police. Hatin's three brothers, aged eighteen to twenty-five, were arrested and formally charged with the murder.

In 2004, an eighteen-year-old Turkish woman, "Jasmin," who was also a German citizen, narrowly escaped an arranged marriage to a wealthy Pakistani man who wanted to gain German residency and citizenship. Her parents stalked her at work. They threatened to kill her if she did not leave her job and agree to the marriage. A supervisor hid her for a week. Her parents cased the building. Co-workers did not call the police. (Since Jasmin was a minor, the police might have turned her over to her parents.) Friends helped her sneak out through the garage and escape to a shelter in Berlin. Jasmin said: "I'm not going to get married to somebody that I don't know just because of my parents. I never even saw a picture."

Jasmin escaped the arranged marriage, but she has lost her entire family and her freedom as well. Were she to surface and return to her family, she risks being murdered for her refusal.

As Turkey becomes more and more radically Islamic and as women are increasingly seen as unequal, different, subordinate, how does PM Davutoğlu plan to transform the honor-shame consciousness that traditionally accompanies this mindset? How much of a budget will he allow for "safe houses," and for the prosecution of honor killers?

Turkey needs a pro-Western, European Enlightenment-style revolution but, despite a large, secular and sophisticated population in Istanbul, that possibility seems more and more remote.

Breitbart
2/16/15

- 91 -

Pakistani Man Convicted of Ordering Honor Killing on Daughter's In-Laws in Pakistan from Brooklyn Cab

The long arm of American justice has prevailed against a heinous overseas revenge-honor killing—one that was orchestrated by cell phone from the front seat of a taxi in Brooklyn, New York.

Muslims driving taxis in American and European cities have been
known to park them illegally when it is time for prayer, and also to help
lead families to daughters on the run. At least one "horror"/honor killing was carried out in a Dallas-based taxi when Yasir Said murdered his
two academically promising and vivacious daughters, Sarah and Amina,
in cold blood.

In the case of Mohammad Choudhry, a taxi was used as a command center to terrorize a daughter as well as the people who helped
rescue her from captivity. It was the moving vehicle from which Chouh-
dry ordered a vigilante hit on those who had shamed him.

First, Mohammad Ajmal Choudhry ordered his daughter into the
marriage. She testified that "[My father] told me he would kill me if [I]
do anything wrong now." She obeyed him. But she also escaped and returned to America with the help of the State Department and with the
help of the man she loved, Shujat Abbas.

After Amina escaped, she was in telephone contact with her father.
She recorded these damning conversations. Her father told her: "If you
don't come back, I will kill each and every one of them... As long as
you're outside the home, my honor is at stake... Getting humiliated and

living is not a life."

Mohammad Choudhry could not find—and therefore could not kill—his American-reared daughter Amina, so he threatened to kill those who had helped her escape from the forced, loveless marriage to her cousin in Pakistan where Amina had been held captive for three years. She immediately went into hiding. She had to do so. Women are "horror"/honor killed for far less than abandoning a forced cousin-marriage and for freely choosing a marriage partner.

Amina surfaced from hiding only to testify against her father at trial. Mohammad was shamed. He had planned, through this marriage, to be able to bring his nephew to America so that he could become a citizen.

Mohammad Ajmal Choudhry had his own brother slaughter his daughter's new father-in-law and sister-in-law. Witnesses observed them do so—and saw them desecrate the bodies afterwards. The daughter and sister of the two victims, Seemab Abbas, submitted a statement to the court which read: "Ajmal (Choudhry) played with us as if we were non-living toys… [He] played with the blood of my family."

Last week, Choudhry was sentenced to life in prison following a nine-day trial which took place in June and July 2014. The judge, William Kuntz, told Choudhry: "You were an egomaniacal force who revealed yourself to be self-absorbed in your merciless pursuit of evil." Choudhry was convicted by a jury of "conspiracy to commit murder in a foreign country, making threats and immigration fraud."

Amina displayed courage and daring. She felt it was her right to marry the man she loved. This so-called "right" is considered heretical and often constitutes a capital crime among Hindus in India, among some Sikhs, and among Muslims globally. Her choice is a heroic one–but it also means that she can never again risk seeing her extended family. It may mean that she will have to live in hiding under a pseudonym for the rest of her life. Her children will have no maternal cousins, aunts, uncles, or grandparents. This is the terrible price of her freedom.

Pakistani-American Choudhry followed tribal a shame-and-honor code. This code is not Western but, clearly, it still exists in immigrant communities. America, Canada, and Europe's daunting task is to educate such families about Western values, to help rescue those who would otherwise be "horror"/honor killed, and to punish the perpetrators and the accomplices.

Breitbart
5/12/15

- 92 -

Another Romeo and Juliet: Brutally Beaten to Death and Burned Before a Mob in India

Earlier this week, an Indian man, Jairam Manjhi, aged either 36 or 25, and Parvati Kumari, a 16-year-old girl related to her lover's wife, were kidnapped by the girl's family and brutally beaten to death; the girls' family publicly burned their corpses while 100 villagers stood by and watched the entire grisly episode.

Although accounts are unclear, it seems that both were members of the same caste: Dalits, formerly known as "untouchables." Also, the teenaged Parvati was related through marriage to her alleged lover: she was the niece of her lover's wife, who was therefore possibly her paternal aunt. If so, their crime was not one of caste violation which, according to my pioneering study on this subject, was found to be the dominant reason for "horror"/honor killings among Hindus in India.

However, a love match is considered a filthy and unacceptable option both among Hindus and Muslims. This Romeo and Juliet scenario, whether it is adultery or not, is seen as a capital crime among tribal people.

Shockingly, the mob who beat the couple to death was composed of more women than men. The police have already arrested six members of Parvati's family including Baby Devi, her aunt. The women said that the girl had brought disgrace to the society. Also puzzling among the early reports is the fact that Jairam Manjhi, the older married lover, has been defended by his wife, Sharda Devi, who claims he was "innocent and was killed for no fault of his." She is quoted as saying "My husband told me over the phone that he was at the residence of a relative with the girl and would be returning on Wednesday." If this is true, it suggests that something else (perhaps something related to envy or greed) might have been going on.

Perhaps the girl's female relatives, possibly long used to unhappy and very abusive arranged marriages, could have been seized by a mad envy which turned them murderous.

However, thus far, the reports remain either contradictory or unclear as to whether this illicit relationship truly existed; whether it was condemned because it was too "incestuous," a forbidden love choice, or an opportunity for someone's hidden economic advancement.

Hopefully, the Indian police and the court will discover the truth of the matter.

Breitbart
5/14/15

Yazidi Victims of Mass Rape Threatened with Death upon Release from ISIS Captivity

According to Kurdish media network Rudaw, seventeen-year-old "Suzan," a Kurdish Yazidi girl was kidnapped, gang-raped, enslaved, and impregnated by ISIS warriors. Incredibly, she managed to escape and has told her story to Delal Sindy, a Swedish-Kurdish activist living in a Kurdish region.

"Suzan's" story is surreal but alarmingly typical. She and other female sex slaves were lined up naked every morning, "smelled," and then chosen either by ISIS militant Al-Russiyah, or by his bodyguards. They were beaten and gang-raped daily. When "Suzan" was sold to Al-Russiyah, she was held in a hotel in Mosul in a building full of half-naked girls and women.

The virgins were highly prized; as such, they were examined to make sure that their hymens were intact and then taken to a room filled with 30-40 men who chose among them.

Based on "Suzan's" and other reports, sexually repressed Jihadic misogynists are treating innocent, virgin children as if they are sophisticated prostituted women, the kind of women that jihadists watch, addictively, in pornography. Among the recently released 216 Yazidi women, there was a nine-year-old Yazidi girl who was pregnant; she had been raped by at least ten Islamic jihadists.

ISIS fighters are also torturing the girls as if sadistic torture is synonymous with sexual expression. They are killing the girls, even burning them alive, when they resist or cannot perform.

"Suzan" reports that she was forced to "say things from the Quran" during the rapes. If she refused, they whipped her or burned her thighs with boiling water. ISIS fighters cut off the legs of one girl who tried to escape.

"Suzan's" father is dead and she cannot find her mother, but her uncle has threatened to honor/"horror" kill her "if he finds out that she has been sexually abused or her honor 'tainted.'"

Tragically, this is typical. The raped Kurdish and Yazidi women and their Sunni Arab babies will probably never be accepted—not even though the "highest Yazidi cleric [has urged] families to accept and welcome the women who had fled ISIS."

Rape is no longer merely a spoil of war. It has become a major weapon of war. Think Bosnia, Rwanda, Sudan, and Nigeria. The repeated public gang-rapes of female children and women is meant to drive these victims out of their minds—which it does. They become depressed, insomniac, and suicidal. "Suzan" is haunted by flashbacks and wishes she was dead. "I want to kill myself," she says.

According to United Nations' Special Representative on Sexual Violence in Conflict, Zainab Bangura, although women are required to cover their heads under sharia law, ISIS fighters "have reportedly banned the captive girls from using headscarves after some of them used the scarves to hang themselves."

This barbaric behavior during war is not new.

According to Algerian-American attorney Karima Bennoune, from 1992 on, Algerian fundamentalist Muslim men committed a series of "terrorist atrocities" against Algerian women. Bennoune describes the "kidnapping and repeated raping of young girls as sex slaves for armed fundamentalists. The girls were also forced to cook and clean for God's warriors... one 17-year-old girl was repeatedly raped until pregnant. She was kidnapped off the street and held with other young girls, one of whom was shot in the head and killed when she tried to escape."

Rape is "gender cleansing." The intended effect of rape is always the same: to utterly break the spirit of the rape victim, to drive her out of her body and out of her mind so as to render her incapable of resistance.

According to Bennoune: "Terrorist attacks on women (in Algeria had) the desired effect: widespread psychosis among the women; internal exile—living in hiding, both physically and psychologically, in their own country." In Bennoune's view, "the collective psychosis" was due to the "escalation of violence" by the "soldiers of the Islamic state." According to Michael Curtis, M.D., an American volunteer-physician for Doctors Without Borders, "In Bosnia's Tuzla camp, the leading cause of death [was] suicide, probably the only refugee camp in the world where that is the case."

But some Muslim families refuse to demonize or kill the rape victim. In 2007, in Pakistan, thirteen-year old Kainat Soomro was chloroformed, drugged, kidnapped, and then gang-raped for three or four days by four men who threatened to kill or sell her. Kainat escaped, in her bare feet and without her headscarf.

Amazingly, her loving family refused to kill her. On the contrary: Kainat's mother wept and kissed her. Her father and older brother proudly supported Kainat's search for justice.

This family deserves a prize for having the courage and the sanity to stand up to tribal misogyny.

A grassroots feminist group, War Against Rape, found Kainat a pro bono lawyer. Bravely, Kainat agreed to endure a 5- to 10-year legal process, one in which she will be grilled in humiliating ways by sophisticated and politically powerful attorneys.

Kainat's lawyer managed to have the four men jailed and held in jail without bail for three years. This, too, is amazing. Ultimately, the accused rapists prevailed. Dozens of villagers descended on the courthouse yelling that "Kainat is a whore." Their winning defense argument was ingenious: They claimed that Kainat married one of them; the rapist produced Kainat's thumbprint on a marriage document and a photo of the two of them, smiling. Kainat insisted that she was drugged and does not remember this. Her presumed bridegroom demanded that she return to him.

Kainat was only 13 and did not have the right to consent to a marriage under secular law. However, under Sharia law, if she has reached puberty, she can do so. Sharia law prevails in the matter and the accused were all freed.

For a poor girl and her family to have four powerful men jailed for three years is extraordinary. The price: The rapists allegedly killed her supportive brother. And despite national headlines, the police closed the murder investigation. Kainat quietly says that her "life is a living hell."

As of 2013, Kainat and her family still lived under police protection.

Breitbart
5/28/15

- 94 -
Injustice as Usual: Malala Assassins Secretly Acquitted in Pakistan

The Pakistani courtroom proceedings were secret. Despite what reporters were previously told this past April—that ten men had been convicted—Pakistani authorities secretly acquitted eight of the men charged with conspiracy and attempted murder in the case of teenager Malala Yousafzai, who was targeted because she wanted girls to receive an education.

In 2012, the world was up in arms when a Pakistani Taliban gunman shot fifteen-year-old Malala Yousafzai in the head for having promoted education for girls. She survived dangerous and delicate surgery, moved to Britain with her family for reasons of security—and, along the way, received the Nobel Peace Prize, Europe's Sakharov prize for Freedom of Thought, and was named one of *TIME* magazine's most influential people.

But Pakistan—the country that sheltered Bin Laden for years—allowed the world to believe that justice was possible in this lawless country, that all the men who conspired to murder Malala and who wounded two other school girls had been convicted and sent to jail for 25 years each.

Today, the judgement of the secret military court was revealed together with contradictory explanations. Some sources said that there had not been enough evidence to convict all ten; others claimed "misreporting" for the confusion.

According to an unnamed security official, cited by *The Independent* and pegged to the *Daily Mirror*, "This was a tactic to get the media pressure away from the Malala case because the whole world wanted convictions for the crime." However, this view is upheld by the BBC's Ilyas Khan, who wrote that "even if Pakistani officials did not purpose-fully spread misinformation, they allowed it to stand."

The *Guardian* quotes yet another unnamed army officer who be-lieved that there "had been enough evidence to convict all of the men" but due to "longstanding weaknesses of Pakistan's judicial system," eight men were acquitted. This officer reported that witnesses were "intim-idated into not giving evidence and the court dropped many of the charges against them." This same officer "denied claims made by the *Daily Mirror* that any of the men had been released. He said they were still being held and would be brought back to court."

The *Guardian* also claims that the ten men were part of a "group tasked by Pakistani Taliban leader Mullah Fazlullah with killing, or at-tempting to kill, a series of high-profile people, including Yousafzai."

NPR's reporter, Philip Reeves, believes that it is "common for po-lice to respond to public pressure by arresting large numbers of people who turn out to be unrelated to the crime in question, including rela-tives of suspects."

Pakistan is a tribal, highly corrupt, increasingly violent and Isla-mist country, in which Christians and women are severely persecuted. Unlike neighboring India, Pakistani honor killings are usually unpun-ished and rarely reported. Pakistan is strategically located between In-dia, Iran, and Afghanistan. It also happens to have nuclear power.

Thus, it is America's ally.

But, if you think that reporters are not on the same page about facts on the ground in Pakistan, just imagine the thin ice upon which diplomats skate.

In 2013 and again in 2015, Secretary of State John Kerry confirmed our alliance with this Wild East state. On a visit to Pakistan, Kerry an-nounced "the reinvigoration of a Strategic Dialogue with Pakistan to foster a deeper, broader, and more comprehensive partnership and [to] facilitate concrete cooperation on core shared interests ranging from en-ergy to counterterrorism."

Good luck to us.

Breitbart
6/5/15

- 95 -
Dukhtar: Award-Winning Film Highlights Struggle of Pakistani Women

In the wild, wild East, in the tribal "badlands" between Pakistan and Muslim India, few girls or women willingly risk being honor killed for refusing an arranged marriage or for wanting to leave an exceptionally violent husband.

Women do not usually run away in search of freedom. No one will help them. It is their own families who are after them—and women are viewed as the property of their families. Whoever dares help a runaway, an allegedly "disobedient" woman, immediately becomes prey as well.

This is precisely what happens in Afia Serena Nathaniel's very beautiful, very gripping, and very tragic film: *Dukhtar* (Daughter). The award-winning film, which opens in New York October 9th and in Los Angeles on October 16th, is a road-trip thriller about a heroic Pakistani mother, Allah Rakhi, who risks almost certain death in an attempt to spare her ten-year-old daughter, Zainab, from having to marry a tribal warlord old enough to be her grandfather; Zainab's father, Daulat Khan, has arranged this in order to end a blood feud.

The film is thrilling and fast-paced. It is like a fable or a folk tale, fraught with forbidden potential romance and ever-present danger. However, despite exceptions such as Samia Sarwar, Mukhtar Bibi, and Malala Yousefzai, our heroine, however inspiring, is fictional and does not represent your average Urdu or Pashto-speaking tribal woman.

On the contrary.

In a new study of mine, just out in *Middle East Quarterly*, I found that female accomplices play an essential role in such family conspiracies and the minority of mothers who personally and physically play a hands-on role in murdering their daughters, also tend to commit torture-murders. Equally significant: Worldwide, the accomplices are arrested significantly less often than the male or female hands-on perpetrators.

While there are an amazing number of feminists in Pakistan and Afghanistan, there are also a far larger number of women who have internalized the values of a shame and honor culture and function as enforcers—as a matter of survival.

Like men, women internalize tribal shame-and-honor codes. The honor killing family views their crime as one of "self-defense." Had they not murdered the girl, no one would marry their other children. They would be shunned both socially and economically. This fear is based in reality.

The film's fictional ten-year-old, Zainab, believes that if "you look at a boy you get pregnant." Absolutely no freedom of choice in terms of a marriage mate is allowed. As I've pointed out, a girl's virginity and fertility are resources that belong to her family and tribe, not to herself.

Tribal councils in Pakistan consider honor killing justifiable; mostly, the local police turn a blind eye. If ever questioned, families say: "She is missing," "she ran away," or "she killed herself."

The film challenges this reality by imagining a rebel: A mother who loves her daughter enough to risk being killed for violating the honor codes; a daughter who loves her mother enough to risk being killed for running away from her father's house. Finally, in *Dukhtar*, a former (and very soulful) *mujahid*, Soheil, is initially duped into rescuing both mother and daughter but over time he actively decides to protect them.

Clearly, his character has come a long way.

Allah Rakhi is an inspiring heroine—and a surprising one too. She is illiterate, and was herself subjected to an arranged marriage to a much older man when she was fifteen years old. The film reverses reality—and challenges tribal imagination by portraying three generations of spirited heroines and woman-loving women: Allah Rakhi, her daughter, and her daughter's maternal grandmother.

The filmmaker was inspired by a story of a Pakistani mother who once kidnapped her two daughters to ensure a better future for them. It took ten years for Nathaniel to write, produce, and direct this amazing film; she shot it in 30 days, working 12-14 hours a day, "under freezing conditions mostly in the disputed territory between Pakistan and India." There were also "bomb blasts and sectarian killings" along their route as well as "extreme weather conditions and warlord threats." The film is a unique co-production between the United States and Pakistan and one directed by a woman with a 40 man crew.

The acting is superb (thank you Samia Mumtaz, Mohib Mirza, and Saleha Aref) and the cinematography breath-taking. Cinematographers Armughan Hassan and Najaf Bilgrami capture the awesome and treacherous beauty of the South Asian mountains, narrow mountain passes— and the sheer grandeur of the sky.

Breitbart
9/14/15

96

When Women Commit Honor Killings

F emale-on-female violence has been minimized because male-on-female violence is far more visible, dramatic, and epidemic. However, women sometimes kill infants, spouses, and adult strangers, including other women. Indeed, as this study shows, women play a very active role in honor-based femicide, both by spreading the gossip underlying such murders and by acting as conspirator-accomplices and/or hands-on-killers in the honor killing of female relatives.

Female perpetrators and accomplices in honor killings, like their male counterparts, can be calculating, brutal, and without remorse. Tooba Yahya Shafia of Canada was directly involved with her husband and son in the murder of three of her biological daughters and her husband's first wife.

In order to explore this phenomenon, this author conducted an original, non-random, qualitative study of 31 honor killings (26 cases) in North America, Europe, India, and Muslim-majority countries, where women were named as hands-on killers and/or conspirator-accomplices in the media.

All of these honor killings took place between 1989 and 2013. Eighty-seven per-cent were Muslim-on-Muslim crimes; the remaining 13 percent were committed by Hindus, Sikhs, and Yazidis. Women were hands-on killers in 39 percent of these cases and served as conspirator-accomplices 61 percent of the time. In India, women were hands-on killers 100 percent of the time.[1] (See Chart 1, below.)

The average age of all victims was twenty years old. When wom-

---

1 There were five Muslim and one Hindu hands-on killers in India.

en were the hands-on killers, the average age of their victims was 18.3; although conspirator-accomplices killed victims whose average age was 21, this age difference was of no statistical significance.[2] (See Chart 2, below.)

Forty-two percent of the honor killings in which women participated were torture-murders. Torture-murders are those in which victims are attacked in multiple ways—drugged/slowly poisoned, beaten, tied up, suffocated, wrists or throats slashed, stabbed many times, hacked to death, or burned with acid—in short, victims are subjected to a slow and painful death. However, in the case of female hands-on killers, the victims were torture-murdered 92 percent of the time as compared to women who served as conspirator-accomplices with a male hands-on killer; in that case the torture-murder rate was 11 percent.[3] Torture-murders were most frequent in India[4] (83 percent) and in Europe (57 percent). The rate of torture-murder in Muslim-majority countries was 43 percent while in North America it was 9 percent.

The legal outcomes of 25 of these cases are known: 92 percent led to arrests, trials, and/or convictions. This is not surprising as an arrest is probably what triggered the media coverage that brought these cases to light. However, as with incest and other "hidden" family crimes, only a minority of such cases may attract media or legal attention. One hundred percent (100%) of the female and 90 percent of the male hands-on killers were arrested, tried, and/or convicted. Only 53 percent of the female conspirator-accomplices were arrested, tried and/or convicted. The differential arrest rate for (male and female) hands-on killers vs. (female) conspirator-accomplices was statistically significant (p=0.010).

Hands-on killers and conspirator-accomplices killed for the same reasons: They saw their victims as "too Western" or as "sexually inappropriate." Motive varied as a function of region. Both hands-on killers and conspirator-accomplices viewed their victims as "too Western" 77 percent of the time. Sixty-seven percent of female hands-on killers and 84 percent of conspirator-accomplices perceived their victims this way. (See Charts 2 and 3, below.) In Muslim-majority countries, only 43 percent of victims were killed for this reason. However, in the West, the mainly Muslim victims in North America were viewed as "too Western" 91 percent of the time and 100 percent of the time in Europe. (See Chart

2 The mean age difference between the groups was 3 years, SD +/2.888.

3 According to Fisher's exact test, this was a statistically significant difference, p<0.0001.

4 There were four Muslim victims and one Hindu victim.

1 for definitions of "too Western.")

Twenty-three percent of victims were killed for committing an act of "sexual impropriety." However, in Muslim-majority countries, 57 percent of victims, and, in predominantly Muslim areas of India, 33 percent of victims, were killed for this reason as compared to only 9 percent in North America; there were no honor killings for this reason in Europe.[5]

The above statistics tell only part of the story. What emerges from the narratives of these cases is that the majority of both hands-on killers and conspirator-accomplices blamed their victims for their gruesome fates and are calculating, cold, and self-righteous women. Both female hands-on killers and conspirator-accomplices physically and verbally abused, monitored, and stalked their victims, warning them of dire consequences if they failed to obey the rules. Some issued clear death threats. A few examples:

On the day Aqsa Parvez, a 16-year-old Pakistani-Muslim-Canadian girl, was killed, her mother said in a police interview that she "thought her husband was only going to 'break legs and arms,' but instead [he] 'killed her straight away.'" Distraught, she said, "Oh God, Oh God...Oh my Aqsa, you should have listened. Everyone tried to make you understand. Everyone begged you, but you did not listen."[6] Although seemingly in anguish, the mother appears to have had no problem with having her daughter's bones broken. Aqsa's father and brother received life sentences with eligibility for parole after 18 years. The mother was not arrested or tried.

Shafilea Ahmed was a 17-year-old Pakistani-Muslim-British girl. Her parents carried out her slow suffocation murder in front of their other young children, warning them that they "would be killed if they ever revealed the truth."[7] Almost a decade later, perhaps fearing for her own life, Shafilea's sister Alesha approached the police. She said their mother "began the attack with the words 'Just finish it here.'"[8] During the murder, the mother said to one of her younger daughters, "You will

---

5 Included in this study are three rape victims since being raped is often viewed as "sexual impropriety" within the Muslim world. See, for example, Phyllis Chesler, "Punished for Being Raped and for Accusing Rapists: Women's Burden under Sharia," *Breitbart*, Oct. 28, 2014; idem, "The Price of Justice for a Raped Pakistani Girl," *The Huffington Post* (New York), May 30, 2014.

6 *The Toronto Star*, June 26, 2010.

7 *The Telegraph* (London), Aug. 3, 2012.

8 *The Daily Mail* (London), Aug. 12, 2012.

be next" and "Shut up, or you are dead."[9]

A 19-year-old Indian-Muslim girl, Zahida, was strangled to death by her mother who said, "This should be the treatment meted out to young people from our religion who marry into families of other faiths."[10] The mother also said that she "killed her because [she] brought shame to our community. How could [she] elope with [a] Hindu? She deserved to die. I have no remorse."[11]

Noor Almaleki was a 20-year-old Iraqi-Muslim-American living in Arizona. Her father ran her over with a two-ton Jeep Cherokee. When her mother was informed that her daughter was dying, she said, "Thank you, thank you ... That's what she needs."[12]

Sixteen-year-old Indian-Muslim Rekha Yadav was hacked to death by her mother who claimed she did so "in a bid to save her family's prestige."[13] The mother confessed to the murder and expressed no remorse.

Married at sixteen, 27-year-old Surjit Athwal was treated like a despised servant by her mother-in-law Bachan Kaur, a domineering but respected matriarch within the Sikh community in London. Kaur called Surjit a "murderer" when she had a miscarriage. According to Surjit's sister-in-law, Bachan intimated publicly that she was going to have the offending daughter-in-law—who wanted to divorce Kaur's son—eliminated: "I've spoken to someone in India ... It's her own fault. She is out of control ...We're the laughing-stock of the community ... It's decided. I won't have her shaming our family."[14]

Seventeen-year-old Rofayda Qaoud was raped and impregnated in her West Bank home by her two brothers. According to news reports, "Relatives and friends refused to speak to her family. Her elder daughters' husbands wouldn't allow them to visit [the family] because [Rofayda] had returned home."[15] Finally, her mother Amira perpetrated a torture-murder and then "purged her home of all pictures of her older children."[16]

However, the perpetrators of these crimes were not only un-

9 Chief Crown Prosecutor Nazir Afzal, personal communication, July 15, 2013.
10 India Today (New Delhi), May 15, 2011.
11 The New York Daily News, May 15, 2011.
12 Abigail Pesta, "An American Honor Killing," Marie Claire, July 8, 2010.
13 Indian Express (New Delhi), June 30, 2010.
14 Sarbjit Athwal, Shamed (London: Virgin, 2013), pp. 148-9.
15 Soraya Sarhaddi Nelson, "Culture of Death? Palestinian Girl's Murder Highlights Growing Number of 'Honor Killings,'" Jewish World Review, Nov. 18, 2003.
16 The Guardian (London), June 22, 2005.

schooled women brought up in tribal settings. In the case of Samia Sarwar Imran, an educated 28-year-old Pakistani-Muslim woman, Imran's wealthy physician-mother hired a hit man, accompanied him to her daughter's divorce lawyer's office, and made sure he shot her daughter dead: "The paralegal said that Mrs. Sarwar was 'cool and collected during the getaway, walking away from the murder of her daughter as though the woman slumped in her own blood was a stranger.'"[17]

Strikingly, from among these 26 cases, only two women came forward—many years later—to testify against their families. Both lived in Britain. One was a sister, Alesha Ahmed, who may have feared for her own life, and the second, Hatim Goren, a mother, had a guilty conscience and, after testifying, was shunned by her family and placed into witness protection.[18]

Gossip and Honor Killing

Honor killings are not merely individual family matters; extended family and community-cultural pressures often demand that dishonorable female behavior be dealt with in this way. Female gossip plays a critical role in these murders.[19]

Roland Barthes once described gossip as "murder by language."[20] Anthropologist Joseph Ginat theorized that

Anthropological literature claims that offenses against 'ird' are only punished when they become public knowledge. However... not all instances of illicit sexual relations that become the subject of rumor and gossip result in a killing. Murder occurs only when there is not only gossip or rumor, but [also] accusation by an injured party.[21]

Anthropologists Ilsa Glazer and Wahiba Abu Ras tested Ginat's

17 Kwame Anthony Appiah, *The Honor Code* (New York: W. W. Norton and Company, 2010), pp. 148-9.

18 Chief Crown Prosecutor Nazir Afzal, personal communication, July 15, 2013.

19 Max Gluckman, "Papers in Honor of Melville J. Herskovits: Gossip and Scandal," *Current Anthropology*, no. 3, 1962, pp. 307-16; Alexander Rysman, "How the 'Gossip' Became a Woman," *Journal of Communication*, no. 1, 1977, pp. 176-80.

20 Roland Barthes, *Roland Barthes by Roland Barthes* (Berkeley: University of California Press, 1977), p. 169.

21 Joseph Ginat, *Women in Muslim Rural Society* (New Brunswick, N.J.: Transaction Books, 1982), p. 184.

hypothesis by conducting a careful analysis of the honor killing of a young Arab-Muslim Israeli woman named Jamila and by tracking the gossip that led to her honor killing.[22]

The 2,200 inhabitants of Jamila's village were related to each other in multiple ways both by marriage and blood. When the men were away at work during the day, the women of the village would monitor each other's behavior. Jamila was a young, secluded, uneducated, unemployed, and unmarried girl who lived with her impoverished, widowed mother. As a result, she was at risk of being approached by higher-status boys in the village. One sent her a love letter, which she could not read, and trinkets that she had someone else return; another boy, Younis, drugged and raped her.

At least six women, including her friends, relatives, and the village herbalist, gossiped about Jamila's plight, and her shame became public. Younis was forced by the village elders to marry the lower-status Jamila. Not long thereafter, he locked up his bride, starved, and anally raped her, thereafter, he had her killed by her brothers, telling them that he "had not married a virgin." Indeed, he had not, since he himself had drugged and raped her prior to their marriage.

Upon learning of her death, Jamila's mother reportedly wept, saying, "Why did [my] daughter behave in a manner which made her death necessary?" The authors concluded that "women's gossip creates the climate in which the [honor killing] of a young woman is inevitable."[23]

Similar hostile gossip was probably involved in the twenty-six cases studied here, but the media rarely mentions this phenomenon. However, a full-length book about one of the cases did so.[24] This honor killing took place in 1989 in St. Louis, Missouri. Palestina (Tina) Isa, a Palestinian-Muslim-American, was an academically promising and vivacious 16-year-old girl who was routinely beaten, cursed, and overworked by her parents who viewed her as too "Americanized." Three of Tina's envious and unhappily married sisters kept nagging their father to do something. One said: "Tie her down in the basement of the store. Tape her mouth all day; go buy her passport; send her to the homeland, and over there it is neither forbidden nor against the law." Another sis-

---

22 Ilsa M. Glazer and Wahiba Abu Ras, "On Aggression, Human Rights, and Hegemonic Discourse: The Case of a Murder for Family Honor in Israel," *Sex Roles*, no. 3-4, 1994, p. 269.

23 Ibid.

24 Ellen Harris, *Guarding the Secrets: Palestinian Terrorism and a Father's Murder of His Too-American Daughter* (New York: Scribner, 1995).

ter said: "A person should shoot her and throw her into the sea."[25] Tina had been encircled and rendered vulnerable by such chilling hatred. While her mother held her down, Tina's father planted his foot on Tina's mouth and stabbed her multiple times. Her mother told the judge that it was all Tina's fault: "My daughter was very rebellious, disobedient …We shouldn't have to pay for it with our lives for what she did."[26] The murder was recorded by a hidden FBI wire-tap in the Isas' home as the father was under surveillance as a terrorism suspect.[27]

Trends and Implications

The author's review of fifty studies, reports, and books about honor killing (1968-2013), found that a surprising 54 percent of this literature reported no female participation in this gruesome practice while the other 46 percent reported such participation, focusing primarily on conspirator-accomplices and more rarely on hands-on killers.[28] (See "Source Material" below.) One previous review of the literature examined 161 cases of honor killing in the West Bank and Gaza, as well as among Israeli Arabs (1973-2000) and charted the percentage of female involvement at an estimated 8-17 percent.[29]

Compared to these previous findings, this study found a higher percentage of female participation in honor killings than has ever been documented. This is hardly surprising since this study considered only those cases in which women played a role. Thus, it cannot claim to have documented a real increase in female participation.

Some of the male-perpetrated "overkill" styles of torture murders documented in the author's previous studies involve a perverted sexual dimension similar to what Western serial killers do to prostituted stranger-women.[30] An element of male sexual ownership coupled with rage for having been shamed by a mere woman may combine to explain

25 Ibid., pp. 129, 212.

26 Ibid., p. 255.

27 *The New York Times*, Oct. 27, 1991.

28 This total sample size is derived from four studies, which took place in Arab Israel, Lebanon, the West Bank and Gaza. Andrzej Kulczycki and Sarah Windle, "Honor Killings in the Middle East and North Africa: A Systematic Review of the Literature," *Violence against Women*, no. 11, 2011, Table 2.

29 Phyllis Chesler, "Worldwide Trends in Honor Killings," *Middle East Quarterly*, Spring 2010, pp. 3-11; Phyllis Chesler and Nathan Bloom, "Hindu vs. Muslim Honor Killings," *Middle East Quarterly*, Summer 2012, pp. 43-52.

30 Chesler, "Worldwide Trends in Honor Killings," pp. 3-11.

this.

What can one explain the torture rate among female hands-on killers? This study found a 39 percent rate of female hands-on killers and a high rate of torture-murder among them. Female hands-on killers torture-murdered 92 percent of the time, compared to an 11 percent rate among female conspirator-accomplices. (See Chart 4.) Although this difference is statistically significant, it is important to remember that this is a small population of victims (N=12 vs. N=19).

One possible explanation for this difference is that female conspirator-accomplices may exert a restraining impact on their male counterparts leading to less tortuous and more "merciful" killings. In comparison, a female torture-killer may be enraged with her intimate female relative who, she believes, has forced her into so extreme a response. These women know that the "dishonoring" relatives, daughters in particular, have potentially brought social and economic "death" upon the family. A mother might be furious that her own daughter has driven her to such an ugly act and thus may behave even more brutally.

On the other hand, women have been routinely beaten and bullied by men (and by other, older women) and have not been permitted to express any anger toward them. In such situations, they may be projecting all their anger and aggression against younger women whom they are allowed to persecute and even kill, especially if they are family intimates.

In general, motive varies as a function of region but not as a function of gender.[31] Both men and women honor kill for the same reasons.

Female chastity and fertility is considered a family-owned asset and one that no individual woman dares to claim as her own. Thus, any girl or woman who refuses or wants to leave an arranged marriage or who chooses her own spouse or the father of her child has, by definition, dishonored her family and is seen as "too Western" for having put her "self" first. There is no concept of "self" in these societies as it has evolved in Western terms.

Conclusions and Recommendations

Female-on-female aggression is wrongfully viewed as a minor problem. However, such aggression can have serious, even lethal consequences. People may recoil from the knowledge that, like men, women have also internalized sexist and tribal codes of behavior; that a mother, grandmother, or mother-in-law can instigate, serve as a conspirator-ac-

---

31 *The National Post* (Toronto), Dec. 19, 2013.

complice in, or perpetrate the hands-on killing of her daughter, grand-daughter, or daughter-in-law; and that female hands-on killers and conspirator-accomplices are, like their male counterparts, calculating, brutal, and without remorse.

The entire community upholds and enforces tribal-religious-ethnic concepts of shame and honor. No family can risk "dishonor" without incurring economic and social disaster. The respective society dictates that if an allegedly deviant daughter is not eliminated, then the family will be shamed and shunned; no one will marry its daughters or sons; it will be condemned to poverty and ostracism.

For example, Thamar Zeidan, a 33-year-old Muslim woman from the West Bank divorced her abusive husband and lost custody of her children. In response, fifty relatives signed a petition to punish Thamar for disgracing the family by divorcing. According to one news account, "For some of the relatives, [her killing] was a cause for celebration. Zeidan's aunt held a feast celebrating that the family's honor had been restored."[32]

Can one change traditional, tribal thinking? Certainly not easily. One might conduct a pilot project to reach out to families whose children are eligible to marry each other. If reframing the honor codes is presented as being in the best interests of the family and the community, such an approach might work. It may be argued that female literacy and education contributes to a family's economic survival and that "choices" about veiling have an honorable place in Muslim history. Choosing one's own spouse (as opposed to arranged or first-cousin marriage) may enlarge an inbred gene pool and contribute to family and communal connectedness in new ways. Unfortunately, in the current atmosphere of multicultural relativism in which blaming all that is Western and modern and honoring all that is anti-Western and tribal has become sacred, it is unlikely that such an initiative could gain much ground in the West without being pilloried as racist and "colonialist."

It is important to hold accomplices liable for their criminal acts. Too often, they have escaped the consequences of their actions. In this study, conspirator-accomplices were arrested significantly less often than hands-on killers of both genders. If Western society is serious about ending honor killings, it must punish all culpable parties including conspirator-accomplices—without whom many honor killings could not take place.

Social workers, physicians, teachers, lawyers, and judges in the

---

32 Ibid.

West should also be made aware that when girls who come from shame-and-honor cultures are being monitored or beaten, far more serious consequences may follow. Legislators must be educated to understand that those who flee being killed for honor or who agree to testify against their families may require lifelong security and new lives under false names. This is a huge and difficult undertaking, and ideally, it might be necessary to find alternative, extended families for them since these potential victims are often individuals whose identities are moored in collectivity, not individualism.

Those in the West who want to help girls and women in flight from being killed for honor must understand that psychologically such girls are used to living with the knowledge that, while outsiders cannot be trusted, their own parents or siblings may one day kill them. This terrible duality means that tribal girls in flight may choose to return home, may not be able to accept outside help, and may ultimately spurn the kindness of strangers. A number of girls do escape, do testify, and do seek asylum. They are the subject of a future study of mine; they should be offered compassionate assistance in escaping this scourge of femicide.

Source Material

Gideon M. Kressel, et al., "Sororicide/Filiacide: Homicide for Family Honour," Current Anthropology, no. 2, 1981, p. 141; Joseph Ginat, Women in Muslim Rural Society (New Brunswick, N.J.: Transaction Publishers, reprint ed., 2013); Ilsa M. Glazer and Wahiba Abu Ras, "On Aggression, Human Rights, and Hegemonic Discourse: The Case of a Murder for Family Honor in Israel," Sex Roles, no. 3-4, 1994, p. 269; Kathryn Christine Arnold, "Are the Perpetrators of Honor Killings Getting away with Murder? Article 340 of the Jordanian Penal Code Analyzed under the Convention on the Elimination of All Forms of Discrimination against Women," American University International Law Review, no. 5, 2001, p. 1343; Nadera Shalhoub-Kevorkian, "Femicide and the Palestinian Criminal Justice System: Seeds of Change in the Context of State Building?" Law & Society Review, no. 3, 2002, p. 577; Niaz A. Shah Kakakhel, "Honour Killings: Islamic and Human Rights Perspectives," Northern Ireland Legal Quarterly, no. 1, 2004, p. 78; Aida Touma-Sliman, "Culture, National Minority and the State: Working against the 'Crime of Family Honour' within the Palestinian Community in Israel," in Lynn Welchman and Sara Hossain, Honour (London: Zed Books, 2005), p. 181; Danielle Hoyek, Rafif Rida Sidawi, and Amira Abou Mrad, "Murders of Women in Lebanon: 'Crimes of Honour' between Reality and the Law." in Welchman and Hossain, Honour, p. 111; Abdessamad Dialmy, "Sexuality in Contemporary Arab Society," Social Analysis, no. 2, 2005, p. 16; Purna Sen, "'Crimes of Honour,' Value and Meaning," in Welchman and Hossain, Honour, p. 42; Nazand Begikhani, "Honour-Based Violence among the Kurds: The Case of Iraqi Kurdistan," in Welchman and Hossain, Honour, p. 209; Centre for Egyptian Women's Legal Assistance, "'Crimes of Honour' as Violence against Women in Egypt," in Welchman and Hossain, Honour, p. 137; Valerie Plant, "Honor Killings and the Asylum Gender Gap," Journal of Transnational Law & Policy, no. 1, 2006, pp. 109-29; "Bibliography on 'Crimes of Honour' – Case Summaries," Centre of Islamic and Middle Eastern Law and International Centre for the Legal Protection of Human Rights, Sept. 2006; Veena Meeto and Heidi Safia Mirza, "There Is Nothing 'Honourable' about Honour Killings: Gender, Violence and the Limits of Multiculturalism," Women's Studies International Forum, no. 3, 2007, pp. 187-200; David Rosen, "Honour Killings: An Expression of Immigrant Alienation," Eureka Street, no. 6; James Brandon and Salam Hafez, "Crimes of the Community: Honor-based Violence in the UK," Centre for Social Cohesion; Aisha Gill, "Honor Killings and the Quest for Justice in Black and Minority Ethnic Communities in the United Kingdom," Criminal Justice Policy Review, no. 4, 2009, pp. 475-94; Kenneth Lasson, "Bloodstains on a 'Code of Honor': The Murderous Marginalization of Women in the Islamic World," Women's Rights Law Reporter, no. 3-4, 2009, p. 407; Kwame Anthony Appiah, The Honor Code (New York: W. W. Norton and Company, 2010), pp. 147-61, 167-9.; Brooklynn A. Welden, "Restoring Lost 'Honor': Retrieving Face and Identity, Removing Shame, and Controlling the Familial Cultural Environment through 'Honor' Murder," Journal of Alternative Perspectives in the Social Sciences, no. 1, 2010, pp. 380-98; John Alan Cohan, "Honor Killings and the Cultural Defense," California Western International Law Journal, no. 2, 2010, pp. 178-249; Andrzej Kulczycki and Sarah Windle, "Honor Killings in the Middle East and North Africa: A Systematic Review of the Literature," Violence against Women, no. 11, 2011, pp. 1442-64.

CHART 1: Female Hands-on Killer and Conspirator Accomplices

	Worldwide	North America	Europe	India	Muslim Majority Countries
# of Victims, N=	31	11	7	6	7
Victim's Average Age	20	19.8	20.1	19.7	20
Religion= Muslim[1]	87%	92%	71%	83%	100%
Hands-on Killers[2]	39%	9%	29%	100%	43%
Conspirator/ Accomplices[3]	61%	91%	71%	0%	57%
Motive: "Too Western"[4]	77%	91%	100%	67%	43%
Motive: "Sexual Impropriety"[5]	23%	9%	0%	33%	57%
Method: Torture	42%	9%	0%	83%	43%
Average # of Perpetrators	2	3	2	2	1

1 Victims and perpetrators who were not Muslim were Sikh, Hindu or Yazidi

2 Hands-on killers have a direct, hands-on role in the murders and may also have planned the honor killings.

3 Conspirator-accomplices initiated gossip of participated in family council meetings in which honor killings were arranged, or they lured the victims, did not warn the victim beforehand, did nothing to prevent such killings from taking place, helped the killers get away, and/or covered up for the killers after the fact.

4 "Too Western" means a girl refuses to wear varieties of Islamic clothing (including forms of the veil), wants an advanced education and a career, has friends, a boyfriend, or a husband who is not Muslim (or Sikh, Hindu or Yazidi), refuses an arranged marriage or wants to choose her own husband, tries to leave an abusive husband, is actually living with a boyfriend, or is viewed as acting too independently.

5 This accusation refers to victims who have been raped, were allegedly or actually having an extramarital affair, or who was viewed, rightly or wrongly, as "promiscuous." This might involve any sexual activity, but could consist of merely looking at a boy on a motorbike.

CHART 2: Female Hands on Killers

	Worldwide	North America	Europe	India[1]	Muslim Majority Countries[2]
N=	12	1	2	6	3
Average Age	18.3	16	18	19.7	16.3
Religion= Muslim	92%	100%	100%	83%	100%
Method: Torture	92%	100%	100%	83%[3]	100%
Motive: "Too Western"	67%	100%	100%	67%	33%
Motive: "Sexual Impropriety"	33%	0%	0%	33%	67%
Average # of Perpetrators	2	2	2	2	2

1 Muslims = 5, Hindus = 1
2 West Bank, Pakistan and Somalia
3 Muslims = 4, Hindus = 1

CHART 3: Female Hands-on Killers

	Worldwide	North America	Europe	India[1]	Muslim Majority Countries[2]
N=	19	10	5	0	4
Average Age	21	20.2	21	/	22.8
Religion= Muslim	84%	90%	60%	/	100%
Method: Torture	11%	0%	40%	/	0%
Motive: "Too Western"	84%	90%	100%	/	50%
Motive: "Sexual Impropriety"	16%	10%	0%	/	50%
Average # of Perpetrators	2	3	2	/	1

1 Muslims = 5, Hindus = 1
2 West Bank, Pakistan and Turkey

CHART 4: Female Hands-on Killers vs. Conspirator-Accomplices

	Worldwide	North America	Europe	India[1]	Muslim Majority Countries[2]
Killers, N=	12	1	2	6	3
Average Age	18.3	16	18	19.7	16.3
Method: Torture	92%	100%	100%	83%[3]	100%
Accomplices, N=	19	10	5	0	4
Average Age	21	20.2	21	/	22.8
Method: Torture	11%	0%	40%	/	0%

1 Muslims = 5, Hindus = 1
2 West Bank, Pakistan, Somalia and Turkey
3 Muslims = 4, Hindus = 1

Middle East Quarterly
Fall 2015

97

How Academia Whitewashes Muslim Honor Killings

The whitewashing of Muslim honor killings in America has seeped into academia. And the PC police have found a new scapegoat: Hindu Americans.

In January, the *Journal of Family Violence* published "An Exploratory Study of Honor Crimes in the United States" by Brittany E. Hayes, Joshua D. Froelich and Steven M. Chermak. It was an act of cowardice as well as a shoddy piece of research. It broke absolutely no new ground, either theoretically or statistically, and is so "politically correct" that it completely misses an entire forest for a tree.

The study's first error consists of comparing violence against women in general with femicide. Being battered is not the same as being murdered. The reason Hayes et al. place honor killings within the broader context of "violence against women" is clear. They don't want to be accused of "Islamophobia" or of targeting any one ethnic or religious group.

They don't tell us the names of any of the 16 honor-killing perpetrators or the names of their victims. The phrase "Muslim perpetrator" and "Muslim honor killing" appear nowhere. In 10,000 words, the words: "Islam," "Muslims," "Arabs" or "Middle Easterners" appear only 14 times.

Three times, Hayes et al. rail against "Western media coverage." They write: "Significantly, media reporters in the United States may be more inclined to cover honor crimes, especially those committed by Middle Easterners, compared to other fatal crimes because they may be perceived as more 'exotic' and news worthy." They insist, "Reporters may search for an honor crime angle when the victim and/or offender are of a particular ethnicity or religion ... there is a need to study honor crimes in the United States that involve victims and perpetrators from other cultures, like India, or extremist ideologies."

Wrong.

The New York Times, for example, has published a series of articles on Hindu honor killings in India and has published very few articles about Muslim honor killings in the United States, Canada, or Europe. Ironically, my study's comparison of Hindu and Muslim honor killings quietly supports a "politically correct" point of view: The origin of honor killings probably resides in shame-and-honor tribalism, not necessarily in a particular religion. I don't understand why other scholars have not yet absorbed this point. However, as I've noted, neither Islam nor Hinduism, as religious institutions, have worked very hard to abolish honor killing. The Indian Hindu government has tried to do so. The Pakistani government has not.

Nevertheless, Hayes, Freilich and Chermak bend over backward not to single out any one ethnicity, religion or nationality — except, perhaps, Hindu India.

New York Post
2/22/16

- 98 -
Horrific Domestic Terrorism in Pakistan

Her name was Ambreen Riasat. Ambreen is a quite a lovely name and now that is all we have left of her.

Ambreen was only fifteen, almost sixteen years old, when the local religious council (known as the *"jirga"* or *"panchayat"*) ordered that she be bound, perhaps sedated, (perhaps not), strangled, and then burned alive in a bus.

Her crime? She presumably helped a friend elope with a man her family had not chosen for her.

Ambreen's village, Makol, is not far from Islamabad and is even closer to Abbotobad, the very place where Osama bin Laden was kept safe-and-sound by the Pakistani government, America's military ally.

This act of tribal murder is an act of domestic terrorism and should be treated accordingly.

It is being called an "honor killing." It is a version of what may be understood as a classic honor killing. Ambreen's murder was ordered by an Islamic tribal council, long relied upon to settle disputes among poor people. In both Pakistan and India, the governments are at odds with the Muslim and Hindu religious councils that have ordered punishments ranging from public gang-rapes to murder.

This is a murder in the name of Islam—at least, as Islam is being interpreted by a religious council whose power is now being challenged by the government. This is also a murder in the name of a barbaric misogyny; the all-male tribal council does not want other local girls to get the idea that a love match is acceptable.

This is a classic honor killing with one unique and welcome feature: Ambreen's mother has been charged along with thirteen council

343

members in her death. She is accused of knowing about this horrific order but failing to notify her daughter or to aid in her daughter's escape.

Ambreen's father, Sardar Riasat, has asked: "How can a mother aid in the murder of her own daughter?"

In this particular case, Ambreen's mother committed a crime by proxy. Either the council could not find the eloped pair—or they decided to inflict the maximum haunting guilt upon them by murdering their innocent friend.

Prime Minister Nawaz Sharif has vowed to end honor killings. Playing the "Islamic Card," he said: "Such a barbaric act is not only Un-Islamic but also inhuman."

Bilawal Bhutto Zardari, the Chairman of the opposition PPP party, and Benazir Bhutto's son, has called for a "revolt" against these religious councils.

Ambreen's father has demanded that the Council members suffer the same death that they inflicted upon his daughter.

The village, Makol, where this took place, has claimed that there have never before been any honor killings.

I highly doubt that. The problem is daunting. The Pakistani Human Rights Commission has admitted that 8,694 girls and women have been known to have been honored murdered in the last eleven years. The "unknown" number is probably far higher than that.

What is the United Nations doing about this crime against humanity? And about the ruthless slaughter of Christians and dissidents in Muslim Pakistan?

Absolutely nothing. Other than providing an address for all sorts of global do-gooders who are not on the UN payroll, all the UN has done is further legalize Jew hatred; sexually abuse their female employees; sexually abuse and traffic the most vulnerable women whom they are charged to protect in hot war zones, and party hard in Western capitals.

FrontPage Magazine
5/11/16

- 99 -

Is Vetting Immigrants or Refugees for Honor-Based Gender Violence "Islamophobic"?

F eminists, Hollywood celebrities, academic, pundits, and Democratic legislators have denounced President Trumps Executive Order titled, "Protecting the Nation From Foreign Terrorist Entry
Into the United States." Demonstrators have surged at airports, class-ac-
tion lawsuits have been filed, judicial restraining orders have been issued.

I do not necessarily view this Act as a "Muslim Ban" since 43 other
Muslim-majority countries are not included. Only Iran and six failed,
and war-torn Muslim states, (Iraq, Libya, Somalia, Syria, Sudan, Yemen), well known for training Jihadists, and for producing pro-Jihad
propaganda, are named. Neither Afghanistan, Saudi Arabia, or Pakistan
are named here and one can only wonder why.

Whether or not the Trump administration prepared people for
what was coming; made all the necessary humane exceptions; crafted it
in a way that upholds our Constitution; and "rolled it out" carefully in
terms of explaining it to We, the People, is another question. That, they
did not do.

However, I want to focus on something else that no one else seems
to have discussed.

[Section 1] In order to protect Americans, the United States
must ensure that those admitted to this country do not bear

345

> hostile attitudes towards it and its founding principles....
> [Section 10. Transparency and Data Collection] (iii) in-
> formation regarding the number and type of acts of gen-
> der-based violence against women, including honor killings,
> in the United States by foreign nationals, since the date of
> this order or the last reporting period, whichever is later."

This clause seems to address acts of honor based violence committed in the United States by foreign-born nationals. It may also hope to
exclude would-be immigrants based on their records of past gender violence—information that might be almost impossible to obtain. Finally,
how can we prevent an immigrant from coming if he or she has yet to
commit an act of gender-based violence on American soil?

Thus, this Act has been poorly planned and even more poorly
written. However, the inclusion of this concept and language interests
me greatly. One can argue that America already has laws in place that,
if enforced, can punish such crimes if and when they are committed
within our sovereign boundaries.

For example, the Ethiopian father who genitally mutilated his 2
year old daughter in Atlanta in 2001, was sentenced to ten years in jail,
after which he was deported back to Ethiopia.

If we are "vetting" or seeking transparency in terms of an immigrant's past history as a way of predicting what he or she might do in
America—we will have a serious problem. American immigration authorities would have no way of knowing whether an immigrant or a
refugee from a tribal culture had or had not previously engaged in gender based violence, including honor killing. Desperate people have been
known to lie on their immigration applications.

Families who believe in and who have practiced FGM, forced veiling, daily battering, child marriage, first-cousin marriage, forced marriage and polygamy—and who honor kill their daughters—do not admit
that they've done so.

As we have seen, such killers genuinely feel that they have been
sinned against and that they've only acted in self-defense.

Only after a jail sentence has been obtained and time served, can
we consider deportation after the fact. That would not prevent the entry
of such an immigrant.

Is this Act a flat-out ban on Muslims? Many seem to think so.
However, we might remember that, to date, most recorded honor killings in the United States have been Muslim-on-Muslim crimes.

Many feminists insist that some American men are also domestically violent; they consider focusing on honor killings to be "Islamophobic." But as my research has shown, honor killing femicides are not the same as Western-style domestic violence. Here's why I also welcome the language in this Executive Order even as I despair over whether it is constitutional and whether it will or will not be upheld.

In my view, forced face veiling constitutes gender-based violence. Wherever we find women in niqab, (face-veiled), or wearing burqas, we must consider, perhaps even assume, that they are living in families in which daughter- and wife-beating, close monitoring and supervision, as well as forced marriages, and death threats, are normalized.

I also fear that today, hijab (the Islamic headscarf), increasingly signifies one's acceptance of Islamic supremacism and woman's subordinate status. Contrary to the recent Women's March against President Trump in D.C., where non-Muslim women donned hijab (made of American flags), I view this non-Muslim Donning of Hijab as a form of appeasement, not as a sign of political resistance to racism, fascism, Nazism, or totalitarianism.

The same feminists who've betrayed those Muslim feminists, dissidents, and gays who are fighting Islamic fundamentalism and totalitarianism, are the very feminists who are proudly donning hijab and vowing to register as Muslims. They are sadly misguided.

America is a country of immigrants. Many immigrants of yore were hated and feared: The Irish, the Italians, the Jews. They all assimilated and yet all also kept some or all of their traditions. That is the genius of America. However, the immigrants who came to this country mainly came from Christian and Jewish Europe. They were all Westerners. Those who are coming from war-torn Muslim countries like Syria, Iraq, Somalia, Yemen, and Afghanistan are coming from a very different culture. Many want to become "Americans;" many may not.

Europe is currently reaping the whirlwind in terms of their embrace of large, immigrant, mainly male and mainly Muslim immigrants who have created their own separate and hostile "no-go" zones in which they terrorize their own people as well as infidels.

Can Americans read this handwriting on the sky or will we remain willfully blind, consumed with guilt about America's past institution of slavery; confusing Arabs and Muslims with African-American slaves; believing that repentance and atonement mean absorbing and subsidizing a large number of potentially anti-American and misogynistic immigrants from tribal cultures.

It is true: Many Islamic terrorists have been born in America and radicalized abroad, via the internet and videos, or in their American mosques. So far, American law enforcement has been able to prevent countless terrorist attacks. We may not always be so lucky—and the question of what to do about this is a serious one.

The United States has successfully prosecuted some honor killings—but have not prevented them when, arguably, they could have done so.

Careful, knowledgeable, anti-Islamist vetting of refugees and immigrants, but in a way that satisfies our Constitution, will not be easy, but this and subsequent perfected orders are necessary first steps in that process.

Israel National News
1/30/17

www.ingramcontent.com/pod-product-compliance
Lightning Source LLC
Chambersburg PA
CBHW020455270326
41926CB00008B/608